Hands-On Full Stack Web Development with Angular 6 and Laravel 5

Become fluent in both frontend and backend web development with Docker, Angular and Laravel

Fernando Monteiro

BIRMINGHAM - MUMBAI

Hands-On Full Stack Web Development with Angular 6 and Laravel 5

Commissioning Editor: Kunal Chaudhari
Acquisition Editor: Larissa Pinto
Content Development Editor: Aishwarya Gawankar
Technical Editor: Leena Patil
Copy Editor: Safis Editing
Project Coordinator: Sheejal Shah
Proofreader: Safis Editing
Indexer: Aishwarya Gangawane
Graphics: Jason Monteiro
Production Coordinator: Nilesh Mohite

First published: July 2018

Production reference: 1300718

Published by Packt Publishing Ltd.
Livery Place
35 Livery Street
Birmingham
B3 2PB, UK.

ISBN 978-1-78883-391-2

www.packtpub.com

Eu dedico este livro a minha mãe Paschoalina Patrizzi da Silva, que luta contra o mau de Parkinson's e a Polineuropatia - durante os últimos anos e nunca perdeu o brilho no olhar de esperar por dias melhores e lutar a todo instante contra todos os efeitos colaterais das medicações e limitações impostas por essas terríveis doenças.

Mãe, você me inspira todos os dias da minha vida.

Do fundo do meu coração, muito obrigado,... Sou o que sou graças a você.

The previous paragraphs are to thank and honor my dear mother, who fights against Parkinson's disease and polyneuropathy. It was written in Portuguese so she can read and understand.

In addition, I thank my family for all support and understanding.

`mapt.io`

Mapt is an online digital library that gives you full access to over 5,000 books and videos, as well as industry leading tools to help you plan your personal development and advance your career. For more information, please visit our website.

Why subscribe?

- Spend less time learning and more time coding with practical eBooks and Videos from over 4,000 industry professionals

- Improve your learning with Skill Plans built especially for you

- Get a free eBook or video every month

- Mapt is fully searchable

- Copy and paste, print, and bookmark content

PacktPub.com

Did you know that Packt offers eBook versions of every book published, with PDF and ePub files available? You can upgrade to the eBook version at `www.PacktPub.com` and as a print book customer, you are entitled to a discount on the eBook copy. Get in touch with us at `service@packtpub.com` for more details.

At `www.PacktPub.com`, you can also read a collection of free technical articles, sign up for a range of free newsletters, and receive exclusive discounts and offers on Packt books and eBooks.

Contributors

About the author

Fernando Monteiro is a full-stack engineer, speaker, and open source contributor. He has built and made some of his personal projects open source, such as Responsive Boilerplate, Frontend Boilerplate, Angm-Generator, and TrelloMetrics, written in Angular, and Node.js. With around 16 years of experience in information technology and software development, his current focus is on web and hybrid mobile enterprise JavaScript applications.

He began his career as a graphic designer and worked in the music industry for many years, performing creation and layout work for several record labels around the world such as; Nuclear Blast, Century Media, Listenable Rec, Hellion Records, and many others.

In addition, Fernando is a packt pub author, since 2013, and has published the following books - *Instant HTML5 Responsive Table Design, Learning Single-page Web Application Development, AngularJS Directives Cookbook, Node.JS 6.x Blueprints*, and *Node.JS Projects*. When not programming, he enjoys riding motorcycles, making his own beer, and watching movies with his family.

About the reviewer

Sonny Recio is experienced developer with a five-year track record of commended performance in modular and object-oriented programming. He is well-versed in all phases of the software development life cycle, with a strong working knowledge of algorithms and data structures.

He gained five years of solid experience in C# and .NET/ASP.NET, along with writing web APIs and JavaScript in different industries.

You can find him on Twitter (YellowFlashDev), Instagram (yellowflashdev), GitHub (reciosonny).

I would like to personally thank my family, my loved ones, and my closest friends who pushed me further, and for their continued support throughout my career. Above all, I would like to thank God for everything I have. Without them, my accomplishments wouldn't have been possible.

Packt is searching for authors like you

If you're interested in becoming an author for Packt, please visit `authors.packtpub.com` and apply today. We have worked with thousands of developers and tech professionals, just like you, to help them share their insight with the global tech community. You can make a general application, apply for a specific hot topic that we are recruiting an author for, or submit your own idea.

Table of Contents

Preface   1

Chapter 1: Understanding the Core Concepts of Laravel 5   7
  Setting up the environment   8
    Installing Composer package manager   9
    Installing Docker   9
    Configuring PHPDocker.io   11
    Setting up PHPDocker and Laravel   12
    Installing VS Code text editor   15
  The basic architecture of Laravel applications   16
    Laravel directory structure   16
    The MVC flow   18
  Laravel application life cycle   19
  Artisan command-line interface   21
  MVC and routes   23
    Creating models   24
    Creating controllers   24
    Creating views   25
    Creating routes   25
  Connecting with a database   27
    Setting up the database inside a Docker container   27
    Creating a migrations file and database seed   29
    Using the resource flag to create CRUD methods   33
    Creating the Blade template engine   36
  Summary   38

Chapter 2: The Benefits of TypeScript   39
  Installing TypeScript   40
    Creating a TypeScript project   41
    Benefits of TypeScript   43
  Writing JavaScript code with static types   46
    Creating a tuple   46
    Using the void type   48
    The opt-out type checking - any   49
    Using enum   50
    Using the never type   51
    Types: undefined and null   52
  Understanding interfaces, classes, and generics in TypeScript   52
    Creating a class   52
    Declaring an interface   54

Creating generic functions   55
Working with modules   57
Using the class export feature   57
Importing and using external classes   58
Summary   58

Chapter 3: Understanding the Core Concepts of Angular 6   59
Angular 6 – smaller, faster, and easier   60
**Angular and the component method for developing modern web
applications**   60
Angular's main building blocks   61
The component life cycle   63
Installing the tools – Git, the Angular CLI, and VS Code plugins   64
Installing Git   64
Installing the Angular CLI   65
Installing VS Code Angular plugins   67
Creating a simple Angular application   70
The structure of an Angular application   70
The package.json file   72
Dotfiles – .editorconfig, .gitignore, and .angular-cli.json   73
Environments   75
Running the sample application   75
Adding a new module   76
Adding a new component   78
Adding a new route   79
Creating an Angular service   79
Template data binding   83
Simple deployment   84
Summary   86

Chapter 4: Building the Baseline Backend Application   87
Additional notes about Laravel with Docker   88
Creating the Docker Compose foundation   88
Configuring nginx   88
Configuring php-fpm   89
Creating a docker-compose configuration file   90
Building the application container   92
Using PHP Composer to scaffold a Laravel application   94
Creating the application scaffold   95
Running the application   97
Setting up a MySQL database   98
Adding a storage folder   98
Configuring the .env file   99
Using a MySQL external client   101
Migrations and database seed   104
Creating the migration boilerplate   104

Creating our first database seed | 106
Exploring the Workbench table view | 108
API documentation with the Swagger framework | 109
Installing the L5-Swagger library | 110
Creating the application API controller | 111
Generating and publishing the API documentation | 112
Adding Swagger definitions | 113
Summary | 115
Chapter 5: Creating a RESTful API Using Laravel - Part 1 | 117
Preparing the application and understanding what we are building | 118
Refactoring the application files | 119
What we are building | 120
The application's summary | 122
Creating models and migrations files | 123
Adding content to migration files | 125
Eloquent ORM relationship | 129
One-to-one relationship | 131
One-to-many relationship | 134
Many-to-many relationship | 134
Seeding our database | 139
Querying the database using Tinker | 144
Creating controllers and routes | 149
Creating and updating the controller function | 149
Creating the API routes | 164
Generating Swagger UI documentation | 165
Summary | 165
Chapter 6: Creating a RESTful API Using Laravel - Part 2 | 167
Dealing with request validation and error messages | 167
HTTP status code | 169
Implementing the Controllers validation | 169
Adding custom error handling | 171
Checking API URLs with the Swagger UI | 173
Get all records | 175
Get record by ID | 175
Checking API response errors | 176
Token-based authentication | 177
Installing tymon-jwt-auth | 178
Updating the User model | 179
Setting up the auth guard | 180
Creating the authController | 181
Creating user routes | 186
Protecting API routes | 187
Creating and logging in a User | 187
Dealing with Laravel resources | 190

Creating BikesResource   190
Creating BuildersResource   191
Creating ItemsResource   192
Creating ratingResource   193
Adding resources to controllers   194
Summary   207
Chapter 7: Progressive Web Applications with the Angular CLI   209
Starting a web application with the Angular CLI   209
Preparing the baseline code   210
Scaffolding a web application with the Angular CLI   212
Creating the directory structure   215
Building the baseline for a PWA   217
Adding PWA features using ng add   218
Understanding the key files in PWA   218
PWA in action   219
Running the application in production mode   222
Angular service – workers in action   223
Debugging a progressive web application   225
Creating boilerplate Angular components   227
Creating the home module and component   228
Creating the bikes module and component   229
Creating the builders module and component   231
Preparing Auth routes – login, register, and logout components   232
Creating a layout component   235
Summary   236
Chapter 8: Dealing with the Angular Router and Components   237
Preparing the baseline code   237
Adding components to our application   239
Dealing with Angular routes   242
Creating authentication routes   243
Creating home routing   244
Configuring child routes for details pages   245
Adding builders child routes   245
Adding bikers child routes   246
Refactoring app.component.html   248
Building frontend views   248
Creating the navigation component   249
Creating the home view and template   251
Creating the bikes router-outlet   252
Creating the bike-list view and template   253
Creating the bike-detail view and template   255
Creating the builders router-outlet   256
Creating the builder-list view and template   256
Creating the builder-detail view and template   257

Creating the login view and template	258
Creating the register view and template	259
Testing routes and views	260
Summary	261
Chapter 9: Creating Services and User Authentication	263
Preparing the baseline code	264
Dealing with models and classes	265
Creating the User class model	266
Creating the builders class model	266
Creating the Bike class model	268
Using the new HttpClient to deal with XHR requests	269
Creating the auth service	270
Creating the Register function	271
Creating the Login function	272
Creating the Logout function	273
Creating the setToken and getToken functions	274
Creating the getUser function	274
Creating the isAuthenticated function	275
Creating the handleError function	275
Creating the bikes service	276
Creating CRUD functions	277
Creating the voteOnBike function	278
Creating the handleError function	278
Creating the builders service	279
Dealing with the HttpErrorHandler service	282
Creating a handler error service	282
Importing HttpErrorHandler into app.module.ts	284
Refactoring the builders service	285
Refactoring the bikes service	287
How to use authorization headers	289
Creating an HTTP interceptor	290
Adding AppHttpInterceptorService to the main module	292
How to protect application routes with route guards	294
Creating the route guard for bike-detail	295
Summary	296
Chapter 10: Frontend Views with Bootstrap 4 and NgBootstrap	297
Preparing the baseline code	297
Installing the Bootstrap CSS framework	299
Removing the Bootstrap CSS import	300
Adding Bootstrap SCSS imports	301
Overriding Bootstrap variables	302
Writing Angular templates with Bootstrap	304
Adding template bindings to the navigation component	305
Adding template bindings to the login page	306

Adding template bindings to the register page   307
Adding template bindings to the bike-detail page   308
Adding template bindings to the bike-list page   312
Adding template bindings to the builder-detail page   313
Adding template bindings to the builder-list page   316
Setting up CORS on a Laravel backend   **317**
Setting up Laravel CORS   318
Connecting Angular services with application components   **319**
Adding environment configuration   319
Creating the navigation methods   320
Creating the bike-detail methods   321
Creating the bike-list methods   326
Creating the builder-detail methods   328
Creating the builder-list methods   330
Dealing with Angular pipes, forms, and validation   **332**
Creating a pipe filter   332
Intoducing Angular forms   334
Understanding Angular template-driven forms   335
Reviewing the login form template and component   335
Understanding Angular reactive/model-driven forms   337
Reviewing the register form template and component   337
Adding frontend form validation   340
Dealing with form validation on template-driven forms   340
Dealing with form validation on model-driven forms   342
Summary   **348**
Chapter 11: Building and Deploying Angular Tests   **349**
Preparing the baseline code   **349**
Setting application linters   **351**
Adding stylelint for SCSS files   352
Adding new scripts to the package.json file   352
Adding the .stylelintrc configuration   352
Installing the Stylelint plugin for VS Code   354
Setting VS Code for the new linter   354
Applying stylelint rules on style.scss   355
Fixing SCSS errors   357
Adding TSLint-angular to the package.json file   359
Creating linter tasks in package.json   361
Understanding Angular tests   **361**
Writing unit and e2e tests   **363**
Fixing unit tests   366
Fixing authGuard tests   371
Fixing authService tests   372
Fixing login tests   373
Fixing register tests   374
Fixing bike service tests   375
Fixing bike-detail tests   376

Fixing bike-list tests   377
Fixing bike tests   378
Fixing builders service tests   378
Fixing builder-detail tests   379
Fixing builder-list components   380
Fixing builders tests   381
Fixing home tests   382
Fixing app tests   383
Fixing app interceptor tests   384
Adding unit tests   384
Fixing e2e tests   386
Application deployment   387
Creating Docker images for frontend applications   387
Creating a Dockerfile   388
Creating an nginx file   388
Creating npm building tasks   389
Creating the bash script   390
Running npm build scripts   390
Reviewing Docker commands   391
Building the application for production   392
Testing Docker images   392
Summary   394
Other Books You May Enjoy   395
Index   399

Preface

Web Development has come a long way since its inception. Today we want web applications that are fast, robust, and engaging, and Progressive Web Applications (PWA) is the way to go ahead. In this book we are going to build powerful web applications using two of the most popular frameworks at our disposal, Angular and Laravel.

Angular is one of the most popular frontend JavaScript frameworks for creating modern and fast PWA. In addition to being very versatile and complete, Angular also includes the Angular CLI tool for generating modules, components, services, and many more utilities. On the other hand we have Laravel framework, a powerful tool for the development of web applications which explores the use of the paradigm convention over configuration.

This book gives you a practical knowledge of building modern full-stack web apps from scratch using Angular with a Laravel RESTful backend. It takes you through the most important technical facets of developing with these two frameworks and demonstrates how to put those skills into practice.

Who this book is for

This book is for developers who are new to Angular and Laravel. Knowledge of HTML, CSS, and scripting languages such as JavaScript and PHP is required.

The book's content covers all of the phases of the software engineering life cycle by looking at modern tools and techniques, including – but not limited to – RESTful APIs, token-based authentication, database configurations, and Docker containers and images.

What this book covers

Chapter 1, *Understanding the Core Concepts of Laravel 5*, introduces the Laravel framework as a powerful tool for the development of web applications and explores the use of the paradigm convention over configuration. We will see how, out of the box, Laravel has all of the features that we need to build modern web applications, token-based authentication, routes, resources, and more. Also, we will find out why the Laravel framework is one of the most popular PHP frameworks for developing web applications today. We will learn how to set up the environment, look at the Laravel application lifecycle, and see how to use the Artisan CLI.

Chapter 2, *The Benefits of TypeScript,* looks at how TypeScript enables you to write consistent JavaScript code. We examine the features that it includes, such as static typing and other features that are very common in object-oriented languages. Also, we look at using the new features of the latest version of ECMAScript, and find out TypeScript helps us to write clean and well-organized code. In this chapter, we will see the benefits of TypeScript over traditional JavaScript, discover how to use static typing, and understand how to use Interfaces, Classes, and Generics, as well as Import and Export classes.

Chapter 3, *Understanding the Core Concepts of Angular 6, dives* into Angular, which is one of the most popular frameworks for the development of frontend web applications. In addition to being very versatile and complete, Angular also includes the Angular CLI tool for generating modules, components, services, and many more utilities. In this chapter, we will learn how to use the new version of the Angular CLI, understand the core concepts of Angular, and get to grips with the component lifecycle.

Chapter 4, *Building the Baseline Backend Application,* is where we will start building the sample application. In this chapter, we are going to create a Laravel application using the RESTful architecture. We will take a closer look at some points that we mentioned briefly in the first chapter, such as the use of Docker containers to configure our environment and also how to keep our database populated. we will even check out how to use the MySQL Docker container, how to use migrations and database seed, and also how to create consistent documentation with Swagger UI.

Chapter 5, *Creating a RESTful API Using Laravel - Part 1,* will introduce RESTful APIs. You will learn how to build a RESTful API using the core elements of the Laravel framework—controllers, routes, and eloquent Object Relational Mapping (ORM). We also show some basic wireframes for the application we are building. In addition, we will look more closely at some relationships that you will need to be familiar with, such as one-to-one, one-to-many, and many-to-many.

Chapter 6, *Creating a RESTful API Using Laravel - Part 2,* continues our project of building a sample API, though, at that point, we will still have a long way to go in Laravel. We will learn how to use some features that are very common among web applications, such as token-based authentication, request validation, and custom error messages; we will also see how to use Laravel resources. Also, we will see how to use the Swagger documentation to test our API.

Chapter 7, *Progressive Web Applications with Angular CLI*, covers the changes that have affected angular-cli.json since the previous Angular version. The angular-cli.json file has now improved its support for multiple applications. We will see how to use the *ng add* a command to create a PWA and how we can organize our project structure to leave a single basis for a scalable project. Also, we will see how to use the Angular CLI to create service-work and manifest files.

Chapter 8, *Dealing with Angular Router and Components*, is where we come to one of the most important parts of Single-Page Applications (SPAs), which is the use of routes. Luckily, the Angular framework provides a powerful tool for dealing with application routing: the @angular/router dependency. In this chapter, we will learn how to use some of these features, such as router outlets and child-views, and we will see how to create master-detail pages. Also, we will start to create the frontend views.

Chapter 9, *Creating Services and User Authentication*, is one where we will create many new things, and we will be performing some refactoring to memorize import details. This is a great way to learn new things in a regular and progressive way. Also, we will dig deeper into the operation and use of the HTTP module of the Angular framework, now known as httpClient. In addition, we will look at interceptors, handling errors, using authorization headers, and how to protect application routes using *route guards*.

Chapter 10, *Frontend Views with Bootstrap 4 and NgBootstrap*, explains how to include the Bootstrap CSS framework and NgBootstrap components inside a running Angular application using the new *ng add* command from Angular CLI. Also, we will see how to connect our Angular services with components and how to use the backend API to put it all together. We will learn to configure CORS on our backend API, and how to use it with our Angular client-side application. We will also learn to deal with the Angular pipe, template-driven forms, model-driven forms, and form validations.

Chapter 11, *Building and Deploying Angular Tests*, covers how to install, customize, and extend the Bootstrap CSS framework, as well as how to use NgBootstrap components and how to connect Angular services with components and UI interfaces. We will learn to write Angular unit tests, configure application linters (for SCSS and Tslint) to maintain code consistency, create NPM scripts, and also create a Docker image and deploy the application.

To get the most out of this book

Some knowledge of the command line, Docker, and MySQL would be very helpful; however, it is not fully required, as all commands and examples are accompanied by brief instructions.

You need to have the following tools installed on your machine:

- Node.js and NPM
- Docker
- A code editor—we recommend that you use Visual Studio Code
- Git source control is recommend but not required

Download the example code files

You can download the example code files for this book from your account at `www.packtpub.com`. If you purchased this book elsewhere, you can visit `www.packtpub.com/support` and register to have the files emailed directly to you.

You can download the code files by following these steps:

1. Log in or register at `www.packtpub.com`.
2. Select the **SUPPORT** tab.
3. Click on **Code Downloads & Errata**.
4. Enter the name of the book in the **Search** box and follow the onscreen instructions.

Once the file is downloaded, please make sure that you unzip or extract the folder using the latest version of:

- WinRAR/7-Zip for Windows
- Zipeg/iZip/UnRarX for Mac
- 7-Zip/PeaZip for Linux

The code bundle for the book is also hosted on GitHub at `https://github.com/PacktPublishing/Hands-On-Full-Stack-Web-Development-with-Angular-6-and-Laravel-5`. In case there's an update to the code, it will be updated on the existing GitHub repository.

We also have other code bundles from our rich catalog of books and videos available at `https://github.com/PacktPublishing/`. Check them out!

Download the color images

We also provide a PDF file that has color images of the screenshots/diagrams used in this book. You can download it here `https://www.packtpub.com/sites/default/files/downloads/HandsOnFullStackWebDevelopmentwithAngular6andLaravel5_ColorImages.pdf`.

Conventions used

There are a number of text conventions used throughout this book.

`CodeInText`: Indicates code words in text, database table names, folder names, filenames, file extensions, pathnames, dummy URLs, user input, and Twitter handles. Here

is an example: "All PHP projects that use Composer have a file called `composer.json` at the root project."

A block of code is set as follows:

```
{
  "require": {
      "laravel/framework": "5.*.*",
  }
}
```

Any command-line input or output is written as follows:

```
composer create-project --prefer-dist laravel/laravel chapter-01
```

Bold: Indicates a new term, an important word, or words that you see onscreen. For example, words in menus or dialog boxes appear in the text like this. Here is an example: "

"Search for the `chapter-01` folder, and click **Open**."

 Warnings or important notes appear like this.

 Tips and tricks appear like this.

Get in touch

Feedback from our readers is always welcome.

General feedback: Email feedback@packtpub.com and mention the book title in the subject of your message. If you have questions about any aspect of this book, please email us at questions@packtpub.com.

Errata: Although we have taken every care to ensure the accuracy of our content, mistakes do happen. If you have found a mistake in this book, we would be grateful if you would report this to us. Please visit www.packtpub.com/submit-errata, selecting your book, clicking on the Errata Submission Form link, and entering the details.

Piracy: If you come across any illegal copies of our works in any form on the Internet, we would be grateful if you would provide us with the location address or website name. Please contact us at copyright@packtpub.com with a link to the material.

If you are interested in becoming an author: If there is a topic that you have expertise in and you are interested in either writing or contributing to a book, please visit authors.packtpub.com.

Reviews

Please leave a review. Once you have read and used this book, why not leave a review on the site that you purchased it from? Potential readers can then see and use your unbiased opinion to make purchase decisions, we at Packt can understand what you think about our products, and our authors can see your feedback on their book. Thank you!

For more information about Packt, please visit packtpub.com.

1
Understanding the Core Concepts of Laravel 5

As the title of this chapter suggests, we will be providing a general overview of the Laravel framework, covering the main concepts related to the development of web applications using a web services architecture. More precisely, we will use a RESTful architecture in this book.

We assume that you already have a basic understanding of the RESTful architecture and how web services (here, we call them **Application Programming Interface (API)** endpoints) work.

However, if you are new in this concept, don't worry. We will help you get started.

The Laravel framework will be a helpful tool because with it, all of the data inside our controllers will be converted to the JSON format, by default.

The Laravel framework is a powerful tool for the development of web applications, using the paradigm *convention over configuration*. Out of the box, Laravel has all of the features that we need to build modern web applications, using the **Model View Controller (MVC)**. Also, the Laravel framework is one of the most popular PHP frameworks for developing web applications today.

From now until the end of this book, we will refer to the Laravel framework simply as Laravel.

The Laravel ecosystem is absolutely incredible. Tools such as Homestead, Valet, Lumen, and Spark further enrich the experience of web software development using PHP.

There are many ways to start developing web applications using Laravel, meaning that there are many ways to configure your local environment or your production server. This chapter does not favor any specific way; we understand that each developer has his or her own preferences, acquired over time.

Regardless of your preferences for tools, servers, virtual machines, databases, and so on, we will focus on the main concepts, and we will not assume that a certain way is right or wrong. This first chapter is just to illustrate the main concepts and the actions that need to be performed.

Keep in mind that regardless of the methods you choose (using Homestead, WAMP, MAMP, or Docker), Laravel has some dependencies (or server requirements) that are extremely necessary for the development of web applications.

 You can find more useful information in the official Laravel documentation at `https://laravel.com/docs/5.6`.

In this chapter, we will cover the following points:

- Setting up the environment
- The basic architecture of a Laravel application
- The Laravel application life cycle
- Artisan CLI
- MVC and routes
- Connecting with the database

Setting up the environment

Remember, no matter how you have configured your environment to develop web applications with PHP and Laravel, keep the main server requirements in mind, and you will be able to follow the examples in this chapter.

It is important to note that some operating systems do not have PHP installed. As this is the case with Windows machines, here are some alternatives for you to create your development environment:

- HOMESTEAD (recommended by Laravel documentation): `https://laravel.com/docs/5.6/homestead`
- MAMP: `https://www.mamp.info/en/`
- XAMPP: `https://www.apachefriends.org/index.html`
- WAMP SERVER (only for Windows OS): `http://www.wampserver.com/en/`
- PHPDOCKER: `https://www.docker.com/what-docker`

Installing Composer package manager

Laravel uses **Composer**, a dependency manager for PHP, very similar to **Node Package Manager (NPM)** for Node.js projects, PIP for Python, and Bundler for Ruby. Let's see what the official documentation says about it:

> *"A Composer is a tool for dependency management in PHP. It allows you to declare the libraries your project depends on and it will manage (install/update) them for you."*

So, let's install Composer, as follows:

Go to `https://getcomposer.org/download/` and follow the instructions for your platform.

 You can get more information at `https://getcomposer.org/doc/00-intro.md.`

Note that you can install Composer on your machine locally or globally; don't worry about it right now. Choose what is easiest for you.

All PHP projects that use Composer have a file called `composer.json` at the root project, which looks similar to the following:

```
{
  "require": {
      "laravel/framework": "5.*.*",
  }
}
```

This is also very similar to the `package.json` file on Node.js and Angular applications, as we will see later in this book.

 Here's a helpful link about the basic commands: `https://getcomposer.org/doc/01-basic-usage.md`

Installing Docker

We will use Docker in this chapter. Even though the official documentation of Laravel suggests the use of Homestead with virtual machines and Vagrant, we chose to use Docker because it's fast and easy to start, and our main focus is on Laravel's core concepts.

You can find more information about Docker at `https://www.docker.com/what-docker`.

As the Docker documentation states:

Docker is the company driving the container movement and the only container platform provider to address every application across the hybrid cloud. Today's businesses are under pressure to digitally transform, but are constrained by existing applications and infrastructure while rationalizing an increasingly diverse portfolio of clouds, datacenters, and application architectures. Docker enables true independence between applications and infrastructure and developers and IT ops to unlock their potential and creates a model for better collaboration and innovation.

Let's install Docker, as follows:

1. Go to `https://docs.docker.com/install/`.
2. Choose your platform and follow the installation steps.
3. If you have any trouble, check the getting started link at `https://docs.docker.com/get-started/`.

As we are using Docker containers and images to start our application and won't get into how Docker works behind the scenes, here is a short list of some Docker commands:

Command:	Description:
`docker ps`	Show running containers
`docker ps -a`	Show all containers
`docker start`	Start a container
`docker stop`	Stop a container
`docker-compose up -d`	Start containers in background
`docker-compose stop`	Stop all containers on `docker-compose.yml` file
`docker-compose start`	Start all containers on `docker-compose.yml` file
`docker-compose kill`	Kill all containers on `docker-compose.yml` file
`docker-compose logs`	Log all containers on `docker-compose.yml` file

You can check the whole list of Docker commands at `https://docs.docker.com/engine/reference/commandline/docker/`. And Docker-compose commands at `https://docs.docker.com/compose/reference/overview/#command-options-overview-and-help`.

Configuring PHPDocker.io

PHPDocker.io is a simple tool that helps us to build PHP applications using the Docker/Container concept with Compose. It's very easy to understand and use; so, let's look at what we need to do:

1. Go to `https://phpdocker.io/`.
2. Click on the **Generator** link.
3. Fill out the information, as in the following screenshot.
4. Click on the **Generate project archive** button and save the folder:

PHPDocker interface

The database configuration is as per the following screenshot:

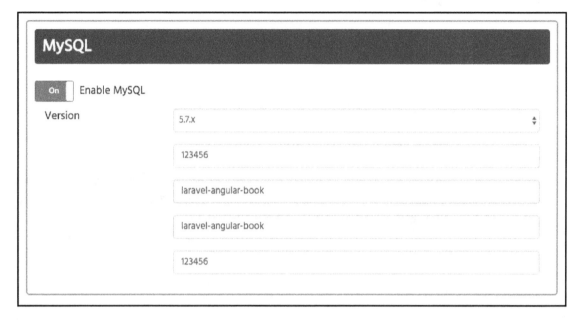

Database configuration

 Note that we are using the latest version of the MYSQL database in the preceding configuration, but you can choose whatever version you prefer. In the following examples, the database version will not matter.

Setting up PHPDocker and Laravel

Now that we have filled in the previous information and downloaded the file for our machine, let's begin setting up our application so as to delve deeper into the directory structure of a Laravel application.

Execute the following steps:

1. Open `bash/Terminal/cmd`.
2. Go to `Users/yourname` on Mac and Linux, or `C:/` on Windows.

3. Open your Terminal inside the folder and type the following command:

```
composer create-project --prefer-dist laravel/laravel chapter-01
```

At the end of your Terminal window, you will see the following result:

```
Writing lock file
Generating autoload files
> Illuminate\Foundation\ComposerScripts::postUpdate
> php artisan optimize
Generating optimized class loader
php artisan key:generate
```

4. In the Terminal window, type:

```
cd chapter-01 && ls
```

The results will be as follows:

```
app            composer.json   database       phpunit.xml    resources      tests
artisan        composer.lock   gulpfile.js    public         server.php     vendor
bootstrap      config          package.json   readme.md      storage
```

Terminal window output

Congratulations! You have your first Laravel application, built with the `Composer` package manager.

Now, it's time to join our application with the file downloaded from PHPDocker (our PHP/MySQL Docker screenshot). To do so, follow the next steps.

5. Grab the downloaded archive, `hands-on-full-stack-web-development-with-angular-6-and-laravel-5.zip`, and unzip it.

6. Copy all of the folder content (a `phpdocker` folder and a file, `docker-compose.yml`).

7. Open the `chapter-01` folder and paste the content.

Now, inside the `chapter-01` folder, we will see the following files:

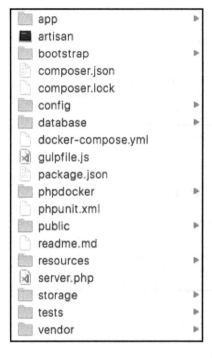

chapter-01 folder structure

Let's check to make sure that everything will go well with our configuration.

8. Open your Terminal window and type the following command:

```
docker-compose up -d
```

It's important to remember that at this point, you need to have Docker up and running on your machine. If you are completely new to how to run Docker on your machine, you can find more information at `https://github.com/docker/labs/tree/master/beginner/`.

9. Note that this command may take more time to create and build all of the containers. The results will be as follows:

```
hands-on-full-stack-web-development-with-angular-6-and-laravel-5-memcached ... done
hands-on-full-stack-web-development-with-angular-6-and-laravel-5-webserver ... done
hands-on-full-stack-web-development-with-angular-6-and-laravel-5-mysql     ... done
hands-on-full-stack-web-development-with-angular-6-and-laravel-5-php-fpm   ... done
```

Docker containers up and running

The preceding screenshot indicates that we have started all containers successfully: `memcached`, `webserver` (**Nginx**), `mysql`, and `php-fpm`.

Open your browser and type `http://localhost:8081`; you should see the welcome page for Laravel.

At this point, it is time to open our sample project in a text editor and check all of the Laravel folders and files. You can choose the editor that you are used to, or, if you prefer, you can use the editor that we will describe in the next section.

Installing VS Code text editor

For this chapter, and throughout the book, we will be using **Visual Studio Code (VS Code)**, a free and highly configurable multiplatform text editor. It is also very useful for working with projects in Angular and TypeScript.

Install VS Code as follows:

1. Go to the download page and choose your platform at `https://code.visualstudio.com/Download`.
2. Follow the installation steps for your platform.

VS Code has a vibrant community with tons of extensions. You can research and find extensions at `https://marketplace.visualstudio.com/VSCode`. In the next chapters, we will install and use some of them.

For now, just install VS Code icons from `https://marketplace.visualstudio.com/items?itemName=robertohuertasm.vscode-icons`.

The basic architecture of Laravel applications

As mentioned previously, Laravel is an MVC framework for the development of modern web applications. It is a software architecture standard that separates the representation of information from users' interaction with it. The architectural standard that it has adopted is not so new; it has been around since the mid-1970s. It remains current, and a number of frameworks still use it today.

 You can read more about the MVC pattern at https://en.wikipedia. org/wiki/Model-view-controller.

Laravel directory structure

Now, let's look at how this pattern is implemented within an application with Laravel:

1. Open the VS Code editor.
2. If this is the first time you are opening VS Code, click on the top menu and navigate to **File** | **Open.**
3. Search for the chapter-01 folder, and click **Open.**
4. Expand the app folder at the left-hand side of VS Code.

The application files are as follows:

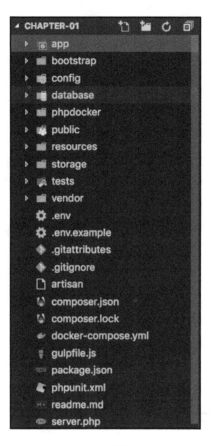

Laravel root folder

The `phpdocker` folder and `docker-compose.yml` files are not part of the Laravel framework; we added these files manually, earlier in this chapter.

The MVC flow

In a very basic MVC workflow, when a user interacts with our application, the steps in the following screenshot are performed. Imagine a simple web application about books, with a search input field. When the user types a book name and presses *Enter*, the following flow cycle will occur:

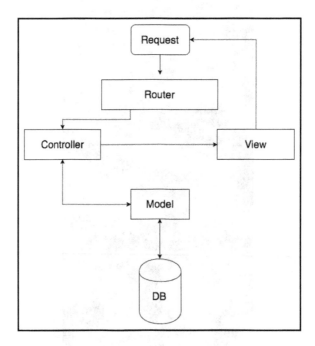

MVC flow

The MVC is represented by the following folders and files:

MVC Architecture	Application Path	File
Model	app/	User.php
View	resources/views	welcome.blade.php
Controller	app/Http/Controllers	Auth/AuthController.php Auth/PasswordController.php

Note that the application models are at the root of the app folder, and the application already has at least one file for MVC implementation.

Also note that the `app` folder contains all of the core files for our application. The other folders have very intuitive names, such as the following:

Bootstrap	Cache, autoload, and bootstrap applications
Config	Application's configuration
Database	Factory, migrations, and seeds
Public	JavaScript, CSS, fonts, and images
Resource	Views, SASS/LESS, and localization
Storage	This folder has separated apps, frameworks, and logs
Tests	Unit tests using PHPunit
Vendor	Composer dependencies

Now, let's see how things work in the Laravel structure.

Laravel application life cycle

In a Laravel application, the flow is almost the same as in the previous example, but a little more complex. When the user triggers an event in a browser, the request arrives on a web server (Apache/Nginx), where we have our web application running. So, the server redirects the request into `public/index.php`, the starting point for the entire framework. In the `bootstrap` folder, the `autoloader.php` is started and loads all of the files generated by the composer retrieving an instance to the Laravel application.

Let's look at the following screenshot:

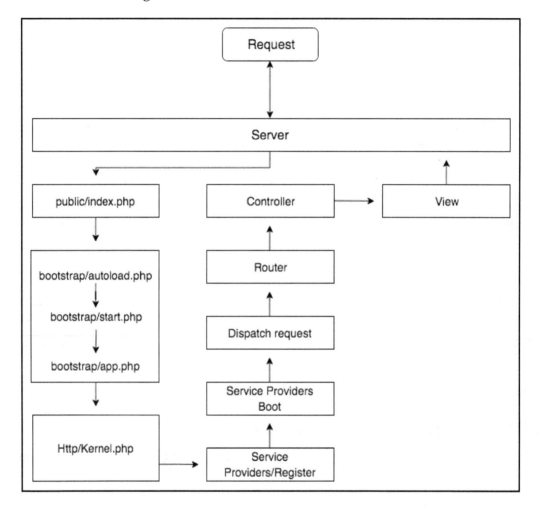

Laravel application cycle

The diagram is complex enough for our first chapter, so we will not get into all of the steps performed by the user's request. Instead, we will go on to another very important feature that is a main concept in Laravel: the Artisan **command-line interface (CLI)**.

 You can read more about the request life cycle in Laravel in the official documentation at `https://laravel.com/docs/5.2/lifecycle`.

Artisan command-line interface

Nowadays, it is common practice to create web applications by using the command line; and, with the evolution of web development tools and technologies, this has become very popular.

We will mention that NPM is one of the most popular. However, for the development of applications using Laravel, we have an advantage. The Artisan CLI is automatically installed when we create a Laravel project.

Let's look at what the official documentation of Laravel says about the Artisan CLI:

> *Artisan is the name of the command-line interface included with Laravel. It provides a number of helpful commands for your use while developing your application.*

Inside of the `chapter-01` folder, we find the Artisan bash file. It's responsible for running all of the commands available on the CLI, and there are many of them, to create classes, controllers, seeds, and much more.

After this small introduction to the Artisan CLI, there would be nothing better than looking at some practical examples. So, let's get hands on, and don't forget to start Docker:

1. Open your Terminal window inside the `chapter-01` folder, and type the following command:

   ```
   docker-compose up -d
   ```

2. Let's get inside the `php-fpm container` and type the following:

   ```
   docker-compose exec php-fpm bash
   ```

   We now have all of the Artisan CLI commands available in the Terminal.

   This is the simplest way to interact with the Teminal within our Docker container. If you are using another technique to run the Laravel application, as mentioned at the beginning of the chapter, you do not need to use the following command:

   ```
   docker-compose exec php-fpm bash
   ```

   You can just type the same commands from the next steps into the Terminal.

3. Still in the Terminal, type the following command:

   ```
   php artisan list
   ```

You will see the framework version and a list of all available commands:

```
Laravel Framework version 5.2.45
Usage:
  command [options] [arguments]
Options:
  -h, --help              Display this help message
  -q, --quiet             Do not output any message
  -V, --version           Display this application version
      --ansi              Force ANSI output
      --no-ansi           Disable ANSI output
  -n, --no-interaction    Do not ask any interactive question
      --env[=ENV]         The environment the command should run
under.
  -v|vv|vvv, --verbose    Increase the verbosity of messages: 1 for
normal output, 2 for more verbose output and 3 for debug
...
```

As you can see, the list of commands is very large. Note that the above code snippet, we did not put all the options available with the php artisan list command, but we will see some combinations on next lines.

4. In your Terminal, type the following combination:

```
php artisan -h migrate
```

The output will explain exactly what the migrate command can do and what options we have, as seen in the following screenshot:

```
root@26f56807db17:/application# php artisan -h migrate
Usage:
  migrate [options]

Options:
      --database[=DATABASE]  The database connection to use.
      --force                Force the operation to run when in production.
      --path[=PATH]          The path of migrations files to be executed.
      --pretend              Dump the SQL queries that would be run.
      --seed                 Indicates if the seed task should be re-run.
      --step                 Force the migrations to be run so they can be rolled back individually.
  -h, --help                 Display this help message
  -q, --quiet                Do not output any message
  -V, --version              Display this application version
      --ansi                 Force ANSI output
      --no-ansi              Disable ANSI output
  -n, --no-interaction       Do not ask any interactive question
      --env[=ENV]            The environment the command should run under.
  -v|vv|vvv, --verbose       Increase the verbosity of messages: 1 for normal output, 2 for more verbose output and
3 for debug

Help:
  Run the database migrations
root@26f56807db17:/application#
```

Output of php artisan -h migrate

It's also possible to see what options we have for the `migrate` command.

5. Still in the Terminal, type the following command:

    php artisan -h make:controller

    You will see the following output:

```
root@26f56807db17:/application# php artisan -h make:controller
Usage:
  make:controller [options] [--] <name>

Arguments:
  name                  The name of the class

Options:
      --resource        Generate a resource controller class.
  -h, --help            Display this help message
  -q, --quiet           Do not output any message
  -V, --version         Display this application version
      --ansi            Force ANSI output
      --no-ansi         Disable ANSI output
  -n, --no-interaction  Do not ask any interactive question
      --env[=ENV]       The environment the command should run under.
  -v|vv|vvv, --verbose  Increase the verbosity of messages: 1 for normal output, 2 for more verbose output and 3 for
debug

Help:
  Create a new controller class
root@26f56807db17:/application#
```

Output of php artisan -h make:controller

Now, let's look at how to create the MVC in the Laravel application, using the Artisan CLI.

MVC and routes

As mentioned earlier, we will now create a component each of the model, view, and controller, using the Artisan CLI. However, as our heading suggests, we will include another important item: the routes. We have already mentioned them in this chapter (in our diagram of the request life cycle in Laravel, and also in the example diagram of the MVC itself).

In this section, we will focus on creating the file, and checking it after it has been created.

Creating models

Let's get hands on:

1. Open your Terminal window inside the `chapter-01` folder, and type the following command:

   ```
   php artisan make:model Band
   ```

   After the command, you should see a success message in green, stating: **Model created successfully**.

2. Go back to your code editor; inside the `app` folder, you will see the `Band.php` file, with the following code:

   ```php
   <?php
   namespace App;
   use Illuminate\Database\Eloquent\Model;
   class Band extends Model
   {
       //
   }
   ```

Creating controllers

Now it is time to use the artisan to generate our controller, let's see how we can do that:

1. Go back to the Terminal window, and type the following command:

   ```
   php artisan make:controller BandController
   ```

   After the command, you should see a message in green, stating: **Controller created successfully**.

2. Now, inside `app/Http/Controllers`, you will see `BandController.php`, with the following content:

   ```php
   <?php
   namespace App\Http\Controllers;
   use Illuminate\Http\Request;
   use App\Http\Requests;
   class BandController extends Controller
   {
       //
   }
   ```

As a good practice, always create your controller with the suffix `<Somename>Controller`.

Creating views

As we can see earlier when using the `php artisan list` command, we do not have any alias command to create the application views automatically. So we need to create the views manually:

1. Go back to your text editor, and inside the `resources/views` folder, create a new file, named `band.blade.php`.
2. Place the following code inside the `band.blade.php` file:

```
<div class="container">
    <div class="content">
        <div class="title">Hi i'm a view</div>
    </div>
</div>
```

Creating routes

The routes within Laravel are responsible for directing all HTTP traffic coming from the user's requests, so the routes are responsible for the entire inflow in a Laravel application, as we saw in the preceding diagrams.

In this section, we will briefly look at the types of routes available in Laravel, and how to create a simple route for our MVC component.

At this point, it is only necessary to look at how the routes work. Later in the book, we will get deeper into application routing.

So, let's look at what we can use to handle routes in Laravel:

Code	HTTP | METHOD | Verb
`Route::get($uri, $callback);`	GET
`Route::post($uri, $callback);`	POST
`Route::put($uri, $callback);`	PUT
`Route::patch($uri, $callback);`	PATCH
`Route::delete($uri, $callback);`	DELETE
`Route::options($uri, $callback);`	OPTIONS

Each of the routes available is responsible for handling one type of HTTP request method. Also, we can combine more than one method in the same route, as in the following code. Do not be too concerned with this now; we'll see how to deal with this type of routing later in the book:

```
Route::match(['get', 'post'], '/', function () {
    //
});
```

Now, let's create our first route:

1. On your text editor, open `web.php` inside the `routes` folder, and add the following code, right after the `welcome view`:

```
Route::get('/band', function () {
 return view('band');
});
```

2. Open your browser to `http://localhost:8081/band`, and you will see the following message:

   Hi i'm a view

 Don't forget to start all Docker containers using the `docker-compose up -d` command. If you followed the previous examples, you will already have everything up and running.

Bravo! We have created our first route. It is a simple example, but we have all of the things in place and working well. In the next section, we'll look at how to integrate a model with a controller and render the view.

Connecting with a database

As we saw previously, the controllers are activated by the routes and transmit information between the model/database and the view. In the preceding example, we used static content inside the view, but in larger applications, we will almost always have content coming from a database, or generated within the controller and passed to the view.

In the next example, we will see how to do this.

Setting up the database inside a Docker container

It's now time to configure our database. If you use Homestead, you probably have your database connection configured and working well. To check, open your Terminal and type the following command:

```
php artisan tinker
DB::connection()->getPdo();
```

If everything goes well, you will see the following message:

```
Psy Shell v0.7.2 (PHP 7.2.2-3+ubuntu16.04.1+deb.sury.org+1 - cli) by Justin Hileman
>>> DB::connection()->getPdo();
=> PDO {#639
     inTransaction: false,
     attributes: {
       CASE: NATURAL,
       ERRMODE: EXCEPTION,
       AUTOCOMMIT: 1,
       PERSISTENT: false,
       DRIVER_NAME: "mysql",
       SERVER_INFO: "Uptime: 27  Threads: 1  Questions: 9  Slow queries: 0  Opens: 105  Flush tables: 1  Open tables: 98  Queries
per second avg: 0.333",
       ORACLE_NULLS: NATURAL,
       CLIENT_VERSION: "mysqlnd 5.0.12-dev - 20150407 - $Id: 38fea24f2847fa7519001be390c98ae0acafe387 $",
       SERVER_VERSION: "5.7.21",
       STATEMENT_CLASS: [
         "PDOStatement",
       ],
       EMULATE_PREPARES: 0,
       CONNECTION_STATUS: "mysql via TCP/IP",
       DEFAULT_FETCH_MODE: BOTH,
     },
   }
>>>
```

Database connection message

For this example, however, we are using Docker, and we need to do some configuration to accomplish this task:

1. Inside of the root project, open the `.env` file and look at line 8 (the database connection), which looks as follows:

```
DB_CONNECTION=mysql
DB_HOST=127.0.0.1
DB_PORT=3306
DB_DATABASE=homestead
DB_USERNAME=homestead
DB_PASSWORD=secret
```

Now, replace the preceding code with the following lines:

```
DB_CONNECTION=mysql
DB_HOST=mysql
DB_PORT=3306
DB_DATABASE=laravel-angular-book
DB_USERNAME=laravel-angular-book
DB_PASSWORD=123456
```

Note that we need to change a bit to get the Docker MySQL container directions; if you don't remember what you chose in the `PHPDocker.io` generator, you can copy it from the container configuration.

2. Open `docker-compose.yml` at the root directory.
3. Copy the environment variables from the MySQL container setup:

```
mysql:
  image: mysql:8.0
  entrypoint: ['/entrypoint.sh', '--character-set-server=utf8', '--
  collation-server=utf8_general_ci']
  container_name: larahell-mysql
  working_dir: /application
  volumes:
    - .:/application
  environment:
    - MYSQL_ROOT_PASSWORD=larahell
    - MYSQL_DATABASE=larahell-angular-book
    - MYSQL_USER=larahell-user
    - MYSQL_PASSWORD=123456
  ports:
    - "8083:3306"
```

Now, it's time to test our connection.

4. In your Terminal window, type the following command:

```
docker-compose exec php-fpm bash
```

5. Finally, let's check our connection; type the following command:

```
php artisan tinker
DB::connection()->getPdo();
```

You should see the same message as the previous screenshot. Then, you will have everything you need to go ahead with the example.

Creating a migrations file and database seed

Migration files are very common in some MVC frameworks, such as Rails, Django, and, of course, Laravel. It is through this type of file that we can keep our database consistent with our application, since we cannot versioning the database schemes . Migration files help us to store each change in our database, so that we can version these files and keep the project consistent.

Database seeds serve to populate the tables of a database with an initial batch of records; this is extremely useful when we are developing web applications from the beginning. The data of the initial load can be varied, from tables of users to administration objects such as passwords and tokens, and everything else that we require.

Let's look at how we can create a migration file for the Bands model in Laravel:

1. Open your Terminal window and type the following command:

```
php artisan make:migration create_bands_table
```

2. Open the database/migrations folder, and you will see a file called<timestamp>create_bands_table.php.

3. Open this file and paste the following code inside public function up():

```
Schema::create('bands', function (Blueprint $table) {
    $table->increments('id');
    $table->string('name');
    $table->string('description');
    $table->timestamps();
});
```

4. Paste the following code inside `public function down():`

    ```
    Schema::dropIfExists('bands');
    ```

5. The final result will be the following code:

    ```php
    <?php
    use Illuminate\Support\Facades\Schema;
     use Illuminate\Database\Schema\Blueprint;
     use Illuminate\Database\Migrations\Migration;
    class CreateBandsTable extends Migration
    {
        /**
        * Run the migrations.
        *
        * @return void
        */
        public function up()
        {
            Schema::create('bands', function (Blueprint $table) {
            $table->increments('id');
            $table->string('name');
            $table->string('description');
            $table->timestamps();
            });
        }
        /**
        * Reverse the migrations.
        *
        * @return void
        */
        public function down()
        {
            Schema::dropIfExists('bands');
        }
    }
    ```

6. Inside of the `database/factories` folder, open the `ModalFactory.php` file and add the following code, right after the `User Factory`. Note that we are using a PHP library called `faker` inside a `factory` function, in order to generate some data:

    ```php
    $factory->define(App\Band::class, function (Faker\Generator $faker)
    {
    return [
     'name' => $faker->word,
     'description' => $faker->sentence
    ```

```
];
});
```

7. Go back to your Terminal window and create a database seed. To do this, type the following command:

```
php artisan make:seeder BandsTableSeeder
```

8. In the database/seeds folder, open the BandsTableSeeder.php file and type the following code, inside public function run():

```
factory(App\Band::class,5)->create()->each(function ($p) {
$p->save();
});
```

9. Now, in the database/seeds folder, open the DatabaseSeeder.php file and add the following code, inside public function run():

```
$this->call(BandsTableSeeder::class);
```

 You can read more about Faker PHP at https://github.com/fzaninotto/Faker.

Before we go any further , we need to do a small refactoring on the Band model.

10. Inside of the app root, open the Band.php file and add the following code, inside the Band class:

```
protected $fillable = ['name','description'];
```

11. Go back to your Terminal and type the following command:

```
php artisan migrate
```

After the command, you will see the following message in the Terminal window:

```
Migration table created successfully.
```

The preceding command was just to populate the database with our seed.

12. Go back to your Terminal and type the following command:

```
php artisan db:seed
```

We now have five items ready to use in our database.

Let's check whether everything will go smoothly.

13. Inside of your Terminal, to exit `php-fpm container`, type the following command:

    exit

14. Now, in the application root folder, type the following command in your Terminal:

    docker-compose exec mysql mysql –ularavel-angular-book –p123456

    The preceding command will give you access to the MySQL console inside `mysql Docker container`, almost exactly the same as how we gained access to `php-fpm container`.

15. Inside of the Terminal, type the following command to see all of the databases:

    show databases;

    As you can see, we have two tables: `information_schema` and `laravel-angular-book`.

16. Let's access the `laravel-angular-book` table; type the following command:

    use laravel-angular-book;

17. And now, let's check our tables, as follows:

    show tables;

18. Now, let's `SELECT` all records from the `bands` tables:

    `SELECT * from bands;`

    We will see something similar to the following screenshot:

```
mysql> SELECT * from bands;
+----+--------+----------------------------------------------------------+
| id | name   | description                                              |
+----+--------+----------------------------------------------------------+
|  1 | quidem | Sed sed rerum autem accusamus assumenda quia exercitationem. |
|  2 | at     | Deleniti eos quas eum consectetur.                       |
|  3 | totam  | Voluptates quibusdam non vel quia sed et et.             |
|  4 | alias  | Adipisci mollitia ipsum iste harum maiores.              |
|  5 | libero | Quia tempore quia numquam ad.                            |
+----+--------+----------------------------------------------------------+
5 rows in set (0.00 sec)
```

Database bands table

19. Now, exit the MySQL console with the following command:

```
exit
```

Using the resource flag to create CRUD methods

Let's see another feature of the Artisan CLI, creating all of the **Create**, **Read**, **Update**, **and Delete** (**CRUD**) operations using a single command.

First, in the app/Http/Controllers folder, delete the BandController.php file:

1. Open your Terminal window and type the following command:

   ```
   php artisan make:controller BandController --resource
   ```

   This action will create the same file again, but now, it includes the CRUD operations, as shown in the following code:

   ```php
   <?php
   namespace App\Http\Controllers;
   use Illuminate\Http\Request;
   class BandController extends Controller
     {
         /**
         * Display a listing of the resource.
         *
         * @return \Illuminate\Http\Response
         */
         public function index()
         {
             //
         }
       /**
         * Show the form for creating a new resource.
         *
         * @return \Illuminate\Http\Response
         */
         public function create()
         {
             //
         }
       /**
         * Store a newly created resource in storage.
         *
         * @param \Illuminate\Http\Request $request
         * @return \Illuminate\Http\Response
   ```

```php
     */
    public function store(Request $request)
    {
        //
    }
    /**
     * Display the specified resource.
     *
     * @param int $id
     * @return \Illuminate\Http\Response
     */
    public function show($id)
    {
        //
    }
    /**
     * Show the form for editing the specified resource.
     *
     * @param int $id
     * @return \Illuminate\Http\Response
     */
    public function edit($id)
    {
        //
    }
    /**
     * Update the specified resource in storage.
     *
     * @param \Illuminate\Http\Request $request
     * @param int $id
     * @return \Illuminate\Http\Response
     */
    public function update(Request $request, $id)
    {
        //
    }
    /**
     * Remove the specified resource from storage.
     *
     * @param int $id
     * @return \Illuminate\Http\Response
     */
    public function destroy($id)
    {
        //
    }
}
```

For this example, we will write only two methods: one to list all of the records, and another to get a specific record. Don't worry about the other methods; we will cover all of the methods in the upcoming chapters.

2. Let's edit `public function index()` and add the following code:

```
$bands = Band::all();
return $bands;
```

3. Now, edit `public function show()` and add the following code:

```
$band = Band::find($id);
return view('bands.show', array('band' => $band));
```

4. Add the following line, right after `App\Http\Requests`:

```
use App\Band;
```

5. Update the `routes.php` file, inside the routes folder, to the following code:

```
Route::get('/', function () {
return view('welcome');
});
Route::resource('bands', 'BandController');
```

6. Open your browser and go to `http://localhost:8081/bands`, where you will see the following content:

```
[{
  "id": 1,
  "name": "porro",
  "description": "Minus sapiente ut libero explicabo et voluptas
harum.",
  "created_at": "2018-03-02 19:20:58",
  "updated_at": "2018-03-02 19:20:58"}
...]
```

Don't worry if your data is different from the previous code; this is due to Faker generating random data. Note that we are returning a JSON directly to the browser, instead of returning the data to the view. This is a very important feature of Laravel; it serializes and deserializes data, by default.

Creating the Blade template engine

Now, it's time to create another view component. This time, we will use the Blade template engine to show some records from our database. Let's look at what the official documentation says about Blade:

Blade is the simple, yet powerful, templating engine provided with Laravel. Unlike other popular PHP templating engines, Blade does not restrict you from using plain PHP code in your views. All Blade views are compiled into plain PHP code and cached until they are modified, meaning Blade adds essentially zero overhead to your application.

Now, it's time to see this behavior in action:

1. Go back to the code editor and create another folder inside `resources/views`, called `bands`.

2. Create a file, `show.blade.php`, inside `resources/views/bands`, and place the following code in it:

```
<h1>Band {{ $band->id }}</h1>
<ul>
<li>band: {{ $band->name }}</li>
<li>description: {{ $band->description }}</li>
</ul>
```

 You can find out more about Blade at `https://laravel.com/docs/5.2/blade`.

3. Open your browser to `http://localhost:8081/bands/1`. You will see the template in action, with results similar to the following:

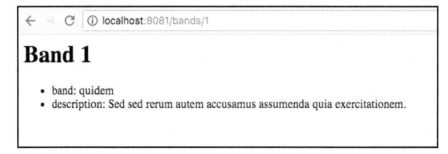

View of the template engine

Note that here, we are using the Blade template engine to show a record from our database. Now, let's create another view to render all of the records.

4. Create another file, called `index.blade.php`, inside `resources/views/bands`, and place the following code in it:

```
@foreach ($bands as $band)
<h1>Band id: {{ $band->id }}</h1>
<h2>Band name: {{ $band->name }}</h2>
<p>Band Description: {{ $band->description }}</p>
@endforeach
```

5. Go back to your browser and visit `http://localhost:8081/bands/`, where you will see a result similar to the following:

View template engine

Summary

We have finally finished the first chapter, and we have covered many of the core concepts of the Laravel framework. Even with the simple examples that we discussed in this chapter, we have provided a relevant basis for all of Laravel's functionality. It would be possible to create incredible applications with only this knowledge. However, we intend to delve deeper into some concepts that deserve separate chapters. Throughout the book, we will create an entire application, using a RESTful API, Angular, and some other tools, such as TypeScript, which we will look at in the next chapter.

The Benefits of TypeScript

2

TypeScript enables you to write JavaScript code. It includes static typing and other features that are very common in object-oriented languages. In addition, with TypeScript, you can use all of the features of ECMAScript 6, because the compiler converts them into readable code for the current browser.

One of the features of TypeScript is that users can create typed variables, like it is done in Java or C# (for example, `const VARIABLE_NAME: Type = Value`), Not only that, but TypeScript helps us to write clean, well-organized code. That is one of the reasons why the Angular team adopted TypeScript for the current version of the framework.

Before we begin, let's look at what the official TypeScript documentation states:

> *"TypeScript is a typed superset of JavaScript that compiles to plain JavaScript.*
> *Any browser. Any host."*

In this chapter, we will install TypeScript in our environment globally, in order to understand what happens with TypeScript files when they are converted to JavaScript. Don't worry; Angular applications already provide us with a TypeScript compiler, built into the Angular CLI.

In this chapter, we will cover the following points:

- Installing TypeScript
- The benefits of using TypeScript
- How to transpile a TypeScript file to a JavaScript file
- Writing JavaScript code with static typing
- Understanding interfaces, classes, and generics in TypeScript

Installing TypeScript

It's pretty simple to install and get started with TypeScript. It is necessary to have Node.js and Node Package Manager (NPM) installed on your machine.

If you don't have them yet, go to `https://nodejs.org/en/download/` and follow the step-by-step installation instructions for your platform.

Let's install TypeScript, as follows:

1. Open your Terminal and type the following command to install the TypeScript compiler:

   ```
   npm install -g typescript
   ```

   Note that the `-g` flag means to install the compiler on your machine globally.

2. Let's check the available TypeScript commands. Type the following command in the Terminal:

   ```
   tsc --help
   ```

The preceding command will provide a lot of information about the TypeScript compiler; we will see a simple example of how we can transpile a TypeScript file to a JavaScript file.

Examples:

```
tsc hello.ts
tsc --outFile file.js file.ts
```

Descriptions of the preceding lines are as follows:

- The `tsc` command compiles the `hello.ts` file.
- Tell the compiler to create an output file, named `hello.js`

Creating a TypeScript project

Some text editors, such as VS Code, give us the ability to deal with TS files as independent units, called File Scope. Although this is very useful for isolated files (as in the following examples), it is recommended that you always create a TypeScript project. You can then modularize your code and use dependency injection between files in the future.

A TypeScript project is created with a file called tsconfig.json, placed at the root of a directory. You will need to indicate to the compiler which files are part of the project, the compile options, and many other settings.

A basic tsconfig.json file contains the following code:

```
{ "compilerOptions":
  { "target": "es5",
   "module": "commonjs"
  }
}
```

Although the preceding code is very simple and intuitive, we are only indicating which compiler we will use in our project, and also what kind of module. If the code snippet indicates that we are using ECMAScript 5, all TypeScript code will be converted to JavaScript, using ES5 syntax.

Now, let's look at how we can create this file automatically, with the help of the tsc compiler:

1. Create a folder, called chapter-02.
2. Open your Terminal inside the chapter-02 folder.
3. Type the following command:

   tsc --init

   We will see the following content, generated by the tsc compiler:

   ```
   {
   "compilerOptions": {
   /* Basic Options */
   /* Specify ECMAScript target version: 'ES3' (default), 'ES5',
   'ES2015', 'ES2016', 'ES2017','ES2018' or 'ESNEXT'. */
   "target": "es5",
   /* Specify module code generation: 'none', 'commonjs', 'amd',
   'system', 'umd', 'es2015', or 'ESNext'. */
   ```

```
    "module": "commonjs",
    ...
    /* Strict Type-Checking Options */
    /* Enable all strict type-checking options. */
    "strict": true,
    ...
    /* Enables emit interoperability between CommonJS and ES Modules
    via creation of namespace objects for all imports. Implies
    'allowSyntheticDefaultImports'. */
    "esModuleInterop": true
    /* Source Map Options */
    ...
    /* Experimental Options */
    ...
    }
}
```

Note that we have omitted some sections. You should see all of the available options; however, most of them are commented. Do not worry about that at this time; later on, we will look at some of the options in more detail.

Now, let's create a TypeScript file, and check that everything goes smoothly.

4. Open VS Code in the `chapter-02` folder and create a new file, called `sample-01.ts`.

5. Add the following code to `sample-01.ts`:

   ```
   console.log('First Sample With TypeScript');
   ```

6. Go back to your Terminal and type the following command:

   tsc sample-01.ts

 In VS Code, you can use the integrated Terminal; on the top menu bar, click on **View | Integrate Terminal [^`]**.

Note that another file appears with the same name, but with a `.js` extension.

If you compare both files, they are exactly the same, because our example is pretty simple, and we are using a simple `console.log()` function.

As TypeScript is a super set of JavaScript, all of the JS features are available here, too.

Benefits of TypeScript

Here's a small list of the benefits of using TypeScript:

- TypeScript is robust, secure, and easy to debug.
- TypeScript code is compiled before being transformed into JavaScript, so we can catch all sorts of errors before running the code.
- IDEs that support TypeScript have the ability to improve code completion and checking static typing.
- TypeScript supports OOP (Object Oriented Programming), including modules, namespaces, classes, and more.

The main point in TypeScript's favor is that it has been adopted by the Angular team; and, since Angular is one of the most important frontend frameworks for the development of modern web applications with JavaScript, this has motivated many developers, who are migrating from Version 1.x of the AngularJS to Version 2/4/5/6, to learn it.

A simple reason for this is that the majority of Angular tutorials and examples are written in TypeScript.

1. Open `sample-01.ts` and add the following code, right after the `console.log()` function:

```
class MyClass {
  public static sum(x:number, y: number) {
  console.log('Number is: ', x + y);
  return x + y;
  }
}
MyClass.sum(3, 5);
```

2. Go back to your Terminal and type the following code:

```
tsc sample-01.ts
```

3. Now, when you open the `sample-01.js` file, you will see the results shown in the following screenshot:

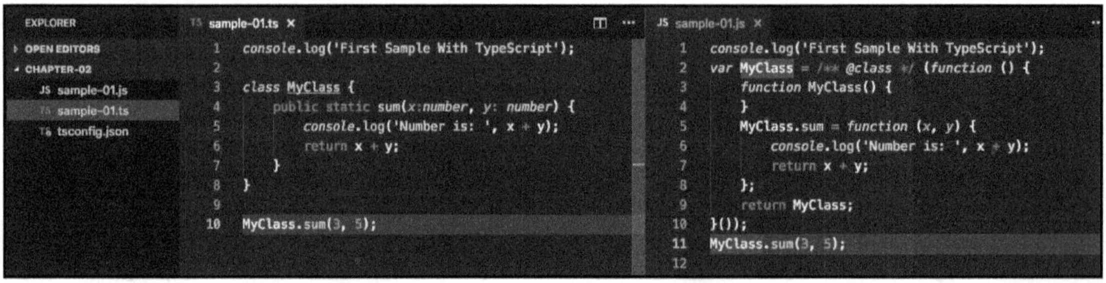

Comparing TypeScript with generated JavaScript

Note that the sum class parameters, (x:number, y:number), are given the type number. This is one of the advantages of TypeScript; however, as we are acting according to typing and using numbers within the function call MyClass.sum(3, 5), we cannot see its power.

Let's make a small change, and see the difference.

4. Change the MyClass.sum() function call to MyClass.sum('a', 5).

5. Go back to your Terminal and type the following command:

```
tsc sample-01.ts
```

Note that we receive a TypeScript error:

```
error TS2345: Argument of type '"a"' is not assignable to parameter
of type 'number'.
```

If you are using VS Code, you will see the message in the following screenshot, before you execute the command to compile the file:

Compiling error message

As previously mentioned, VS Code is a powerful editor for the TypeScript language; in addition to having an integrated Terminal, we are able to clearly see the compilation errors.

Instead of typing the same command every time, we can make some modifications to the TS file. We can use the `--watch` flag, and the compiler will run every change that we make to the file automatically.

6. In your Terminal, type the following command:

```
tsc sample-01.ts --watch
```

7. Now, let's fix it; go back to VS Code and replace the `MyClass.sum()` function with the following code:

```
MyClass.sum(5, 5);
```

To stop the TS compiler, just press *Ctrl + C*.

Writing JavaScript code with static types

The first thing that you'll notice when working with TypeScript are its static types, in addition to all of the JavaScript types, indicated on the following table:

Primitives	Objects
String	Function
Number	Array
Null	Prototypes
Undefined	
Boolean	
Symbol	

This means that you can declare the types of variables; it's pretty simple to assign a type to a variable. Let's look at some examples, using JavaScript types only:

```
function Myband () {
   let band: string;
   let active: boolean;
   let numberOfAlbuns: number;
}
```

With TypeScript, we have a few more types, as we'll see in the following sections.

Creating a tuple

A tuple is like an organized typed array. Let's create one to see how it works:

1. Inside the `chapter-02` folder, create a file called `tuple.ts`, and add the following code:

    ```
    const organizedArray: [number, string, boolean] = [0, 'text',
        false];
    let myArray: [number, string, boolean];
    myArray = ['text', 0, false]
    console.log(myArray);
    ```

    The preceding code looks fine for JavaScript, but in TypeScript, we must respect the variable type; here, we are trying to pass a string where we must pass a number.

2. In your Terminal, type the following command:

```
tsc tuple.ts
```

You will see the following error message:

```
tuple.ts(4,1): error TS2322: Type '[string, number, false]' is not
assignable to type '[number, string, boolean]'.
 Type 'string' is not assignable to type 'number'.
```

 In VS Code, you will see the error message before you compile your file. This is a very helpful feature.

When we fix it with the right order (`myArray = [0, 'text', false]`), the error message disappears.

It's also possible to create a tuple type and use it to assign a variable, as we can see in the next example.

3. Go back to your Terminal and add the following code to the `tuple.ts` file:

```
// using tuple as Type
type Tuple = [number, string, boolean];
let myTuple: Tuple;
myTuple = [0, 'text', false];
console.log(myTuple);
```

At this point, you may be wondering why the previous examples have a `console.log` output.

With the help of Node.js, which we installed previously, we can run the examples and view the output of the `console.log()` function.

4. Inside the Terminal, type the following command:

```
node tuple.js
```

 Note that you will need to run the JavaScript version, as in the previous example. If you try to run the TypeScript file directly, you will probably receive an error message.

Using the void type

In TypeScript, it is mandatory to define the type of the return of a function. When we have a function that does not have a return, we use a type called `void`.

Let's see how it works:

Create a new file called `void.ts` inside the `chapter-02` folder, and add the following code:

```
function myVoidExample(firstName: string, lastName: string): string {
    return firstName + lastName;
}
console.log(myVoidExample('Jhonny ', 'Cash'));
```

In the preceding code, everything is OK, because our function returns a value. If we remove the return function, we will see the following error message:

```
void.ts(1,62): error TS2355: A function whose declared type is neither
'void' nor 'any' must return a value.
```

In VS Code, you would see the following:

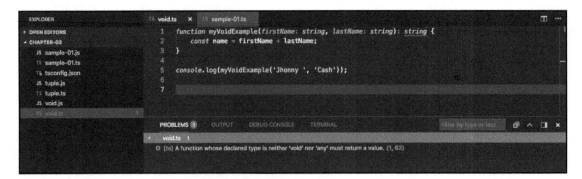

VS Code output error

To fix it, replace the type `string` with `void`:

```
function myVoidExample(firstName: string, lastName: string): void {
const name = firstName + lastName;
}
```

This is very useful, because our functions do not always return a value. But remember, we cannot declare `void` in functions that *do* return a value.

The opt-out type checking - any

The `any` type is very useful when we do not know what to expect from a function (in other words, when we do not know which type we are going to return):

1. Create a new file called `any.ts` inside the `chapter-02` folder, and add the following code:

```
let band: any;
band = {
    name: "Motorhead",
    description: "Heavy metal band",
    rate: 10
}
console.log(band);
band = "Motorhead";
console.log(band);
```

Note that the first `band` assignment is an object, while the second is a string.

2. Go back to your Terminal and compile and run this piece of code; type the following command:

```
tsc any.ts
```

3. Now, let's see the output. Type the following command:

```
node any.js
```

You will see the following message in the Terminal:

```
{ name: 'Motorhead', description: 'Heavy metal band', rate: 10 }
Motorhead
```

Here, we can assign *anything* to our band variable.

Using enum

enum allows us to group values with more intuitive names. Some people prefer to call the enumerated list and some other names. Let's look at an example, so as to make it easier to understand how this works in practice:

1. Create a file called enum.js in the chapter-02 folder, and add the following code:

```
enum bands {
    Motorhead,
    Metallica,
    Slayer
}
console.log(bands);
```

2. In your Terminal, type the following command to transpile the file:

```
tsc enum.ts
```

3. Now, let's execute the file. Type the following command:

```
node enum.js
```

You will see the following result in the Terminal:

```
{ '0': 'Motorhead',
  '1': 'Metallica',
  '2': 'Slayer',
  Motorhead: 0,
  Metallica: 1,
  Slayer: 2 }
```

We can now get the value by using the name instead of the position.

4. Add the following lines of code, right after the console.log() function:

```
let myFavoriteBand = bands.Slayer;
console.log(myFavoriteBand);
```

Now, execute the commands in *steps 2* and *step 3* to check the results. You will see the following output in the Terminal:

```
{ '0': 'Motorhead',
  '1': 'Metallica',
  '2': 'Slayer',
  Motorhead: 0,
```

```
      Metallica: 1,
      Slayer: 2 }
  My Favorite band is:   Slayer
```

Note that all of the values (band names) declared in the `band` object are converted into strings, inside an indexed object, as you can see in the preceding example.

Using the never type

The never type was introduced in TypeScript 2.0; it implies a value that never occurs. At first glance, it may seem strange, but it can be used in some situations.

Let's look at what the official documentation says about it:

 The `never` type represents the types of values that never occur. Specifically, never is the return type for functions that never return, and never is the type for variables under `type` guards that are never true.

Suppose that a messaging function that is called within another function specifies the callback.

It would look something like the following code:

```
const myMessage = (text: string): never => {
    throw new Error(text);
}
const myError = () => Error('Some text here');
```

Another example would be checking a value that is a string and number at the same time, such as the following:

```
function neverHappen(someVariable: any) {
    if (typeof someVariable === "string" && typeof someVariable ===
    "number") {
    console.log(someVariable);
    }
}
neverHappen('text');
```

Types: undefined and null

In TypeScript, `undefined` and `null` are types themselves; this means that undefined is a type (`undefined`) and null is a type (`null`). Confusing? undefined and null cannot be type variables; they can only be assigned as values to variables.

They are also different: a null variable means that a variable was set to null, while an undefined variable has no value assigned.

```
let A = null;
    console.log(A) // null
    console.log(B) // undefined
```

Understanding interfaces, classes, and generics in TypeScript

Object-Oriented Programming (OOP) is a very old programming concept, used in languages such as Java, C#, and many others.

One of the advantages of using TypeScript is being able to bring some of these concepts into your JavaScript web applications. In addition to being able to use classes, interfaces, and more, we can easily extend import classes and import modules, as we will see in the coming examples.

We know that using classes in pure JavaScript is already an option, with the use of ECMAScript 5. Although it is similar, there are some differences; we will not address them in this chapter, so that we do not confuse our readers. We will only focus on the implementations adopted in TypeScript.

Creating a class

The best way to understand classes in TypeScript is to create one. A simple class looks like the following code:

```
class Band {
    public name: string;
    constructor(text: string) {
    this.name = text;
    }
}
```

Let's create our first class:

1. Open your text editor and create a new file, called `my-first-class.ts`, and add the following code:

```typescript
class MyBand {
    // Properties without prefix are public
    // Available is; Private, Protected
    albums: Array<string>;
    members: number;
    constructor(albums_list: Array<string>, total_members: number)
{
        this.albums = albums_list;
        this.members = total_members;
    }
    // Methods
    listAlbums(): void {
        console.log("My favorite albums: ");
        for(var i = 0; i < this.albums.length; i++) {
            console.log(this.albums[i]);
        }
    }
}
// My Favorite band and his best albums
let myFavoriteAlbums = new MyBand(["Ace of Spades", "Rock and
Roll", "March or Die"], 3);
// Call the listAlbums method.
console.log(myFavoriteAlbums.listAlbums());
```

We added some comments to the previous code to facilitate understanding.

A class can have as many methods as necessary. In the case of the previous class, we gave only one method, to list our favorite band albums. You can test this piece of code on your Terminal, passing any information that you want inside the new `MyBand()` constructor.

This is pretty simple, and if you've had some contact with Java, C#, or even PHP, you will have already seen this class structure.

Here, we can apply the inheritance (OOP) principle to our class. Let's see how to do it:

2. Open the `band-class.ts` file and add the following code, right after the `console.log()` function:

```typescript
////////// using inheritance with TypeScript ///////////
class MySinger extends MyBand {
```

```
        // All Properties from MyBand Class are available inherited
here
        // So we define a new constructor.
        constructor(albums_list: Array<string>, total_members: number)
{
            // Call the parent's constructor using super keyword.
            super(albums_list, total_members);
        }
        listAlbums(): void{
            console.log("Singer best albums:");
            for(var i = 0; i < this.albums.length; i++) {
                console.log(this.albums[i]);
            }
        }
}
// Create a new instance of the YourBand class.
let singerFavoriteAlbum = new MySinger(["At Falson Prision", "Among
out the Stars", "Heroes"], 1);
console.log(singerFavoriteAlbum.listAlbums());
```

In Angular, classes are very useful for defining components, as we will see in the `Chapter 3`, *Understand the core concepts of Angular 6*.

Declaring an interface

Interfaces are our allies when we use TypeScript, since they do not exist in pure JavaScript. They are an efficient way of grouping and typing variables, ensuring that they are always together, maintaining consistent code.

Let's look at a practical way to declare and use an interface:

1. In your text editor, create a new file called `band-interface.ts`, and add the following code:

```
interface Band {
    name: string,
    total_members: number
}
```

To use it, assign the interface to a function type, as in the following example.

2. Add the following code right after the interface code, in the `band-interface.ts` file:

```
interface Band {
    name: string,
    total_members: number
}
function unknowBand(band: Band): void {
    console.log("This band: " + band.name + ", has: " +
band.total_members + " members");
}
```

Note that here, we are using the `Band` interface to type our `function` parameter. So, when we try to use it, we need to keep the same structure in new objects, as in the following example:

```
// create a band object with the same properties from Band interface:
let newband = {
    name: "Black Sabbath",
    total_members: 4
}
console.log(unknowBand(newband));
```

> Note that you can execute all of the sample files by typing the command `tsc band-interface.ts` and the `band-interface.js` node in your Terminal.

So, if you follow the preceding tip, you will see the same result in your Terminal window:

```
This band: Black Sabbath, has: 4 members
```

As you can see, the interfaces in TypeScript are incredible; we can do a lot of things with them. Throughout the course of this book, we will look at some more examples of using interfaces in real web applications.

Creating generic functions

Generics are a very useful way of creating flexible classes and functions. They are very similar to those used in C#. It's very useful to be used in more than one place.

We can create generic functions by adding angle brackets after the function names and enclosing datatypes, as in the following example:

```
function genericFunction<T>( arg: T ): T [] {
    let myGenericArray: T[] = [];
    myGenericArray.push(arg);
    return myGenericArray;
}
```

Note that the t inside the angle brackets (<t>) means that genericFunction() is of the generic type.

Let's see this in practice:

1. In your code editor, create a new file called generics.ts, and add the following code:

```
function genericFunction<T>( arg: T ): T [] {
    let myGenericArray: T[] = [];
    myGenericArray.push(arg);
    return myGenericArray;
}
let stringFromGenericFunction = genericFunction<string>("Some
string goes here");
console.log(stringFromGenericFunction[0]);
let numberFromGenericFunction = genericFunction(190);
console.log(numberFromGenericFunction[0]);
```

Let's see what happens with our generic function.

2. Go back to your Terminal and type the following command:

```
tsc generics.ts
```

3. Now, let's execute the file with the following command:

```
node generics.js
```

We will see the following result:

```
Some string goes here
190
```

Note that the compiler is able to identify the datatype that we are passing as the function argument. In the first case, we explicitly pass the argument as a string, and in the second case, we pass nothing.

Although the compiler is able to identify the type of argument that we are using, it is important to always determine what kind of data we are going to pass. For example:

```
let numberFromGenericFunction = genericFunction<number>(190);
console.log(numberFromGenericFunction[0]);
```

Working with modules

Modules are very important when developing large-scale applications with TypeScript. They allow us to import and export code, classes, interfaces, variables, and functions. These functions are extremely common in applications with Angular.

However, they can only be accomplished by using a library, which could be Require.js for the browser, or Common.js for Node.js.

In the following sections, we will illustrate how we can use these features in practice.

Using the class export feature

Any declaration can be exported, as we mentioned previously; to do so, we just need to add the export keyword. In the following example, we will export the band class.

In your text editor, create a file called export.ts, and add the following code:

```
export class MyBand {
    // Properties without prefix are public
    // Available is; Private, Protected
    albums: Array<string>;
    members: number;
    constructor(albums_list: Array<string>, total_members: number) {
        this.albums = albums_list;
        this.members = total_members;
    }
    // Methods
    listAlbums(): void {
        console.log("My favorite albums: ");
        for(var i = 0; i < this.albums.length; i++) {
            console.log(this.albums[i]);
        }
    }
}
```

We will now have our Myband class available to be imported into another file.

Importing and using external classes

An import can be accomplished with the keyword `import`, and can be declared in different ways, depending on what library you are using. An example of using Require.js is as follows:

- Go back to your text editor, create a file called `import.ts`, and add the following code:

```
import MyBand = require('./export');
console.log(Myband());
```

An example of using Common.js is as follows:

```
import { MyBand } from './export';
console.log(new Myband(['ZZ Top', 'Motorhead'], 3));
```

- The second method has been adopted by the Angular team, because Angular uses Webpack, a module bundler building modern web applications.

Summary

In this chapter, you saw the basic principles of TypeScript. We merely scratched the surface, but we provided you with a solid base for handling Angular applications using TypeScript.

Throughout the course of this book, we will enhance your understanding as we advance with the creation of a web application.

3
Understanding the Core Concepts of Angular 6

The Angular framework has become one of the most popular tools, around the world for the development of frontend applications. In addition to being very versatile (and very different from other libraries, such as `React.js` or `Vue.js`, which serve only one purpose), Angular is a complete framework and, with the new updates for Angular 6, we now have more resources available for creating amazing and fast web applications. In addition, the team behind Angular proposes two major updates annually.

Another strong point in favor of Angular is its inclusion of the Angular **command-line interface** (**CLI**) for creating web applications. This provides us with extra power; with a simple command in the Terminal, we can create our application's boilerplate code very quickly and easily. However, everything is not quite as sweet as we would like it to be, so we need to understand the basic concepts of Angular and know how to avoid some of the issues in our way. This is easily resolved by adopting a mental model of development, based on components and modules. In the following examples, we will carefully create the basic structure of a scalable and modular project.

In this chapter, we will cover the following topics:

- Angular 6 – smaller, faster, and easier
- Angular and the component method for developing modern web applications
- Installing the tools: Git, the Angular CLI, HTTP server, and VS Code plugins
- Creating a simple Angular app
- Simple deployment

Angular 6 – smaller, faster, and easier

The following features are not exclusively for version 6, but were included from version 5; we are just mentioning them here because they are powerful features for building modern web applications:

- **Webpack**: You can now generate smaller modules by using the scope hosting technique.
- You can reduce bundle sizes for common use cases by using the RxJS 6 library for JavaScript.
- The Angular CLI, allowing for commands such as `ng` update, can be used to update all dependencies.
- You will have the option to start your application using Angular material design.
- The `ng add` command supports creating progressive web applications or turning an existing one into a **Progressive Web Application** (**PWA**).
- You will have the opportunity to use Bazel to build your application's libraries and to share libraries with other teams.
- Angular makes it possible to package custom HTML/JavaScript elements for use in third-party applications.

 You can read more about Bazel at `https://bazel.build/`.

Of course, there are many other improvements and features in the Angular 6 release; note that this book was written on the Angular 6 beta 7 version, and the next chapters will have more news about the current Angular version.

Angular and the component method for developing modern web applications

Angular components are similar to web components; they are used to compose web pages, or even other components. There can be dozens of components in a web application.

Components define views and templates, and they belong to a module within an application; every application has, at the very least, a root module, named by the Angular CLI as `AppModule.ts`.

The `app.module.ts` file contains all of the bootstrap code and configurations for an Angular application, as you can see in the following block of code:

```
import { NgModule } from '@angular/core';

@NgModule({
  declarations: [
    AppComponent
  ],
  imports: [],
  providers: [],
  bootstrap: [AppComponent]
})
export class AppModule { }
```

The preceding code is the most basic configuration of an Angular application; we import the `NgModule` from the Angular core library and use it as a decorator: `@NgModule`.

Both components and services are simply classes, with decorators that mark their types and provide metadata that tells Angular how to use them.

 You can read more about web components at `https://www.webcomponents.org/introduction`.

Angular's main building blocks

Every application created using the Angular framework has five very important points that connect to each other and establish the basic architecture of the application:

- **Modules**: Using the decorator `@NgModule`
- **Services**: Using the decorator `@Injectable`
- **Components**: Using the decorator `@component`
- **Templates**: Views with `data-bind` and directives
- **Routes**: Setting URL path to views

Let's look at a simple blog page as an Angular application, built with components:

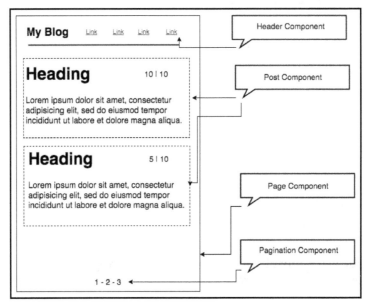

Angular components

The preceding diagram illustrates how components can be used to build a simple application.

A comparison between the preceding diagram and the five basic concepts of an Angular application would look as follows:

- One module: `blog.module.ts`
- A page component: `blog.component.ts`
- A route to the blog page
- A service to load the blog posts

There are also some additional components, such as **Header**, **Post,** and **Pagination.**

Note that the Header component belongs to the main module of the application (in this case, the `AppModule`), and the Post and Pagination components are part of the `BlogModule`.

As we move through this chapter, we will look more closely at the relationship between modules and components. Now, we will look at the life cycle of a component.

The component life cycle

In the life cycle of an Angular component, after instantiating, the component runs a definite path of execution from its beginning until its end. The most basic way to understand this is through observing the following code:

```
export class HelloComponent implements OnInit, OnDestroy {
    constructor() { }

    ngOnInit() {
... Some code goes here
}
ngOnDestroy() {
... Some code goes here
}
}
```

In the preceding example, you can see methods called ngOnInit() and ngOnDestroy; the names are very intuitive, and show us that we have a beginning and an end. The ngOnInit() method is implemented through its OnInit interface, and the same goes for the ngOnDestroy() method. As you saw in the previous chapter, the interfaces in TypeScript are very useful – it's not any different here.

In the following diagram, we will look at the main interfaces that we can implement on a component. In the diagram, after the Constructor() method, there are eight interfaces (also known as hooks); each one is responsible for one thing, at a specific moment:

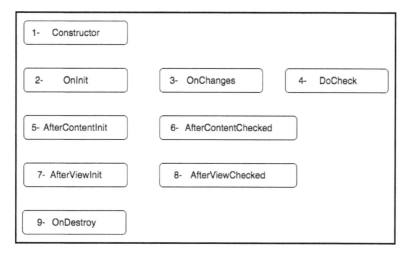

Angular component life cycle

You can learn more about each interface in the official Angular documentation at `https://angular.io/guide/lifecycle-hooks`.

We will not describe the interfaces one by one in this chapter, so as not to overload you, but, throughout the course of the book, we will use them in the application that we will build. Also, the preceding link includes detailed information about each interface and hook.

Installing the tools – Git, the Angular CLI, and VS Code plugins

From this chapter to the end of the book, we will adopt the VS Code text editor – it is free, lightweight, and very powerful for creating web applications.

Also, it is very important to use a version control system for the source code; this will help us to track all of the changes in our code base.

Next, we will introduce Git source control.

Installing Git

As a simple and quick introduction to Git, we can describe it as follows.

Git is a file version control system. By using it, we can develop projects to which many people can simultaneously contribute, editing and creating new files, allowing them to exist without the risk of their changes being overwritten.

A very common case when using Git is to also use a service in the cloud (such as GitHub or Bitbucket), to store the code, so that we can share it.

In addition, almost all open source projects (frameworks and libraries) are in GitHub today. So you can contribute by reporting bugs, or even sending codes and suggestions.

If you are a developer and do not yet have GitHub, you are late – this is the time to start using it. So, let's install Git.

Go to `https://git-scm.com/downloads` and download and install Git for your platform.

After installing, open your Terminal and type the following command:

```
git --version
```

You must see the current version installed on your system.

Also, the `git help` command is very useful, listing all of the commands available.

 You can read more about Git basics at `https://git-scm.com/book/en/v2/Getting-Started-Git-Basics`.

Installing the Angular CLI

In the world of frameworks, regardless of the language, we often find tools that can help us with day-to-day software development, especially when there are repetitive tasks.

The Angular CLI is a command-line interface for creating, developing, and maintaining Angular applications in a very productive way. It is an open source tool developed by the Angular team itself.

With the use of the Angular CLI, we are able to create the entire base structure of an Angular application, as well as the modules, components, directives, services, and more. It has its own server for development and helps us with the application build.

Now, it's time to install it:

1. Open your Terminal and type the following command:

   ```
   npm install -g @angular/cli@latest
   ```

   After the installation, you will see the following output in your Terminal:

   ```
   + @angular/cli@1.7.3 added 314 packages, removed 203 packages,
   updated 170 packages and moved 7 packages in 123.346s
   ```

   The number of packages removed and updated and the Angular CLI version may be different. Don't worry.

2. You can remove your old version of the Angular CLI and install the latest version with the following commands:

```
npm uninstall -g angular-cli
npm cache verify
npm install -g @angular/cli@latest
```

If you experience some npm issues when you try to update your Angular CLI version on a Windows machine, you can check https://docs.npmjs. com/troubleshooting/try-the-latest-stable-version-of-npm#upgrading-on-windows for information.

Note that the preceding command will install the Angular CLI globally on your environment/machine. Frequently, when we develop using the Angular framework and the Angular CLI, we see warning messages about the differences between versions. This means that, even if you have installed the latest version of the Angular CLI in your environment, the Angular CLI will check the version used in the current project and compare it to the version installed on your machine, and will use the current project version.

This is very useful when you work on third-party projects and need to keep dependencies consistency between the globally Angular CLI installed on your machine and the local project version installed on node_modules project folder.

3. Inside of your current Angular project, type the following commands:

```
rm -rf node_modules
npm uninstall --save-dev angular-cli
npm install --save-dev @angular/cli@latest
npm install
```

Like the other commands that we are using in our book, the Angular CLI has a command called ng help. With it, we can access a vast list of options.

One of these commands is particularly useful when we are developing applications with Angular and need to consult something in the official documentation, without leaving the Terminal.

4. Go back to your Terminal and type the following command:

```
ng doc HttpClient
```

The preceding command will open your default browser right at the `HttpClient` documentation API, using `https://angular.io/api?query=HttpClient`. So, you can combine the `ng doc` command with anything from the API that you want to search.

We now have everything we need to start developing web applications using the Angular CLI, but, before we get deeper into building a sample application, we're going to update our toolkit with some very useful tools.

Installing VS Code Angular plugins

As mentioned in the previous chapters, the VS Code text editor is a fantastic IDE for developing web applications using JavaScript and TypeScript, and the same goes for Angular.

In this section, we will look at some extensions (also called plugins) that can help us with our development.

Let's look at the package names and repository URLs:

- **Angular Language Service**: `https://github.com/angular/vscode-ng-language-service`. Provided by the official Angular team, this extension helps us with completions in template files and template strings, and diagnostics for templates and Angular annotations.
- **Angular v5 Snippets**: `https://github.com/johnpapa/vscode-angular-snippets`. The extension name is Angular v5; the GitHub project repository doesn't specify a name. So, we can expect snippets for future versions of Angular from the plugin author. This is a powerful tool that can help us to create almost everything within an Angular application; you can see the complete list in the GitHub repository.
- **Angular Support**: `https://github.com/VismaLietuva/vscode-angular-support`.

Go to and peek definition from:

```
interpolation {{ someVar }}
input [(...)]="someVar"
output (...)="someMethod"
templateUrl or styleUrls in @Component decorator
component <some-component></some-component>
```

Last but not least, we recommend that you use the GitLens plugin. This extension is extremely important, because it helps us to visualize our code in the Git repository, while also providing integration with GitHub or Bitbucket.

- **GitLens**: `https://github.com/eamodio/vscode-gitlens`.

    Supercharge the Git capabilities built into Visual Studio Code.
    – Gitlens

    - You can explore the navigation for repositories and file histories
    - You can also explore commits and visualize comparisons between branches, tags, and commits
    - There is an authorship code lens, showing the most recent commits and number of authors to the top of files and/or on code blocks
- **GitLens Plugin**: `https://gitlens.amod.io/`. This extension is extremely important, because it helps us to visualize our code in the Git repository, while also providing integration with GitHub or Bitbucket.

Also, it's possible to install any extension through the IDE itself. To do that, follow these steps:

    1. Open VS Code.

2. Click on the last icon on the left-hand sidebar; you can see it in the following screenshot:

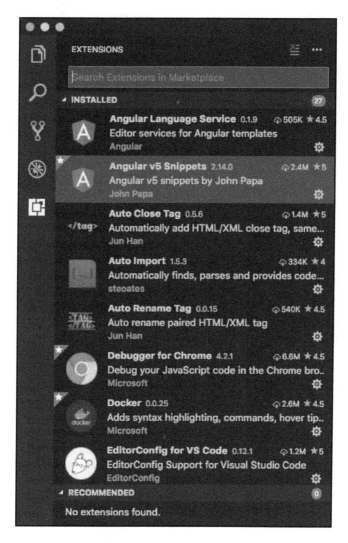

VS Code extension installation

Just type what you want to search for in the search input field, and click **install**.

We now have everything we need to start developing Angular applications. In the next section, we will look at how to create an Angular application using the Angular CLI.

Creating a simple Angular application

In this chapter, we will cover all of the main points for the development of web applications using the Angular framework and the Angular CLI. Now, it's time to get in touch with the code and develop an application from start to finish.

In this example project, we will develop a simple frontend application to consume the data of an API and display it on the screen – something like a simple blog. Open your Terminal and type the following command:

```
ng new chapter03 --routing
```

Note that the `--routing` flag is optional, but, since our next example will use routes, it is a good practice to start an application with that flag. After the Angular CLI has installed, you should see the following message on your Terminal:

```
Testing binary
Binary is fine
added 1384 packages in 235.686s
You can `ng set --global packageManager=yarn`.
Project 'chapter03' successfully created.
```

The structure of an Angular application

Now that we have created our application, let's examine some important files. Although these files have already been set up and and are ready for use, we often need to add settings, and even other modules, in real-world applications.

Open the `chapter03` folder in VS Code; you will see the following screen in the VS Code **explore** tab:

Angular project structure

So, inside the `/src/app` folder, we have the five main blocks of an Angular application, except for the service (which we will see soon):

`app.routing.module.ts`	Route
`app.component.css`	Style sheet
`app.component.html`	Template
`app.component.spec.ts`	Test
`app.component.ts`	@Component
`app.module.ts`	@NgModule

The package.json file

The `package.json` file is very common in web applications that use Node.js modules. It is often found in frontend applications nowadays, in addition to server-side applications with Node.js. With the Angular framework, it is not different; this is one of the great advantages of the new version of Angular, since we can only import modules that are extremely necessary for the application, reducing the size and build time. Let's look at the contents of the `package.json` file. We added some comments before each important section:

```
{
"name": "chapter03",
"version": "0.0.0",
"license": "MIT",
// Npm commands, based on Angular/Cli commands, including: test and
build.
"scripts": {
"ng": "ng",
"start": "ng serve",
"build": "ng build --prod",
"test": "ng test",
"lint": "ng lint",
"e2e": "ng e2e"
  },
"private": true,
// Dependencies to work in production, including:
@angular/core, @angular/common, @angular/route and many more.
"dependencies":{
...
},
// Dependencies only in development environment, including modules for
test, TypeScript version, Angular/Cli installed locally and others.
"devDependencies": {
...
}
}
```

This file is automatically changed when we install a new module. And, we often add some commands inside the tag scripts, as you will see in the next chapters. You can read more about the `package.json` file in the official npm documentation at `https://docs.npmjs.com/files/package.json`.

Dotfiles – .editorconfig, .gitignore, and .angular-cli.json

Dotfiles are the configuration files that start with a dot; they are always in the background of the project, but they are very important. They are used to customize your system. The name dotfiles is derived from the configuration files in Unix-like systems. In an Angular project, we will see three of these files:

- `.editorconfig`: This file configures the text editor to use a particular style of code, so that the project is consistent, even though it is being edited by several people and in several types of text editors.
- `.gitignore`: As the name suggests, it ignores determined folders and files, so that they are not tracked by source control. We often find `node_modules` and a `dist` folder that do not require version control, because they are generated every time we install the application or run build commands.
- `.angular-cli.json`: Stores the project settings and is constantly used when executing build or server commands. There can be several Angular applications in a single project. Let's look at some details and inspect `.angular-cli.json`:

```
{
    "$schema":
"./node_modules/@angular/cli/lib/config/schema.json",
    "project": {
    "name": "chapter03"
    },
    // Here we determinate the projects, for this example we have
only one app.
    "apps": [
    {
    "root": "src",
    "outDir": "dist",
    "assets": [
    "assets",
    "favicon.ico"
    ],
    "index": "index.html",
    "main": "main.ts",
    "polyfills": "polyfills.ts",
    "test": "test.ts",
```

```
    "tsconfig": "tsconfig.app.json",
    "testTsconfig": "tsconfig.spec.json",
    "prefix": "app",
    "styles": [
    "styles.css"
    ],
    "scripts": [],
    "environmentSource": "environments/environment.ts",
    // Configuration for both environment, developing and
production
    "environments": {
    "dev": "environments/environment.ts",
    "prod": "environments/environment.prod.ts"
    }
    }
    ],
    // Configuration for end to end tests and unit tests
    "e2e": {
    "protractor": {
    "config": "./protractor.conf.js"
    }
    },
    "lint": [
    {
    "project": "src/tsconfig.app.json",
    "exclude": "**/node_modules/**"
    },
    {
    "project": "src/tsconfig.spec.json",
    "exclude": "**/node_modules/**"
    },
    {
    "project": "e2e/tsconfig.e2e.json",
    "exclude": "**/node_modules/**"
    }
    ],
    "test": {
    "karma": {
    "config": "./karma.conf.js"
    }
    },
    // Stylesheet configigiration, for this example we are using CSS
    "defaults": {
    "styleExt": "css",
    "component": {}
    }
    }
```

Environments

Inside of the `src/environments` folder, we find two configuration files. One is called `environment.prod.ts`, and the other is `environment.ts`. The Angular CLI will know what to use, depending on the command that we use; for example, consider the following command:

```
ng build --env = prod
```

If we use it, then Angular will use the `environment.prod.ts` file, and, for the other commands, such as `ng serve`, it will use `environment.ts`. This is very useful, especially when we have a local API and one in `production`, using different paths.

Both files have almost the same code; see `environment.prod.ts`, as follows:

```
export const environment = {
    production: true
};
```

The `environment.ts` file is as follows:

```
export const environment = {
    production: false
};
```

Note that the Boolean `true` (on production) and `false` (on development) is the only difference between the two files, at this first stage. It is clear that, in addition to the files that we mentioned, we have a lot of other files within an Angular application, and all of them are extremely important. But, for now, let's focus on these. Don't worry; throughout the course of the book, we will look at more of them in detail, during the development of our example application. For now, we are going to focus on creating the simple example that we are using in this chapter.

Running the sample application

Now that we have started our project, we will run the built-in Angular CLI server to see how our application looks:

1. Open VS Code in the project root to the `chapter03` folder.
2. For this example, we will use the integrated Terminal for the code; for this, click on the top menu in `view`, and then click `Integrated Terminal`.

3. Type the following command in the Terminal:

```
npm start
```

You will see a message similar to the following:

```
** NG Live Development Server is listening on localhost:4200, open
your
browser on http://localhost:4200/ **
Date: xxxx
Hash: xxxx
Time: 16943ms
chunk {inline} inline.bundle.js (inline) 3.85 kB [entry]
[rendered]
chunk {main} main.bundle.js (main) 20.8 kB [initial] [rendered]
chunk {polyfills} polyfills.bundle.js (polyfills) 549 kB [initial]
[rendered]
chunk {styles} styles.bundle.js (styles) 41.5 kB [initial]
[rendered]
chunk {vendor} vendor.bundle.js (vendor) 8.45 MB [initial]
[rendered]
```

4. Behind the scenes, the Angular CLI will use the webpack module manager. Later in this book, you will see how to export and customize the webpack file.

5. Now, go to `http://localhost:4200` and check the result; you will see the welcome page from the boilerplate application that we created previously. You can find the code behind this page at `src/app/app.component.html` – it's our template.

Now, it's time to add a new module to our application.

Adding a new module

In this example, we will, so that you can see how to build applications using the Angular CLI. Even in this very basic example, we will cover the following points:

- How to organize an Angular application
- Creating modules
- Creating services
- Template data binding
- Running an application in production

Now, let's create a module that shows us a list of beers:

1. Open VS Code, and, inside the integrated Terminal, type the following command:

    ng g module beers

    Note that the command ng g module is a shortcut to ng generate module <module-name>, and this command just creates the module; we need to add routes, components, and templates, and also import the beers module in app.modules.ts, at the root of the app folder. The preceding command will generate the following structure and file content inside of our project: src/app/beers/beers.module.ts. The beers.module.ts contents are as follows:

    ```
    import { NgModule } from '@angular/core';
    import { CommonModule } from '@angular/common';
        @NgModule({
        imports: [
        CommonModule
        ],
        declarations: []
        })
    export class BeersModule { }
    ```

    This is a pretty simple boilerplate code, but it is very useful. Now, we will add the missing pieces.

2. Add the beers module to your app module; open app.module.ts and replace the code with the following lines:

    ```
    import { BrowserModule } from '@angular/platform-browser';
    import { NgModule } from '@angular/core';
    import { HttpClientModule } from '@angular/common/http';
    import { AppRoutingModule } from './app-routing.module';
    import { AppComponent } from './app.component';
    import { BeersModule } from './beers/beers.module';
        @NgModule({
        declarations: [
            AppComponent
        ],
        imports: [
        BrowserModule,
        AppRoutingModule,
        HttpClientModule,
        BeersModule
    ```

```
    ],
    providers: [],
    bootstrap: [AppComponent]
})
export class AppModule { }
```

Note that we imported `BeersModule` and added it to the `imports` array.

Adding a new component

Now, we need a component to show a list of beers, since we just created a module called `Beers`.

Later, you will see how to use an API and an Angular service to load a list of beers; for now, we will focus on the creation of our component.

Inside of the root folder, and with the integrated VS Code Terminal, type the following command:

```
ng g component beers
```

The preceding command will generate the following structure:

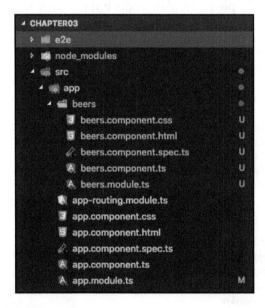

The `BeersModule` and `Component` files have been created. We now have our module, template, and component file. Let's add a new route.

Adding a new route

As you saw previously, routes are part of every web application. Now, we will add a new route, so that we can access the content of our `beers` module. Open `src/app/app-routing.module.ts` and replace the code with the following:

```
import { NgModule } from '@angular/core';
import { Routes, RouterModule } from '@angular/router';
import { AppComponent } from './app.component';
import { BeersComponent } from './beers/beers.component';
const routes: Routes = [
    { path: '', redirectTo: 'beers', pathMatch: 'full' },
    { path: 'beers', component: BeersComponent }
];
@NgModule({
    imports: [RouterModule.forRoot(routes)],
    exports: [RouterModule]
})
export class AppRoutingModule { }
```

Note that we are just adding the new route to an existing route file (in this case, `app.routing.module.ts`), as this example is extremely simple. But, in larger applications, it is recommended that you create individual route files for each application module.

Creating an Angular service

Angular services are used to handle data; it can be internal data (from one component to another) or something external, such as communicating with an API endpoint. Almost all frontend applications with JavaScript frameworks use this technique. In Angular, we call this a service, and we use some modules built into the Angular framework to complete the task: `HttpClient` and `HttpClientModule`.

Let's look at how the Angular CLI can help us:

1. Open VS Code, and, inside the integrated Terminal, type the following command:

   ```
   ng g service beers/beers
   ```

   The previous command will generate two new files in the `beers` folder:

   `beers.service.spec.ts` and `beers.service.ts`.

2. Add the newly created `Service` as a dependency provider to `beers.module.ts`. Open `src/app/beers/beers.module.ts` and add the following lines:

   ```
   import { BeersService } from './beers.service';
   @NgModule({
       providers: [BeersService]
   })
   ```

   In VS Code, we have import module support, so, when you start to type the module's name, you will see the following help screen:

```
1   import { NgModule } from '@angular/core';
2   import { CommonModule } from '@angular/common';
3   import { BeersComponent } from './beers.component';
4
5
6   @NgModule({
7     imports: [
8       CommonModule          NgModule(obj?: NgModule): TypeDecorator
9     ],
10    declarations: [Be     Defines an NgModule.
11    providers: [Beers]
12  })                    ⊛ BeersComponent          [AI] import BeersService (Auto-Impo ×
13  export class Beer ⚛ BeersComponent          rt)
14                    ⚛ BeersComponent
                      ⚛ BeersModule            [AI] Import BeersService from ./beers.service
                      ⚛ BeersModule
                      ⚛ BeersModule
                      ⚛ BeersModule
                      ⚛ BeersModule
                      ⚛ BeersService
                      ⚛ BeersService
                      ⊛ Z_BEST_COMPRESSION
                      ☐ ELEMENT_PROBE_PROVIDERS
```

The final `beers.module.ts` code will look as follows:

```
import { NgModule } from '@angular/core';
import { CommonModule } from '@angular/common';
import { BeersComponent } from './beers.component';
import { BeersService } from './beers.service';
@NgModule({
    imports: [
        CommonModule
    ],
    declarations: [BeersComponent],
    providers: [BeersService
    ]
})
export class BeersModule { }
```

Now, it's time to connect with an API using a service. To get as close to a real application as possible, we'll use a public API in this example. In the next steps, we will effectively create our service and add data binding to our template.

For this example, we will use the free `https://punkapi.com/` API:

1. Open `beers.service.ts` and replace the code with the following lines:

```
import { Injectable } from '@angular/core';
import { HttpClient, HttpHeaders, HttpErrorResponse } from
'@angular/common/http';
import { Observable } from 'rxjs/Observable';
import 'rxjs/add/observable/throw';
import { catchError } from 'rxjs/operators';
@Injectable()
export class BeersService {
    private url = 'https://api.punkapi.com/v2/beers?';
    constructor(private http: HttpClient) { }
/**
* @param {page} {perpage} Are Page number and items per page
*
* @example
* service.get(1, 10) Return Page 1 with 10 Items
*
* @returns List of beers
*/
    get(page: number, per_page: number) {
        return this.http.get(this.url + 'page=' + page +
         '&per_page=' + per_page)
        .pipe(catchError(error => this.handleError(error)));
    }
```

```
        private handleError(error: HttpErrorResponse) {
            return Observable.throw(error);
        }
    }
```

Now, we need to tell the component that we need to use this service to load the data and transmit it to our template.

2. Open `src/app/beers/beers.component.ts` and replace the code with the following:

```
import { Component, OnInit } from '@angular/core';
import { BeersService } from './beers.service';
@Component({
    selector: 'app-beers',
    templateUrl: './beers.component.html',
    styleUrls: ['./beers.component.css']
})
export class BeersComponent implements OnInit {
    public beersList: any [];
    public requestError: any;
    constructor(private beers: BeersService) { }
    ngOnInit() {
        this.getBeers();
    }
    /**
    * Get beers, page = 1, per_page= 10
    */
    public getBeers () {
        return this.beers.get(1, 20).subscribe(
            response => this.handleResponse(response),
            error => this.handleError(error)
        );
    }
    /**
    * Handling response
    */
    protected handleResponse (response: any) {
        this.requestError = null;
        return this.beersList = response;
    }
    /**
    * Handling error
    */
    protected handleError (error: any) {
        return this.requestError = error;
    }
}
```

Template data binding

Now that we have a service that connects to an API endpoint and receives a JSON file, let's make some small changes to our views, known as templates in the Angular world. The templates are the HTML files inside of the `module` folder:

1. Open `src/app/app.component.html` and remove all of the code before the `<router-outlet></route-outlet>` tags.

2. Open `src/app/beers/beers.component.html` and add the following code, right after the `beers` works paragraph:

```
<div class="row">
    <div class="col" href="" *ngFor="let item of beersList">
        <figure>
            <img [src]="item.image_url" [alt]="item.name" />
        <figcaption>
            <h1>{{item.name}}</h1>
                <p>{{item.tagline}}</p>
        </figcaption>
        </figure>
    </div>
</div>
```

Note that we are using the curly brace template tags ({{}}) and a `*ngFor` directive to display our data. Let's look at some Angular data binding types:

```
{{ some.property }} One way Binding
[(ngModel)]="some.value" Two way Binding
(click)="showFunction($event)" Event Binding
```

3. Now, we need to add some style to `beers.component.html`; open `src/app/beers/beers.component.css` and add the following code:

```
body {
    margin: 40px;
}
.row {
    display: grid;
    grid-template-columns: 300px 300px 300px;
    grid-gap: 10px;
    background-color: #fff;
    color: #444;
}
.col {
    background-color: #d1d1d1;
    border-radius: 5px;
```

```
        padding: 10px;
    }
    figure {
        text-align: center;
    }
    img {
        height:250px;
    }
```

We are now very close to completing our example application. The last step is to build our application and see the final result.

Simple deployment

Now that we have everything ready, let's look at how to build our application.

First, we will look at the application after the changes have been made:

1. Open VS Code, click on **view** in the top menu bar, and click **Integrated Terminal**.
2. Type the following command in your Terminal:

   `npm start`

3. Open your default browser and go to http://localhost.com:4200/beers.
4. Congratulations; you should see the following screenshot:

Note that we are running the command for development, using `ng serve` behind the `npm start` command.

Now, let's use the command to build the application, and check the results:

1. Go back to VS Code and type *Ctrl + C* to stop the server.
2. Type the following command:

```
npm run build
```

The preceding command will prepare the application for production; the Angular CLI will do all of the hard work for us. Now, we have a folder at the root of `chapter03`, as shown in the following screenshot:

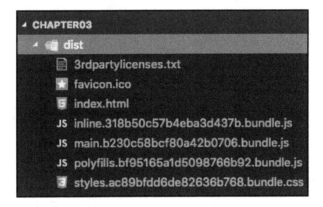

The dist folder

As you can see, all of our application is inside of this folder, as optimized as possible; however, to see the contents, we need a web server. In this example, we will use the `http-server` node package, a very useful Node.js module to make a particular directory on a simple web server. You can find more information about http-server at `https://www.npmjs.com/package/http-server`:

1. Go back to VS Code and the integrated Terminal, and type the following command:

```
npm install http-server -g
```

2. Still in the integrated Terminal, type the following command:

```
cd dist && http-server -p 8080
```

3. You will see the following message in your Terminal:

```
Starting up http-server, serving ./
Available on:
http://127.0.0.1:8080
http://192.168.25.6:8080
Hit CTRL-C to stop the server
```

This means that everything went well, and you can already access the contents of the dist folder in your browser.

4. Open your default browser and go to http://localhost.com:8080/beers.

We're done; now, let's save everything that we did within the chapter03 folder in our local repository, using some Git commands. This step is not required for the next chapters, but it is highly recommended.

5. Open your Terminal in the chapter03 folder and type the following command:

```
git add .git commit -m "chapter03 initial commit"
```

6. After the previous command, you will see the following output in your Terminal:

```
[master c7d7c18] chapter03 initial commit
10 files changed, 190 insertions(+), 24 deletions(-) rewrite
src/app/app.component.html (97%)
create mode 100644 src/app/beers/beers.component.css
create mode 100644 src/app/beers/beers.component.html
create mode 100644 src/app/beers/beers.component.spec.ts
create mode 100644 src/app/beers/beers.component.ts
create mode 100644 src/app/beers/beers.module.ts
create mode 100644 src/app/beers/beers.service.spec.ts
create mode 100644 src/app/beers/beers.service.ts
```

Summary

Well, we have reached the end of another chapter, and you should now understand how to create applications with Angular. In this chapter, we covered the main points that make Angular a powerful framework. You can download the code samples that we used in this chapter directly from GitHub, at https://github.com/PacktPublishing. In the next chapter, we will go deep inside the backend API.

4
Building the Baseline Backend Application

Now, we will start building the baseline of our application. In this chapter, we are going to create a Laravel application using the RESTful architecture. As we saw in the previous chapter, Laravel will provide us with the necessary infrastructure to build a solid and scalable application.

We will take a closer look at some points that we mentioned briefly in Chapter 1, *Understanding the Core Concepts of Laravel 5*, such as using Docker containers to configure our environment, and also how to keep our database always populated, even by using the MySQL Docker container.

As we mentioned before, it is entirely possible to use a different configuration for your development environment, and we mentioned some ways in Chapter 1, *Understanding the Core Concepts of Laravel 5.* However, we strongly recommend that you use Docker.

In this chapter, we will cover the following topics:

- Additional notes about Laravel with Docker
- Using PHP Composer to scaffold a Laravel application
- Setting up a MySQL database
- Migrations and database seed
- API documentation with the Swagger framework

Additional notes about Laravel with Docker

In this section, we will use the same infrastructure we created in Chapter 1, *Understanding the Core Concepts of Laravel 5*. Using the PHPDocker.io generator, we will customize it in order to understand a little more about what is happening inside the Docker container.

So, let's go into a more detailed explanation, and there's nothing better than getting our hands dirty.

Creating the Docker Compose foundation

First, we are going to create the foundation (Dockerfile, docker-compose) files for the application, different from the way we did in the first chapter. Instead, we will create the files manually, but based on the files we used in Chapter 1, *Understanding the Core Concepts of Laravel 5*.

Follow these steps:

1. Create a folder called chapter-04.
2. Inside the chapter-04 folder, create a folder called phpdocker.
3. Inside the phpdocker folder, add two folders, one called nginx, and another called php-fpm.

Configuring nginx

Now, it's time to create the configuration files for the nginx and php-fpm servers, so we will be using the nginx reverse proxy to serve our PHP files to the web.

Inside the nginx folder, create a new file called nginx.conf and add the following code:

```
server {
    listen 80 default;
    client_max_body_size 308M;
    access_log /var/log/nginx/application.access.log;
    root /application/public;
    index index.php;
    if (!-e $request_filename) {
        rewrite ^.*$ /index.php last;
    }
    location ~ \.php$ {
        fastcgi_pass php-fpm:9000;
        fastcgi_index index.php;
```

```
fastcgi_param SCRIPT_FILENAME
 $document_root$fastcgi_script_name;
fastcgi_param PHP_VALUE
 "error_log=/var/log/nginx/application_php_errors.log";
fastcgi_buffers 16 16k;
fastcgi_buffer_size 32k;
include fastcgi_params;
    }
  }
```

The previous file set port 80 as the default port for our web server and set port 9000 to php-fpm, which means that our containers in nginx will communicate with php-fpm through port 9000, and, for communicating with the web, will use the public view through port 80. Later on, in docker-compose.yml, we will configure the internal Docker container ports to the outside world, which, in this case, is our host machine.

Configuring php-fpm

In order to configure php-fpm, follow these steps:

1. Inside the php-fpm folder, create a file called Dockerfile and add the following lines:

```
FROM phpdockerio/php72-fpm:latest
WORKDIR "/application"
# Install selected extensions and other stuff
RUN apt-get update \
    && apt-get -y --no-install-recommends install php7.2-mysql
    libmcrypt-dev \
    && apt-get clean; rm -rf /var/lib/apt/lists/* /tmp/* /var/tmp/*
    /usr/share/doc/*
```

Now, it is time to create our override php.ini file, which is the PHP.ini where we can manually override PHP settings that run on the server.

In the case of Apache servers, it only runs once when the server is started, in our case, as we use nginx with php-fpm. In regards to this, we are using a fastCgi environment, and this file is read with every server invocation.

Some advantages to using fastCgi environment rather than the traditional Apache evironment are as follows:

- Adaptive process growth
- Basic statistics (similar to Apache mod_status)

- Advanced process management with graceful start/stop
- The ability to start workers with different `uid`, `gid`, `chroot`, `environment`, and `php.ini` (replaces `safe_mode`)
- It creates logs for `stdout` and `stderr`
- Emergency restart in case of accidental code destruction (cache)
- Supports accelerated upload
- Several improvements to your facet FastCGI

Other ways to use PHP on servers are as follows:

- Apache module (`mod_php`)
- CGI
- FastCGI
- PHP – **FastCGI Process Manager (FPM)**
- **Command lines (CLI)**

2. Inside the `php-fpm` folder, create a new file called `php-ini-overrides.ini` and add the following code:

```
upload_max_filesize = 300M
post_max_size = 308M
[Xdebug]
zend_extension=/usr/local/lib/php/extensions/no-debug-non-
zts-20151012/xdebug.so
xdebug.remote_enable=1
xdebug.remote_autostart=1
xdebug.remote_host=111.111.11.1 # you must use your own IP address
here
xdebug.remote_port=9009
```

Note that we are only setting up Xdebug here, which is a PHP extension to debug PHP applications.

Creating a docker-compose configuration file

Now, it's time to configure our compose file and mount all the containers that we will use in our application. We will build this file step by step, so the first thing to do is create the file:

1. Inside the root, the `chapter-04` folder creates a file called `docker-compose.yml`.

2. Inside `docker-compose.yml`, add the following piece of code:

```
version: "3.1"
services:
mysql:
  image: mysql:5.7
  container_name: chapter-04-mysql
  working_dir: /application
  volumes:
    - .:/application
  environment:
    - MYSQL_ROOT_PASSWORD=123456
    - MYSQL_DATABASE=chapter-04
    - MYSQL_USER=chapter-04
    - MYSQL_PASSWORD=123456
  ports:
    - "8083:3306"
```

The first block of code here is to configure the MySQL server. We are using the official MySQL image from Docker. We are setting the environment variables and ports, but note that on the host machine, we are accessing MySQL using port `8083` and, inside the container, we are using the `3306` default port. Later on in this chapter, we will see how to connect a MySQL client to our MySQL container.

 You can find out more information from the official Docker website from at `https://hub.docker.com/explore/` and at `https://store.docker.com/`.

Note that we are using a pretty simple password just for the example. In the production environment, we will use global environment variables.

Let's add a new block of code.

3. Still on the `docker-compose.yml` file, add the following code right after the first block:

```
webserver:
  image: nginx:alpine
  container_name: chapter-04-webserver
  working_dir: /application
  volumes:
    - .:/application
    - ./phpdocker/nginx/nginx.conf:/etc/nginx/conf.d/default.conf
  ports:
    - "8081:80"
```

In the previous code, configure our `nginx` container using the internal port 80 as we saw earlier and port `8081` on our host machine. We will also set `nginx.conf` inside the container. Here, we are using the `nginx/alpine` Docker image.

 You can read more about the alpine image here, at the following Docker website: `https://store.docker.com/images/alpine`.

4. Last but not least, let's configure `php-fpm`. Add the following block of code right after the web server configuration block:

```
php-fpm:
build: phpdocker/php-fpm
container_name: chapter-04-php-fpm
working_dir: /application
volumes:
- .:/application
- ./phpdocker/php-fpm/php-ini-
overrides.ini:/etc/php/7.2/fpm/conf.d/99-overrides.ini
```

Here, we just set up `php-ini-overrides.ini` from our machine in the `php-fpm` configuration directory inside the Docker container.

Building the application container

Now, it's time to check whether everything is working as we planned. Let's create the containers that we will use in our application. In `Chapter 1`, *Understanding the Core Concepts of Laravel 5*, we already saw some very useful Docker commands, and now we are going to use them again. Let's see.

First, we will stop any container that is still running from the previous chapter, or on your machine.

 Don't forget that you need to have your Docker Daemon up and running on your local machine.

1. Open your Terminal window and type the following command:

```
docker ps -a
```

If you are using Docker for the first time on your machine, you will see something similar to the following output:

```
CONTAINER ID   IMAGE          COMMAND              CREATED      STATUS          PORTS                 NAMES
e203f89397a8   nginx:alpine   "nginx -g 'daemon of…"   2 days ago   Exited (255)...   0.0.0.0:8081->80/tcp   chapter-01-webserver
...
...
```

Listed Docker containers

But, if you've used Docker on your machine before, the previous command will list all Docker containers on your machine. In this case, be careful with *step 2*, because the command will stop and delete all the containers on your machine.

So, if you want to keep your previous container, we recommend that you just stop and delete the containers created by this book's tutorial using the following command:

```
docker stop <containerId>
```

You can also use the following command instead of the commands that were executed in *steps* 2 and 3:

```
docker rm <containerId>
```

2. Type the following command to stop all containers:

```
docker stop $(docker ps -a -q)
```

3. Let's delete all the containers by typing the following command:

```
docker rm $(docker ps -a -q)
```

Well done! Now, we can create the image that we need to run our application. Let's test the settings we established in the previous session.

4. Inside the `chapter-04` folder, type the following command:

```
docker-compose build
```

At the end of the Terminal window, we will see an output similar to the following:

```
---> 5f8ed0da2be9 Successfully built 5f8ed0da2be9 Successfully
tagged chapter-04_php-fpm:latest mysql uses an image, skipping
```

The previous output tells us that we created a new Docker image called `chapter-04_php-fpm:latest`, so now, let's create the application container.

5. Inside the `chapter-04` folder, on your Terminal, type the following command:

```
docker-compose up -d
```

The output of the previous command will give us the status of all three Docker containers that we set up before, similar to the following output:

```
---> 5f8ed0da2be9
Successfully built 5f8ed0da2be9
Successfully tagged chapter-04_php-fpm:latest
mysql uses an image, skipping
```

6. Now, we can check the new container that's been created with the following command:

```
docker ps -a
```

The output on the Terminal will be very similar to the following message:

CONTAINER ID	IMAGE	COMMAND	CREATED	STATUS	PORTS	NAMES
0ae7f636cfd3	nginx:alpine	"nginx -g 'daemon of…"	minutes ago	Up X minutes	0.0.0.0:8081->80/tcp	chapter-04-webserver
c3dfcf98c6eb	mysql:5.7	"docker-entrypoint.s…"	minutes ago	Up X minutes	0.0.0.0:8083->3306/tcp	chapter-04-mysql
e0eaebc2d57a	chapter-04_php-fpm	"/bin/sh -c /usr/bin…"	minutes ago	Up X minutes	9000/tcp	chapter-04-php-fpm

Docker containers running

Note that we don't have any application code inside the `chapter-04` folder yet, so if we try to access the server using the `http://localhost:8081/` address, we will see a File Not Found message. This is perfectly expected because we don't really have any applications running on our servers yet.

Using PHP Composer to scaffold a Laravel application

We have created a solid base on our servers. The PHP image we used already has all the dependencies that Laravel needs to run the application, including Composer.

Therefore, we will use the Composer that we have inside the `php-fpm` containers instead of using what we installed globally onto our machine.

This is the safest way to avoid conflicts between versions. Let's check what we have inside the `php-fpm` container:

1. Open your Terminal window and type the following command:

```
docker-compose exec php-fpm bash
```

2. Now that we are inside the `php-fpm` bash/terminal, let's check the composer version with the following command:

```
composer --version
```

3. We will see the following output on the Terminal:

```
Composer version 1.6.3
```

Congratulations! We have been able to configure all of our environment and we are ready to start building our application.

Creating the application scaffold

In order to maintain the consistency between this book's application and the moment in when you will use the example code, we will fix the Laravel version that will be installed in your environment.

So, let's continue with the following steps:

1. Open your Terminal window and type the following command:

```
composer create-project laravel/laravel=5.6.12 project --prefer-
dist
```

 At the time of writing this book, we have installed version 5.6.12 of Laravel. Although we should have no problem installing a more current version, we strongly recommend that you keep the version in 5.6. *.

After using the previous command, you will see the following message on your Terminal window:

```
Generating optimized autoload files
> Illuminate\Foundation\ComposerScripts::postAutoloadDump
> @php artisan package:discover
Discovered Package: fideloper/proxy
Package: laravel/tinker
Discovered Package: nunomaduro/collision
Package manifest generated successfully.
> @php artisan key:generate
```

This means that everything went well.

Note that we create the Laravel application inside a directory called `project`. This way, we will have the following application structure:

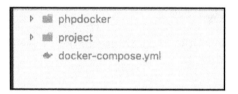

Application folder structure

Notice that we have separated the content of the Laravel application from the Docker configuration folder. This practice is highly recommended since we can make any kind of changes within the project folder without damaging any Docker or `docker-compose` files accidentally.

But with this minor change, we need to adjust the `docker-compose.yml` file in order to fit the new path that's been created.

2. Open `docker-compose.yml` and let's adjust the `php-fpm` volumes tag with the new path, as in the following block of code:

```
php-fpm:
  build: phpdocker/php-fpm
  container_name: chapter-04-php-fpm
  working_dir: /application
  volumes:
    - ./project:/application
    - ./phpdocker/php-fpm/php-ini-
      overrides.ini:/etc/php/7.2/fpm/conf.d/99-overrides.ini
```

Running the application

For the change we just made to take effect, we need to stop and restart our containers:

1. On your Terminal, type `exit` to exit the `php-fpm` bash.
2. Now, at the root of the `chapter-04` folder, still in the Terminal, type the following command:

   ```
   docker-compose kill
   ```

   You will see the following output message:

   ```
   Stopping chapter-04-webserver ... done
   Stopping chapter-04-mysql ... done
   Stopping chapter-04-php-fpm ... done
   ```

3. On your Terminal, type the following command to run the containers again:

   ```
   docker-compose up -d
   ```

   Now, we can see that the `php-fpm` container was recreated and will reflect our changes:

   ```
   Recreating chapter-04-php-fpm ... done
   Starting chapter-04-webserver ... done
   Starting chapter-04-webserver ... done
   ```

   It is highly recommended that you repeat this procedure whenever you make any changes to the `nginx` or `php-fpm` servers.

4. Now, let's check the Laravel installation and configuration. Open your default browser and go to the link `http://localhost:8081/`.

We will see the welcome screen from the Laravel framework, as shown in the following screenshot:

Laravel welcome screen

Setting up a MySQL database

So far, we have come a long way and built a solid foundation for our RESTful application, though we must take a few more steps to finally be able to begin with development.

In this step, we will configure our MySQL database for our application and perform some alterations in our Docker MySQL container in order to make the data of our application persist in our database, even when we disconnect or stop our MySQL container.

Adding a storage folder

A local folder to store MySQL data is very important since our `docker-compose.yml` file does not contain any volume that's been configured to store the data created in our database yet.

Remember, we are using Docker, and our MySQL container is based on an image of a database. This way, every time we finish the container process, our database is erased and the next time we start it, our database will be empty.

Open the `docker-compose.yml` file and add – `./storage-db:/var/lib/mysql` right after the application volumes on the MySQL configuration block, as shown in the following code:

```
mysql:
    image: mysql:5.7
    container_name: chapter-04-mysql
    working_dir: /application
    volumes:
    - .:/application
    - ./storage-db:/var/lib/mysql
```

The previous code sets the `storage-db` folder on our project/machine to store all the MySQL data from the MySQL container. Later in this section, we will see the result of these changes, but for now, let's configure our database.

Configuring the .env file

1. Open the `.env` file at the root of the `project` folder and replace the database configuration with the following lines:

```
DB_HOST=mysql
DB_PORT=3306
DB_DATABASE=chapter-04
DB_USERNAME=chapter-04
DB_PASSWORD=123456
```

Let's check the connection.

2. Inside the Terminal window, type the following command:

   docker-compose exec php-fpm bash

3. Inside the `php-fpm` bash, type the following command:

   php artisan tinker

4. Finally, type the following command:

   DB::connection()->getPdo();

5. You will see something similar to the following output:

```
=> PDO {#760
inTransaction: false,
attributes: {
CASE: NATURAL,
ERRMODE: EXCEPTION,
AUTOCOMMIT: 1,
PERSISTENT: false,
DRIVER_NAME: "mysql",
SERVER_INFO: "Uptime: 2491 Threads: 1 Questions: 9 Slow queries: 0
Opens: 105 Flush tables: 1 Open tables: 98 Queriesper second avg:
0.003",
ORACLE_NULLS: NATURAL,
CLIENT_VERSION: "mysqlnd 5.0.12-dev - 20150407 - $Id:
38fea24f2847fa7519001be390c98ae0acafe387 $",
SERVER_VERSION: "5.7.21",
STATEMENT_CLASS: [
"PDOStatement",
],
EMULATE_PREPARES: 0,
CONNECTION_STATUS: "mysql via TCP/IP",
DEFAULT_FETCH_MODE: BOTH,
},
}
```

This means that everything has gone well. Congratulations! We have a database. Now, it is time to generate our local database folder called `storage-db`.

If you are still inside the `php-fpm` bash, type the `exit` command to get out of it and return to the Terminal.

6. On your Terminal window, type the following command:

```
docker-compose kill
```

7. Let's remove the MySQL container that we created previously:

```
docker-compose rm mysql
```

8. And now, let's recreate the container so that it has the changes up and running. Type the following command:

```
docker-compose up -d
```

You will see the following output on your Terminal:

```
Creating chapter-04-mysql ... done
Starting chapter-04-php-fpm ... done
Starting chapter-04-webserver ... done
```

Note that the MySQL container has been created with the `storage-db` folder properly configured. Our project will have the following structure:

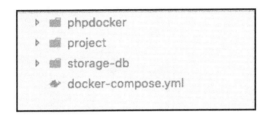

Project folder structure

Using a MySQL external client

Managing a database entirely using the command line may not be an easy task, and, visually speaking, it is not. To assist us in this process, all databases have a tool for this task, and MySQL is no different.

There are several open source and multi-platform tools that help us in this process, and MySQL has its own tool called **Workbench**.

> You can read more about the Workbench at the official MySQL documentation at `https://www.mysql.com/products/workbench/`.

In this session, we will see how to use a tool with the graphical interface to access our database that is inside the Docker container.

1. Go to `https://dev.mysql.com/downloads/workbench/`, choose your platform, and follow the installation steps.
2. Open Workbench, click on the **Database** top menu, and click on **Connect to Database**.

You will see the following screen:

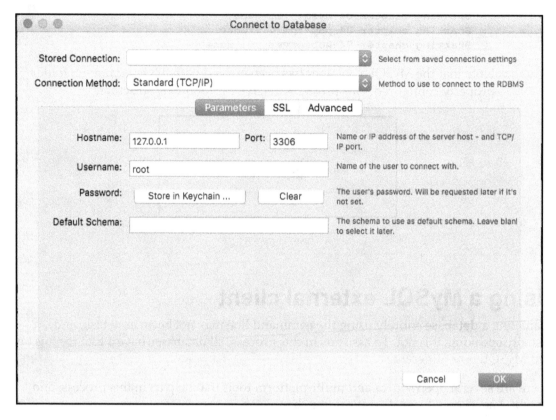

Workbench connection screen

3. Remember that the Workbench is running on the host machine and not inside the MySQL Docker container. Add the following information to it:

Hostname: `127.0.0.1` Port: `8083`
Username: `chapter-04`
Password: `123456`

Note that we are using the same configuration that we used on the Laravel `.env` file.

4. Click the **OK** button. Now, we are connected to the MySQL database running inside the Docker container. You will see something similar to the following screenshot:

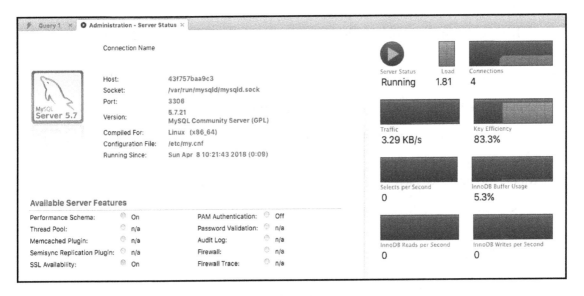

Workbench welcome screen

Notice the left Schema panel. We already have our database created by Docker container and we are ready to use it. At this moment, it is still empty, as can be seen in the following screenshot:

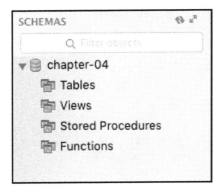

Schema left panel

Migrations and database seed

Now, let's exercise some commands that we briefly saw in the first chapter and create our migrations and seeds in a different way.

1. Open your Terminal window on the `chapter-04` folder and type the following command:

    ```
    docker-compose exec php-fpm bash
    ```

2. Inside the container root bash, type the following command:

    ```
    php artisan make:model Bike —m
    ```

Note that we are using the –m flag to create the migration file together with the creation of Bike Model. So now, we have two new files in our application:

*   `project/app/Bike.php`
*   `project/database/migrations/XXXX_XX_XX_XXXXXX_create_bikes_table.php`

Creating the migration boilerplate

As we saw previously, the new files only have the boilerplate code that's been created by the Laravel engine. Let's add some content to the **Bike** model and migration file.

1. Open `project/app/Bike.php` and add the following code inside the Bike model function:

    ```
    protected $fillable = [
        'make',
        'model',
        'year',
        'mods',
        'picture'
    ];
    ```

2. Now, we need to add the same properties to the migration file we created previously. Open `project/database/migrations/XXXX_XX_XX_XXXXXX_create_bikes_tabl e.php` and add the following code inside the `up()` function:

```
Schema::create('bikes', function (Blueprint $table) {
$table->increments('id');
$table->string('make');
$table->string('model');
$table->string('year');
$table->text('mods');
$table->string('picture');
$table->timestamps();
});
```

Congratulations! You have created our first migration file, and it is time to execute the following command to feed our database.

3. Open your Terminal window and type the following command:

```
php artisan migrate
```

The output of the previous command will be similar to the following:

```
Migration table created successfully. Migrating:
XXXX_XX_XX_XXXXXX_create_users_table Migrated:
XXXX_XX_XX_XXXXXX_create_users_table Migrating:
XXXX_XX_XX_XXXXXX_create_password_resets_table Migrated:
XXXX_XX_XX_XXXXXX_create_password_resets_table Migrating:
XXXX_XX_XX_XXXXXX_create_bikes_table Migrated:
XXXX_XX_XX_XXXXXX_create_bikes_table
```

Now, on the Workbench schema, we can see our new table filled by the `migrate` command, as shown in the following screenshot:

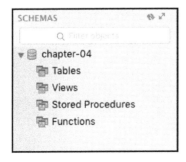

Workbench schema panel

Creating our first database seed

In the previous steps, we basically followed the same procedure as in Chapter 1, *Understanding the Core Concepts of Laravel 5*, so now we are not going to use the Faker library to create our data. Faker is a very useful tool as it's easy to use and quick to create data during the development of applications with Laravel.

In this example, we want to keep the data we have created more consistent with the application we are creating, so we will use an external JSON file with the data we want to insert into our database.

1. Inside the `project/database` folder, create a new folder called `data-sample`.
2. Inside the `project/database/data-sample` folder, create a new file called `bikes.json` and add the following code:

```
[{
  "id": 1,
  "make": "Harley Davidson",
  "model": "XL1200 Nightster",
  "year": "2009",
  "mods": "Nobis vero sint non eius. Laboriosam sed odit hic quia
    doloribus. Numquam laboriosam numquam quas quis.",
  "picture": "https://placeimg.com/640/480/nature
  }, {
  "id": 2,
  "make": "Harley Davidson",
  "model": "Blackline",
  "year": "2008",
  "mods": "Nobis vero sint non eius. Laboriosam sed odit hic quia
   doloribus. Numquam laboriosam numquam quas quis.",
  "picture": "https://placeimg.com/640/480/nature"
 }, {
  "id": 3,
  "make": "Harley Davidson",
  "model": "Dyna Switchback",
  "year": "2009",
  "mods": "Nobis vero sint non eius. Laboriosam sed odit hic quia
   doloribus. Numquam laboriosam numquam quas quis.",
  "picture": "https://placeimg.com/640/480/nature"
 }, {
  "id": 4,
  "make": "Harley Davidson",
  "model": "Dyna Super Glide",
  "year": "2009",
  "mods": "Nobis vero sint non eius. Laboriosam sed odit hic quia
   doloribus. Numquam laboriosam numquam quas quis.",
```

```
    "picture": "https://placeimg.com/640/480/nature"
},{
    "id": 5,
    "make": "Harley Davidson",
    "model": "Dyna Wild Glide",
    "year": "2005",
    "mods": "Nobis vero sint non eius. Laboriosam sed odit hic quia
      doloribus. Numquam laboriosam numquam quas quis.",
    "picture": "https://placeimg.com/640/480/nature"
}]
```

Notice that we keep some placeholder text and an image path. Don't worry about this for now; later on in this book, we will replace all of this data using our frontend application.

3. Now, it's time to create our seed file. On your Terminal window, type the following command:

```
php artisan make:seeder BikesTableSeeder
```

The previous command added a new file called `BikesTableSeeder.php` inside the `project/database/seeds` folder.

4. Open `project/database/seeds/BikesTableSeeder.php` and replace the code inside it with the following:

```
use Illuminate\Database\Seeder;
use App\Bike;
class BikesTableSeeder extends Seeder
    {
    /**
    * Run the database seeds.
    *
    * @return void
    */
    public function run()
    {
        DB::table('bikes')->delete();
        $json = File::get("database/data-sample/bikes.json");
        $data = json_decode($json);
        foreach ($data as $obj) {
        Bike::create(array(
            'id' => $obj->id,
            'make' => $obj->make,
            'model' => $obj->model,
            'year' => $obj->year,
            'mods' => $obj->mods,
```

```
                'picture'=> $obj->picture
        ));
    }
  }
}
```

Note that in the first line, we are using the Eloquent ORM shortcut function (`DB::table()`) to delete the bike tables and are using the `Bike::create()` function to create our records. In the next chapter, we will look deeper at Eloquent ORM, but for now, let's focus on creating our first seed.

5. Open `project/database/seeds/DatabaseSeeder.php` and add the following line of code, right after the `UsersTableSeeder` comment:

    ```
    $this->call(BikesTableSeeder::class);
    ```

   Now, it is time to run our seed and fill the database. We can do this in two ways. We can either run the `BikeSeeder` command `php artisan db:seed --class=BikesTableSeeder` individually, or use the `php artisan db:seed` command, which will run all of the seeds in our application.

   As we are at the beginning of our development, we will execute the command to load all the seeds.

6. Open your Terminal window and type the following command:

    ```
    php artisan db:seed
    ```

   At the end of the previous command, we will see a success message, `Seeding: BikesTableSeeder`, on our Terminal. Bravo! Now, we have our first records on the `chapter-04` database.

Exploring the Workbench table view

Now, we will use the visual interface of the Workbench to visualize the data that we have just placed inside our database. To do this, open the Workbench and perform the following steps:

1. On the right-hand schema panel, click on the **Tables** menu item.
2. Right click on **bikes** and click **Select Rows – Limit 1000**.

   We will see a new panel on the right-hand side, as in the following screenshot:

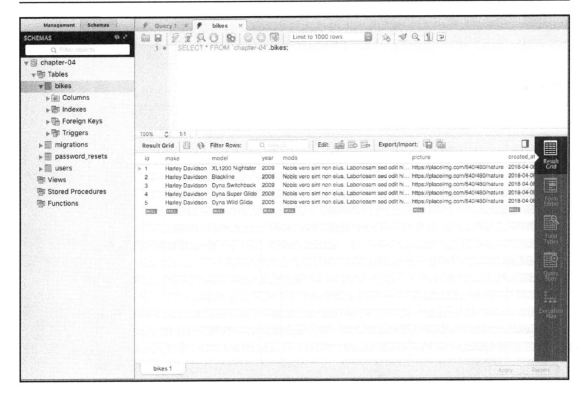

Bike tables on the Workbench interface

Note that we now have five records on our database inside the bike table, which is the same data that we created in the `bike.json` file.

API documentation with the Swagger framework

Let's take a break and tackle an extremely important topic in the development of RESTful applications: documentation on how to use the API endpoints.

Although we have not created any controller or route to be able to view the data of our API in the browser, we will introduce a new tool that will help us develop our frontend application, called the Swagger framework.

Swagger is an open source language-agnostic framework for describing, documenting, consuming, and visualizing REST APIs.

It is very common today to use public and private APIs for creating frontend web applications, and we are familiar with several APIs, such as Twitter, LinkedIn, and many others.

Documenting your application is an important part of the development process. Every API needs to be documented in order to make it easier to use and test, either by your in-house team or by a third-party developer.

The easiest way to do this is at the beginning of the development process.

You can read more about the Swagger framework at the official website: `https://swagger.io/`.

Installing the L5-Swagger library

In this section, we are going to use the L5-Swagger project. A wrapper for Swagger-PHP and Swagger-UI are going to be used with the Laravel 5 framework:

1. Still on your Terminal window, type the following command:

   ```
   composer require "darkaonline/l5-swagger"
   ```

You can read more about L5-Swagger at the official GitHub repository at `https://github.com/DarkaOnLine/L5-Swagger`.

At the end of the command line, we will see the following output:

```
./composer.json has been updated
Loading composer repositories with package information
Updating dependencies (including require-dev)
Package operations: 4 installs, 0 updates, 0 removals
  - Installing swagger-api/swagger-ui (v3.13.3): Downloading (100%)
  - Installing doctrine/annotations (v1.6.0): Downloading (100%)
  - Installing zircote/swagger-php (2.0.13): Downloading (100%)
  - Installing darkaonline/l5-swagger (5.6.3): Downloading (100%)
Writing lock file
Generating optimized autoload files
> Illuminate\Foundation\ComposerScripts::postAutoloadDump
> @php artisan package:discover
Discovered Package: darkaonline/l5-swagger
Discovered Package: fideloper/proxy
Discovered Package: laravel/tinker
Discovered Package: nunomaduro/collision
Package manifest generated successfully.
```

Composer L5-Swagger installation process

2. Open the `project/config/app.php` file and add the following code at the end of package the `ServiceProvider` comment:

```
\L5Swagger\L5SwaggerServiceProvider::class
```

3. Type the following command to publish the package:

```
php artisan vendor:publish --provider
"L5Swagger\L5SwaggerServiceProvider"
```

The output of the previous command will create some new files on our application, as shown in the following screenshot:

```
Copied File [/vendor/darkaonline/l5-swagger/config/l5-swagger.php] To [/config/l5-swagger.php]
Copied Directory [/vendor/darkaonline/l5-swagger/resources/views] To [/resources/views/vendor/l5-swagger]
Publishing complete.
```

L5-Swagger UI

Creating the application API controller

By way of good practice, we will create a new controller in our application just to serve as the basis for the API documentation and hold some basic API information with a Swagger annotation.

1. On your Terminal window, type the following command to create a new controller:

```
php artisan make:controller ApiController
```

2. Open `project/app/Http/Controllers/ApiController.php` and replace `Class ApiController` comments with the following comments:

```
* Class ApiController
*
* @package App\Http\Controllers
*
* @SWG\Swagger(
* basePath="",
* host="localhost:8081",
* schemes={"http"},
* @SWG\Info(
* version="1.0",
* title="Custom Bikes",
* @SWG\Contact(name="Developer Contact",
```

```
      url="https://www.example.com"),
* )
* )
*/
```

Generating and publishing the API documentation

Now, it is time to publish our documentation and access it through a web browser. So, let's do so in the following steps.

Still on your Terminal window, type the following command:

```
php artisan l5-swagger:generate
```

Well done! Now, we have our API documentation ready to be implemented.

Go to `http://localhost:8081/api/documentation` and you will see a result similar to the following screenshot:

Swagger UI

The Swagger framework is up and running on our local machine.

Adding Swagger definitions

Swagger generates the documentation for our notations that use API, a kind of self-writing of the framework itself, where, through tags, we can define what each element does. Let's start building our API documentation.

The first step is to add some definitions to the `Bike` model we just created in the previous steps.

1. Open the `project/app/Bike.php` model file and replace the code with the following lines:

```php
<?php
namespace App;
use Illuminate\Database\Eloquent\Model;
    /**
     * @SWG\Definition(
     * definition="Bike",
     * required={"make", "model", "year", "mods"},
     * @SWG\Property(
     * property="make",
     * type="string",
     * description="Company name",
     * example="Harley Davidson, Honda, Yamaha"
     * ),
     * @SWG\Property(
     * property="model",
     * type="string",
     * description="Motorcycle model",
     * example="Xl1200, Shadow ACE, V-Star"
     * ),
     * @SWG\Property(
     * property="year",
     * type="string",
     * description="Fabrication year",
     * example="2009, 2008, 2007"
     * ),
     * @SWG\Property(
     * property="mods",
     * type="string",
     * description="Motorcycle description of modifications",
     * example="New exhaust system"
     * ),
     * @SWG\Property(
     * property="picture",
     * type="string",
     * description="Bike image URL",
```

```
       * example="http://www.sample.com/my.bike.jpg"
       * )
       * )
       */
class Bike extends Model
{
        /**
         * The attributes that are mass assignable.
         *
         * @var array
         */
        protected $fillable = [
             'make',
             'model',
             'year',
             'mods',
             'picture'
        ];
}
```

The previous annotation is pretty self-explanatory; we just describe each model field and set the data type with a useful example on how to use it.

2. Go back to your Terminal window and type the following command to generate the documentation:

```
php artisan l5-swagger:generate
```

3. Now, let's check our documentation URL and see what happens. Go to `http://localhost:8081/api/documentation` and we will see that our first model has been documented, as shown in the following screenshot:

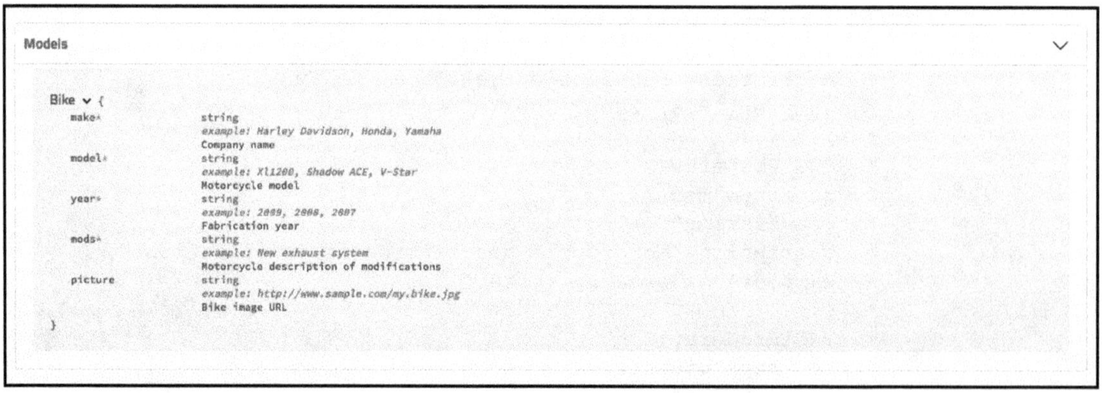

Swagger UI

Note that we have all the model properties explained inside an object, each one with a data type, description, and an example. This was possible due to the `Swagger @SWG\Property` definition:

```
 * @SWG\Property(
 * property="make",
 * type="string",
 * description="Company name",
 * example="Harley Davidson, Honda, Yamaha"
```

As our application grows, we will add all the documentation we need to use our APIs.

 You can find out more information about Swagger's visual interface at the following link `https://swagger.io/swagger-ui/`.

Summary

We have come to the end of another chapter. We put in a lot of hard work here and did a lot of things, such as configuring Docker to maintain the data we are going to create in our MySQL database. We also created a large application and configured the database, and learned how to use the Workbench to view the data loaded by the application.

We created our first model and its migration file, and we also created a seed to perform an initial data load in our database. Finally, we built a solid foundation to scale our RESTful API.

In the next chapter, we will go into more depth in terms of how to create controllers, routes, and relationships between tables using the Eloquent ORM, among other things.

5
Creating a RESTful API Using Laravel - Part 1

Before we get started, let's briefly introduce a software development standard called the RESTful API.

An **Application Programming Interface (API)** is a set of instructions, routines, and programming patterns used to access an internet-based application. This allows a computer or other application to understand the instructions in this application, interpret its data, and use it for integration with other platforms and software, generating new instructions that will be executed by this software or computers.

In this way, we understand that the APIs allow interoperability between applications. In other words, this is communication between applications, in our case, the communication between the client-side and the server-side.

Representational State Transfer (REST) is an abstraction of the web architecture. Briefly, REST consists of principles, rules, and constraints that, when followed, allow the creation of a project with well-defined interfaces.

The features available in a RESTful service can be accessed or manipulated from a set of operations that are predefined by default. The operations make it possible to create (PUT), read (GET), change (POST), and delete (DELETE) resources, and are available from messages using the HTTP protocol.

Although Laravel is an– MVC framework, we can build RESTful apps that are extremely robust and scalable.

In this chapter, you will learn how to build a RESTful API using the core elements of the Laravel framework, such as controllers, routes, and Eloquent **Object Relational Mapping** (**ORM**). Mainly, we will cover the following topics:

- Preparing the application and understanding what we are building
- An Eloquent ORM relationship
- Controllers and routes

Preparing the application and understanding what we are building

Let's start this session using the application that we started to develop in the previous chapter. However, we will make some adjustments before continuing. First, we are going to add our code to the version control. In this way, we will not lose the progress we made in the previous chapter.

1. Inside the `chapter-04` folder, create a new file called `.gitignore` and add the following code:

```
storage-db
.DS_Store
```

- See `https://help.github.com/articles/ignoring-files` for more information about ignoring files
- If you find yourself ignoring temporary files generated by your text editor or operating system, you probably want to add a global ignore instead `git config --global core.excludesfile '~/.gitignore_global'`
- Ignore the `storage` folder's due size

The previous code just added the `storage-db` folder to untracked files.

2. Let's add the changes to source control. Inside the Terminal window, type the following command:

```
git init
```

Finally, let's add our first commit.

3. Inside the Terminal, type the following commands:

```
git add .
git commit -m "first commit"
```

Bravo! We have our code under Git source control.

Refactoring the application files

Now, it is time to change some files to adjust to chapter-05:

1. Copy all the content of chapter-04 and paste it into a new folder called chapter-05.

2. Open the docker-compose.yml file and replace the code with the following lines:

```
version: "3.1"
services:
 mysql:
 screenshot: mysql:5.7
 container_name: chapter-05-mysql
 working_dir: /application
 volumes:
 - .:/application
 - ./storage-db:/var/lib/mysql
 environment:
 - MYSQL_ROOT_PASSWORD=123456
 - MYSQL_DATABASE=chapter-05
 - MYSQL_USER=chapter-05
 - MYSQL_PASSWORD=123456
 ports:
 - "8083:3306"
 webserver:
 screenshot: nginx:alpine
 container_name: chapter-05-webserver
 working_dir: /application
 volumes:
 - .:/application
 - ./phpdocker/nginx/nginx.conf:
 /etc/nginx/conf.d/default.conf
 ports:
 - "8081:80"
 php-fpm:
```

```
build: phpdocker/php-fpm
container_name: chapter-05-php-fpm
working_dir: /application
volumes:
- ./project:/application
- ./phpdocker/php-fpm/php-ini-
overrides.ini:/etc/php/7.2/fpm/conf.d/99-overrides.ini
```

Note that we changed MYSQL_DATABASE and MYSQL_USER and also changed the container names to fit the chapter-05 title.

3. Edit the project/.env file with the new database information, as in the following code:

```
DB_CONNECTION=mysql
DB_HOST=mysql
DB_PORT=3306
DB_DATABASE=chapter-05
DB_USERNAME=chapter-05
DB_PASSWORD=123456
```

4. Now, delete the storage-db folder. Don't worry – we will create a new one with the docker-compose command later.

5. It's time to commit our new changes, but this time we will do it another way. This time, we will use the Git Lens VS Code plugin.

6. Open VS Code. On the left-hand side bar, click on the third icon for source control.

7. Add the following message inside the message box at the top-left sidebar Init chapter 05.

8. Press *Command +Enter* on macOSX, or *Ctrl + Enter* on Windows, and click **Yes**.

Well done. Now, we can start chapter 05 with a new baseline of files.

What we are building

Now, let's talk a bit about the application we have been building since the beginning of this book.

As we can see, we have already built a lot of things so far, but we still don't have a clear idea of what we are doing about the project. And this is the best way to learn and practice web application development.

Many times, when we are learning or doing something for the first time, we tend to pay close attention to the final project and, at this point, there is an anxiety to finish what we started to do and we cannot focus on the building process and details.

Here, we already have *40%* of our project ready. Then, we can reveal more details about what we are doing.

Remember, until now, we have prepared a highly scalable development environment using Docker, installed some very important tools that will help us in our development, and learned how to start a solid Laravel application.

The application will be called **Custom Bike Garage**, a kind of Instagram/Twitter for lovers of custom motorcycle culture. At the end of the development, we will have a web application very similar to the following wire frames screenshot:

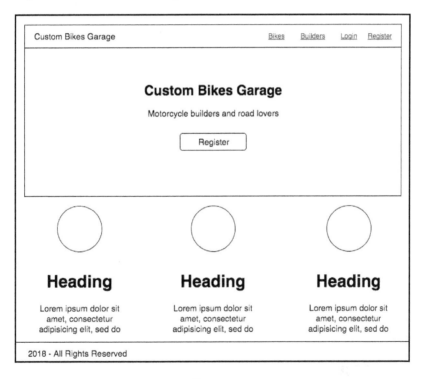

Home page

The previous screenshot is just a basic application home page, with navigation links and a call-to-action button:

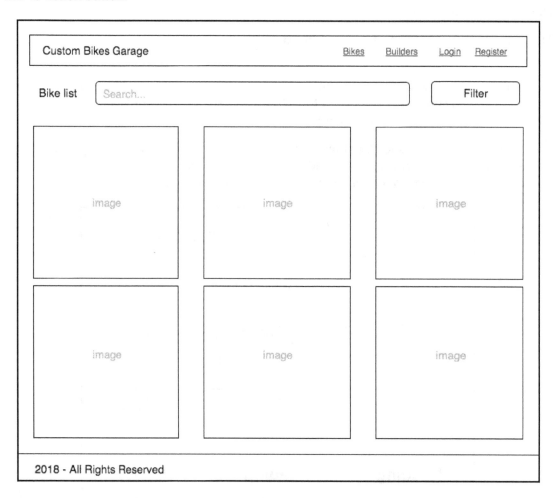

Bike list page

The application's summary

As we can see in the previous screenshot, our application has:

- A home page, which we will call `home` page
- A page of motorcycles, which we will call a `bike-list` page
- A bike detail page, which we will call a `bike-details` page

- A builders page, which we will call a `builders-list` page
- A builder detail page, which we will call a `builder-details` page
- A register page, which we will call a `register-page` page
- A login page, which we will call a `login-page` page
- A rating page, where users can vote on bikes

Imagine that we are building a custom bike application for an exhibition conference. Each conference has a name and customer level.

Users can register, vote on the best bike, and insert their own bike. The conference shows some customized bikes by renowned bike builders, with many custom items for each bike.

So, what we still need to do in order to complete the backend of the application is as follows:

- Create models for `Builder`, `Item`, `Garage`, and `Rating`
- Create migration files for `Builder`, `Item`, `Garage`, and `Rating`
- Seed the database
- Create controllers for `Bike`, `Builder`, `Item`, `Garage`, and `Rating`
- Apply the relationship between models
- Use resources to represent relationships
- Create a token-based authentication

Creating models and migrations files

Let's starting creating the builders model and migration file using the -m flag. Like we did previously in this book, we can create both files at the same time:

1. Open your Terminal window and type the following command:

   ```
   php artisan make:model Builder -m
   ```

2. Still on your Terminal window, type the following command:

   ```
   php artisan make:model Item -m
   ```

3. Still on your Terminal window, type the following command:

   ```
   php artisan make:model Garage -m
   ```

4. Still on your Terminal window, type the following command:

```
php artisan make:model Rating -m
```

Steps 1 to *step 4* will produce the following new files in our application:

```
project/app/Builder.php
project/database/migrations/XXXX_XX_XX_XXXXXX_create_builders_table
.php project/app/Item.php
project/database/migrations/XXXX_XX_XX_XXXXXX_create_items_table.ph
p project/app/Garage.php
project/database/migrations/XXXX_XX_XX_XXXXXX_create_garages_table.
php project/app/Rating.php
project/database/migrations/XXXX_XX_XX_XXXXXX_create_ratings_table.
php
```

Note the XXXX_XX_XX_XXXXXX before the migration file name. It is a timestamp of when the file was created.

At this point, we can see the previous six models on the VS Code left-hand side panel, as in the following screenshot:

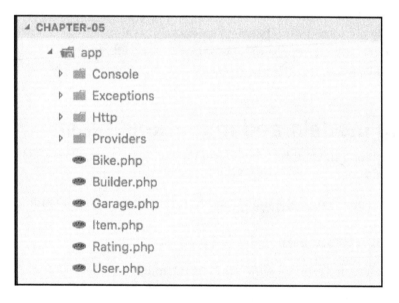

Left-hand side panel

Note that we have already created the Bike model in Chapter 4, *Building the Baseline Application,* and, by default, Laravel's created the User model for us.

5. Now, as we did previously, let's commit the new files created and click the source control icon on the left-hand panel of VS Code.

6. Type the following text inside the message input field: `Added Models and Migration files`.

7. Press *Command* + *Enter* on macOSX, or *Ctrl* + *Enter* on Windows, and click the **Yes** button.

Adding content to migration files

Now, let's create the content of our migration files. Remember that migration files are the simplest and fastest way to create our database schemes using Laravel:

1. Open `project/database/migrations/XXXX_XX_XX_XXXXXX_create_build ers_table.php` and replace the content with the following code:

```php
<?php
use Illuminate\Support\Facades\Schema;
use Illuminate\Database\Schema\Blueprint;
use Illuminate\Database\Migrations\Migration;
class CreateBuildersTable extends Migration
{
    /**
     * Run the migrations.
     *
     * @return void
     */
    public function up()
    {
    Schema::create('builders', function (Blueprint $table) {
        $table->increments('id');
        $table->string('name');
        $table->text('description');
        $table->string('location');
        $table->timestamps();
        });
    }
    /**
     * Reverse the migrations.
     *
     * @return void
     */
    public function down()
    {
        Schema::dropIfExists('builders');
```

```
        }
    }
```

2. Open `project/database/migrations/XXXX_XX_XX_XXXXXX_create_items`
   `_table.php` and replace the content with the following code:

```php
<?php
use Illuminate\Support\Facades\Schema;
use Illuminate\Database\Schema\Blueprint;
use Illuminate\Database\Migrations\Migration;
class CreateItemsTable extends Migration
{
    /**
     * Run the migrations.
     *
     * @return void
     */
    public function up()
    {
        Schema::create('items', function (Blueprint $table) {
        $table->increments('id');
        $table->string('type');
        $table->string('name');
        $table->text('company');
        $table->unsignedInteger('bike_id');
        $table->timestamps();
        });
    }
    /**
     * Reverse the migrations.
     *
     * @return void
     */
    public function down()
    {
        Schema::dropIfExists('items');
    }
}
```

3. Notice the `$table->unsignedInteger('bike_id')` foreign key for the Bike
   table. Later in this chapter, we go deep into model relationships/associations, but
   for now let's focus on migration files.

4. Open `project/database/migrations/XXXX_XX_XX_XXXXXX_create_garag es_table.php` and replace the content with the following code:

```php
<?php
use Illuminate\Support\Facades\Schema;
use Illuminate\Database\Schema\Blueprint;
use Illuminate\Database\Migrations\Migration;
class CreateGaragesTable extends Migration
{
    /**
     * Run the migrations.
     *
     * @return void
     */
    public function up()
    {
        Schema::create('garages', function (Blueprint $table) {
        $table->increments('id');
        $table->string('name');
        $table->integer('customer_level');
        $table->timestamps();
        });
    }
    /**
     * Reverse the migrations.
     *
     * @return void
     */
    public function down()
    {
        Schema::dropIfExists('garages');
    }
}
```

Now, we need another table, just to set up the relationship between `Bike` and `Garage`. We are using the `artisan` command to create a migration file, since, for this kind of relationship, we don't need a model. This table is also known as a pivot table.

5. Open your Terminal window and type the following command:

```
php artisan make:migration create_bike_garage_table
```

6. Open `project/database/migrations/XXXX_XX_XX_XXXXXX_create_bike_garage_table.php` and replace the content with the following code:

```php
<?php
use Illuminate\Support\Facades\Schema;
use Illuminate\Database\Schema\Blueprint;
use Illuminate\Database\Migrations\Migration;
class CreateBikeGarageTable extends Migration
{
    /**
     * Run the migrations.
     *
     * @return void
     */
    public function up()
    {
        Schema::create('bike_garage', function (Blueprint $table) {
        $table->increments('id');
        $table->integer('bike_id');
        $table->integer('garage_id');
        $table->timestamps();
        });
    }
    /**
     * Reverse the migrations.
     *
     * @return void
     */
    public function down()
    {
        Schema::dropIfExists('bike_garage');
    }
}
```

 Remember that the bike migration file was created in the previous chapter.

7. Open your Terminal window and type the following command:

```
php artisan make:migration create_ratings_table
```

8. Open `project/database/migrations/XXXX_XX_XX_XXXXXX_create_ratin
   gs_table.php` and replace the content with the following code:

```php
<?php
use Illuminate\Support\Facades\Schema;
use Illuminate\Database\Schema\Blueprint;
use Illuminate\Database\Migrations\Migration;
class CreateRatingsTable extends Migration
{
    /**
     * Run the migrations.
     *
     * @return void
     */
    public function up()
    {
        Schema::create('ratings', function (Blueprint $table) {
        $table->increments('id');
        $table->unsignedInteger('user_id');
        $table->unsignedInteger('bike_id');
        $table->unsignedInteger('rating');
        $table->timestamps();
        });
    }
    /**
     * Reverse the migrations.
     *
     * @return void
     */
    public function down()
    {
        Schema::dropIfExists('ratings');
    }
}
```

Well, its time to understand a bit more about what we did in this session, so let's go to the next session and understand how `Eloquent` works.

Eloquent ORM relationship

Eloquent is the ORM that is behind Laravel's database queries. It's an abstraction of active record implementation.

As we saw previously, each application model has a respective table in our database. With this, we can query, insert, delete, and update records.

The Eloquent ORM uses the snake case plural name of the class, which will be used as the table name, unless another name is explicitly specified. For example, our `Bike` model class has its own table bikes.

The application models have the following tables:

Application Model	Database Table
`Bike.php`	bikes
`Builder.php`	builders
`Garage.php`	garages
`Item.php`	items
`Rating.php`	ratings
`Builder.php`	builders
`User.php`	users

Note that we keep the table convention name, but it is possible to use a custom table name. For the scope of this book, we will keep the table names generated by Laravel.

You can read more about table names and model conventions in the official Laravel documentation at `https://laravel.com/docs/5.6/eloquent#defining-models`.

The Eloquent ORM supports the following relationships between models:

- One-to-one
- One-to-many
- Belongs to (inverse = one-to-many)
- Many-to-many
- Has-many
- Polymorphic relations
- Many-to-many polymorphic relations

We will see the first four relationships in detail; however, we can't cover all relationships in detail in our book. It is pretty simple to understand the relationships, also known as associations, in many frameworks as well.

You can read more about relationships at `https://laravel.com/docs/5.6/eloquent-relationships`.

One-to-one relationship

Let's set up the one-to-one relationship between `Builder` and `Bike`. This means that a `Bike` will have just one `Builder`.

1. Open `project/app/Builder.php` and replace the content with the following code:

```php
<?php
namespace App;
use Illuminate\Database\Eloquent\Model;
/**
 * @SWG\Definition(
 * definition="Builder",
 * required={"name", "description", "location"},
 * @SWG\Property(
 * property="name",
 * type="string",
 * description="Builder name",
 * example="Jesse James"
 * ),
 * @SWG\Property(
 * property="description",
 * type="string",
 * description="Famous Motorcycle builder from Texas",
 * example="Austin Speed Shop"
 * ),
 * @SWG\Property(
 * property="location",
 * type="string",
 * description="Texas/USA",
 * example="Austin, Texas"
 * ),
 * )
 */
class Builder extends Model
{
    /**
     * The table associated with the model.
     *
     * @var string
     */
    protected $table = 'builders';
    /**
     * The attributes that are mass assignable.
     *
     * @var array
```

```
    */
    protected $fillable = [
        'name',
        'description',
        'location'
    ];
    /**
     * Relationship.
     *
     * @var array
     */
    public function bike() {
        return $this->hasOne('App\Bike');
    }
}
```

Note that we added the Swagger documentation definition as we did in the previous chapter. The `bike()` function creates a one-to-one relationship. You can use any name on the relationship function, but we strongly recommend that you use the same model name, in our case, `Bike` model class.

2. Now, let's add the respective relationship to the `Bike` model. Open `project/app/Bike.php` and add the following code immediately after the protected fillable function:

```
/**
 * Relationship.
 *
 * @var string
 */
public function builder() {
    return $this->belongsTo('App\Builder');
}
```

Notice that `belongsTo` relation is a one-to-many inverse relationship.

3. Open `project/app/Item.php` and replace the content with the following code:

```
<?php
namespace App;
use Illuminate\Database\Eloquent\Model;
/**
 * @SWG\Definition(
```

```
 * definition="Item",
 * required={"type", "name", "company"},
 * @SWG\Property(
 * property="type",
 * type="string",
 * description="Item Type",
 * example="Exhaust"
 * ),
 * @SWG\Property(
 * property="name",
 * type="string",
 * description="Item name",
 * example="2 into 1 Exhaust"
 * ),
 * @SWG\Property(
 * property="company",
 * type="string",
 * description="Produced by: some company",
 * example="Vance and Hines"
 * )
 * )
 */
class Item extends Model
{
    /**
     * The table associated with the model.
     *
     * @var string
     */
    protected $table = 'items';
    /**
     * The attributes that are mass assignable.
     *
     * @var array
     */
    protected $fillable = [
        'type',
        'name',
        'company',
        'bike_id'
    ];
    /**
     * Relationship.
     *
     * @var string
     */
    public function bike() {
        return $this->belongsTo('App\Bike');
```

```
            }
        }
```

One-to-many relationship

The one-to-many relationship will be applied between `Bike` and `Items`, which means that one `bike` will have many custom `items`.

Still in the `project/app/Bike.app` file, let's add the one-to-many relationship between the `Item` and `Bike` models.

Add the following code immediately after the `builder()` function:

```
public function items() {
    return $this->hasMany('App\Item');
}
```

Many-to-many relationship

For the many-to-many relationship, we will have many Bikes in many Garages by using the pivot table.

In the many-to-many relationship, we need to respect some naming rules.

The name of the pivot table should consist of singular names of both tables, separated by underscore symbols, and these names should be arranged in alphabetical order.

By default, there should only be two pivot table fields and the foreign key to each of the tables, in our case, `bike_id` and `garage_id`.

Still in the `project/app/Bike.app` file, let's add the many-to-many relationship between the Bike and Garage models.

Add the following code immediately after the `items()` function:

```
public function garages() {
    return $this->belongsToMany('App\Garage');
}
```

Notice that in the previous code, we are creating the relationship of Bike and Garage in a third table, called the pivot table, which will hold the information relating to the relationship, as we explained previously.

Now, it is time to add the relationship between the user and the ratings with bikes. Add the following code immediately after the `garages()` function:

```php
public function user() {
        return $this->belongsTo('App\User');
public function ratings() {
        return $this->hasMany('App\Rating');
}
```

At this point, we will have the following relationships in the `Bike` model:

```php
/**
 * Relationship.
 *
 * @var string
 */
public function builder() {
    return $this->belongsTo('App\Builder');
}
public function items() {
    return $this->hasMany('App\Item');
}
public function garages() {
    return $this->belongsToMany('App\Garage');
}
public function user() {
    return $this->belongsTo(User::class);
}
public function ratings() {
    return $this->hasMany(Rating::class);
}
```

Now, let's add the relationship in the `project/app/Garage.app` model. Replace its content with the following code:

```php
<?php
namespace App;
use Illuminate\Database\Eloquent\Model;
/**
 * @SWG\Definition(
 * definition="Garage",
 * required={"name", "custumer_level"},
 * @SWG\Property(
 * property="name",
 * type="string",
 * description="Jhonny Garage",
 * example="Exhaust"
 * ),
```

```
 * @SWG\Property(
 * property="customer_level",
 * type="integer",
 * description="Whats the garage level",
 * example="10"
 * )
 * )
 */
class Garage extends Model
{
    /**
     * The table associated with the model.
     *
     * @var string
     */
    protected $table = 'garages';
    /**
     * The attributes that are mass assignable.
     *
     * @var array
     */
    protected $fillable = [
        'name',
        'costumer_level'
    ];
    /
    *
     * @var string
     */
    public function bikes() {
        return $this->belongsToMany('App\Bike', 'bike_garage',
        'bike_id', 'garage_id');
    }
}
 * Relationship.
```

Note that we are using `belongsToMany()` and not `hasMany()`. `hasMany()` is used for one-to-many relationships.

Now, let's add the relationship in the `project/app/User.app` model. Replace its content with the following code:

```
<?php
namespace App;
use Illuminate\Notifications\Notifiable;
use Illuminate\Foundation\Auth\User as Authenticatable;
/**
 * @SWG\Definition(
```

```
 * definition="User",
 * required={"name", "email", "password"},
 * @SWG\Property(
 * property="name",
 * type="string",
 * description="User name",
 * example="John Conor"
 * ),
 * @SWG\Property(
 * property="email",
 * type="string",
 * description="Email Address",
 * example="john.conor@terminator.com"
 * ),
 * @SWG\Property(
 * property="password",
 * type="string",
 * description="A very secure password",
 * example="123456"
 * ),
 * )
*/class User extends Authenticatable
{
    use Notifiable;
    /**
     * The attributes that are mass assignable.
     *
     * @var array
     */
    protected $fillable = [
        'name', 'email', 'password',
    ];
    /**
     * The attributes that should be hidden for arrays.
     *
     * @var array
     */
    protected $hidden = [
        'password', 'remember_token',];
     * Relationship.
     ** @var string
     /
    public function bikes()
    {
        return $this->hasMany(App\Bike);
    }
}
```

Open the `project/app/Rating.app` model, and replace its content with the following code:

```php
<?php
namespace App;
use Illuminate\Database\Eloquent\Model;
/**
 * @SWG\Definition(
 * definition="Rating",
 * required={"bike_id", "user_id", "rating"},
 * @SWG\Property(
 * property="biker_id",
 * type="integer",
 * description="Bike id",
 * example="1"
 * ),
 * @SWG\Property(
 * property="user_id",
 * type="integer",
 * description="User id",
 * example="2"
 * ),
 * @SWG\Property(
 * property="rating",
 * type="integer",
 * description="Vote by rating",
 * example="10"
 * )
 * )
 */
class Rating extends Model
{
    /**
     * The attributes that are mass assignable.
     *
     * @var array
     */
    protected $fillable = [
        'bike_id',
        'user_id',
        'rating'
    ];
    /**
     * Relationship.
     *
     * @var string
     */
    public function bike() {
```

```
            return $this->belongsTo('App\Bike');
    }
}
```

Now that we have our migration files and application models ready, we can create the seeds file to feed our database. But before we go further, let's migrate our tables to our database. Inside your Terminal window, type the following command:

php artisan migrate

Well done! We have successfully migrated all our tables, and now our database is good to go.

If you have some issues when trying to use the `migrate` command, use the `refresh` parameter:

php artisan migrate:refresh

Seeding our database

Remember that, in the last chapter, we already created the Bike seed, so now we just need to create another three seeds, which are going to be `Builders`, `Items`, and `Garage`.

1. Open your Terminal window and type the following command:

   php artisan make:seeder BuildersTableSeeder

2. Add the following code to the `app/database/seeds/BuildersTableSeeder.php` public function `run()`:

   ```
   DB::table('builders')->delete();
   $json = File::get("database/data-sample/builders.json");
   $data = json_decode($json);
   foreach ($data as $obj) {
       Builder::create(array(
           'id' => $obj->id,
           'name' => $obj->name,
           'description' => $obj->description,
           'location' => $obj->location
       ));
   }
   ```

3. Still in your Terminal window, type the following command:

   php artisan make:seeder ItemsTableSeeder

4. Add the following code to `app/database/seeds/ItemsTableSeeder.php`:

```
DB::table('items')->delete();
$json = File::get("database/data-sample/items.json");
$data = json_decode($json);
foreach ($data as $obj) {
    Item::create(array(
        'id' => $obj->id,
        'type' => $obj->type,
        'name' => $obj->name,
        'company' => $obj->company,
        'bike_id' => $obj->bike_id
    ));
}
```

5. In your Terminal window, type the following command:

```
php artisan make:seeder GaragesTableSeeder
```

6. Add the following code to
   the `app/database/seeds/GaragesTableSeeder.php`, `run()` public function:

```
DB::table('garages')->delete();
$json = File::get("database/data-sample/garages.json");
$data = json_decode($json);
foreach ($data as $obj) {
    Garage::create(array(
        'id' => $obj->id,
        'name' => $obj->name,
        'customer_level' => $obj->customer_level
    ));
}
```

7. Add the following code to
   the `app/database/seeds/UsersTableSeeder.php` folder's public
   function, `run()`:

```
DB::table('users')->insert([
'name' => 'Johnny Cash',
'email' => 'johnny@cash.com',
'password' => bcrypt('123456')
]);
    DB::table('users')->insert([
        'name' => 'Frank Sinatra',
        'email' => 'frank@sinatra.com',
        'password' => bcrypt('123456')
    ]);
```

Note that we are using the same function as we did in the previous chapter to load the sample data. Now, it's time to create the JSON files.

8. Inside `project/database/data-sample/`, create a new file called `builders.json` and add the following code:

```
[{
    "id": 1,
    "name": "Diamond Atelier",
    "description": "Diamond Atelier was founded by two fellow
riders
    who grew tired of the same played-out custom bike look and
feel
    they and their friends had grown accustomed to witnessing.",
    "location": "Munich, Germany"
},{
    "id": 2,
    "name": "Deus Ex Machina's",
    "description": "Established in Australia back in 2006. And what
started on the East Coast of Australia has spread across the
    world, building an empire of cafe racers.",
    "location": "Sydney, Australia"
},{
    "id": 3,
    "name": "Rough Crafts",
    "description": "A true testament to how far the custom bike
    world has come since the introduction of motorcycles in the
    early 20th century, Taiwan-based Rough Crafts is a design
    powerhouse.",
    "location": "Taiwan"
},{
    "id": 4,
    "name": "Roldand Sands",
    "description": "Is an American motorcycle racer and designer of
    custom high-performance motorcycles.",
    "location": "California, USA"
},{
    "id": 5,
    "name": "Chopper Dave",
    "description": "An artist, a biker, a builder and an innovator
among other things, but what it comes down to is David
    "ChopperDave" Freston is a motorcycle builder and fabricator
that is passionate about motorcycles",
    "location": "California, USA"
}]
```

9. Inside `project/database/data-sample/`, create a new file called `items.json` and add the following code:

```
[{
    "id": 1,
    "type": "Handlebars",
    "name": "Apes Hanger 16 ",
    "company": "TC Bros",
    "bike_id": 2
},{
    "id": 2,
    "type": "Seat",
    "name": "Challenger",
    "company": "Biltwell Inc",
    "bike_id": 3
},{
    "id": 3,
    "type": "Exhaust",
    "name": "Side Shots",
    "company": "Vance and Hines",
    "bike_id": 3
}]
```

10. Now, we need to create some more seeds so that we have all the database boilerplate for our app. Still in the Terminal window, type the following command:

```
php artisan make:seeder BikesGaragesTableSeeder
```

11. Add the following code to the `app/database/seeds/BikesGaragesTableSeeder.php` public function, `run()`:

```
DB::table('bike_garage')->insert([
    'bike_id' => 1,
    'garage_id' => 2
]);
DB::table('bike_garage')->insert([
    'bike_id' => 2,
    'garage_id' => 2
]);
```

12. Notice that in the previous code, we just inserted the records manually using the Eloquent `insert()` method instead to create a JSON file for this task.

13. Now, open `project/database/data-sample/bikes.json` and replace the content with the following code:

```
[{
    "id": 1,
    "make": "Harley Davidson",
    "model": "XL1200 Nightster",
    "year": "2009",
    "mods": "Nobis vero sint non eius. Laboriosam sed odit hic quia
doloribus. Numquam laboriosam numquam quas quis."
    "picture": "https://placeimg.com/640/480/nature","user_id": 2,
    "builder_id": 1
}, {
    "id": 2,
    "make": "Harley Davidson",
    "model": "Blackline",
    "year": "2008",
    "mods": "Nobis vero sint non eius. Laboriosam sed odit hic quia
doloribus. Numquam laboriosam numquam quas quis.",
    "picture": "https://placeimg.com/640/480/nature",
    "user_id": 1,
    "builder_id": 2
}, {
    "id": 3,
    "make": "Harley Davidson",
    "model": "Dyna Switchback",
    "year": "2009",
    "mods": "Nobis vero sint non eius. Laboriosam sed odit hic quia
doloribus. Numquam laboriosam numquam quas quis.",
    "picture": "https://placeimg.com/640/480/nature",
    "user_id": 2,
    "builder_id": 3
}, {
    "id": 4,
    "make": "Harley Davidson",
    "model": "Dyna Super Glide",
    "year": "2009",
    "mods": "Nobis vero sint non eius. Laboriosam sed odit hic quia
doloribus. Numquam laboriosam numquam quas quis.",
    "picture": "https://placeimg.com/640/480/nature",
    "user_id": 4,
    "builder_id": 4
},{
    "id": 5,
    "make": "Harley Davidson",
    "model": "Dyna Wild Glide",
    "year": "2005",
    "mods": "Nobis vero sint non eius. Laboriosam sed odit hic quia
```

```
doloribus. Numquam laboriosam numquam quas quis.",
    "picture": "https://placeimg.com/640/480/nature",
    "user_id": 5,
    "builder_id": 5
}]
```

In the previous code, we added the `builder_id` and `user_id` to each bike record to make the association between a bike and its builder and the user and their bike. Remember that we created `project/database/data-sample/bikes.json` in the previous chapter.

Note that we assigned bike 4 and 5 to `user_id` as 4 and 5. Don't worry about this now, as later on in the book, you will understand why we did this now.

14. Open `project/database/seeds/databaseSeeder.php` and uncomment the user's seeds.

15. Let's use the `seed` command to fill our database. Type the following command in your Terminal window:

```
php artisan migrate:fresh --seed
```

After using the previous command, we will have the following output:

```
Seeding: UsersTableSeeder
Seeding: BikesTableSeeder
Seeding: BuildersTableSeeder
Seeding: ItemsTableSeeder
Seeding: GaragesTableSeeder
Seeding: BikeGarageTableSeeder
```

This means that everything is correct for now.

The `migrate:fresh` command will drop all tables from the database and then execute the `migrate` command with a fresh install.

Querying the database using Tinker

Tinker is a command-line application that allows you to interact with your Laravel application, including the Eloquent ORM, jobs, events, and more. To get access to the Tinker console, run the `artisan tinker` command that we previously used to check the database connection in Chapter 01, *Understanding the Core Concepts of Laravel 5*.

1. Open your Terminal window and type the following command:

   ```
   php artisan tinker
   ```

   Since we have not created any controllers or routes for our application yet, it's impossible to check our data using the browser to access the API endpoints.

   However, using Tinker, it is possible to interact with our database and check whether everything went well with our migration files and database seed.

   Let's go to the builders table and make sure that everything is set up correctly.

2. Still on your Terminal and inside the Tinker console, type the following command:

   ```
   DB::table('builders')->get();
   ```

   The output on your Terminal will be a builders list that's very similar to the following JSON structure:

   ```
   >>> DB::table('builders')->get();
   => Illuminate\Support\Collection {#810
        all: [
          {#811
            +"id": 1,
            +"name": "Diamond Atelier",
            +"description": "Diamond Atelier was founded by two fellow
            riders who grew tired of the same played-out custom
            bike look and feel they and their friends had grown
            accustomed     to witnessing.",
            +"location": "Munich, Germany",
            +"created_at": "XXXX",
            +"updated_at": "XXXX",
          },
          ...
        }]
   ```

   Note that you omit all the records on the builders list, so do not become repetitive in your code blocks.

3. Still on your Terminal and inside the Tinker console, type the following command:

   ```
   DB::table('builders')->find(3);
   ```

Here, we have just one record with the id 3 inside the `find()` function, as we can see in the following output:

```
>>> DB::table('builders')->find(3);
=> {#817
     +"id": 3,
     +"name": "Rough Crafts",      +"description": "A true testament
to how far the custom bike world has come since the
     introduction      of motorcycles i
     n the early 20th century, Taiwan-based Rough Crafts is a
design        powerhouse.",
     +"location": "Taiwan",
     +"created_at": "XXXX",
     +"updated_at": "XXXX",
   }
```

Now, let's see how we can get the same result from the previous command, but this time using the Where clause and the `Builder` model instance.

4. Still on your Terminal and inside the Tinker console, type the following command:

```
Builder::where('id', '=', 3)->get();
```

We will have the following output as a query result:

```
>>> Builder::where('id', '=', 3)->get();
=> Illuminate\Database\Eloquent\Collection {#825
     all: [
       App\Builder {#828
         id: 3,
         name: "Rough Crafts",
         description: "A true testament to how far the custom bike
world has come since the introduction of motorcycles
         in the early 20th century, Taiwan-based Rough Crafts is a
design powerhouse.",
         location: "Taiwan",
         created_at: "XXXX",
         updated_at: "XXXX",
       },
     ],
   }
```

But wait, you must be asking yourself, where is the bike data? Remember that we attribute a bike to a builder on our seed. Let's introduce the association query.

5. So, imagine that we want to query all customized bikes. Still on your Terminal and inside the Tinker console, type the following command:

```
Builder::with('bike')->find(3);
```

Note that the previous command will return the builder record with id: 3 using the find() method and the ::with() method association. This time, we can see the bike's information, as shown in the following output:

```
>>> Builder::with('bike')->find(3);
=> App\Builder {#811
      id: 3,
      name: "Rough Crafts",       description: "A true testament to
how
      far the custom bike world has come since the introduction of
      motorcycles in t
      he early 20th century, Taiwan-based Rough Crafts is a design
      powerhouse.",
      location: "Taiwan",
      created_at: "XXXX",
      updated_at: "XXXX",
      bike: App\Bike {#831
        id: 3,
        make: "Harley Davidson",
        model: "Dyna Switchback",
        year: "2009",
        mods: "Nobis vero sint non eius. Laboriosam sed odit hic
quia
        doloribus. Numquam laboriosam numquam quas quis.",
        picture: "https://placeimg.com/640/480/nature",
        builder_id: 3,
        created_at: "XXXX",
        updated_at: "XXXX",
      },
    }
```

Now, let's see how we can submit a query to get all model associations, this time using the Builder model instance.

6. Still on your Terminal and inside the Tinker console, type the following command:

```
Bike::with(['items', 'builder'])->find(3);
```

Note that we are using an array inside the `::with()` method to get items and builder associations, as we can see in the following output:

```
>>> Bike::with(['items', 'builder'])->find(3);
[!] Aliasing 'Bike' to 'App\Bike' for this Tinker session.
=> App\Bike {#836
     id: 3,        make: "Harley Davidson",
     model: "Dyna Switchback",
     year: "2009",
     mods: "Nobis vero sint non eius. Laboriosam sed odit hic quia
     doloribus. Numquam laboriosam numquam quas quis.",
     picture: "https://placeimg.com/640/480/nature",
     builder_id: 3,
     created_at: "XXXX",
     updated_at: "XXXX",
     items: Illuminate\Database\Eloquent\Collection {#837
       all: [
         App\Item {#843
           id: 2,
           type: "Seat",
           name: "Challenger",
           company: "Biltwell Inc",
           bike_id: 3,
           created_at: "XXXX",
           updated_at: "XXXX",
         },
         App\Item {#845
           id: 3,
           type: "Exhaust",
           name: "Side Shots",
           company: "Vance and Hines",
           bike_id: 3,
           created_at: "XXXX",
           updated_at: "XXXX",
         },
       ],
     },
     builder: App\Builder {#844
       id: 3,
       name: "Rough Crafts",description: "A true testament to how
       far the custom bike world has come since the introduction of
       motorcycles in the early 20th century, Taiwan-based Rough
       Crafts is a design powerhouse.",
       location: "Taiwan",
       created_at: "XXXX",
       updated_at: "XXXX",
     },
   }
```

Creating controllers and routes

We are almost there, but we have a few steps left so that we can finish our API. Now, is time to create the API controller and API routes.

With the newest version (5.6) from Laravel we have a new command available to do this task. This is the `--api` flag. Let's see how it works in practice.

Creating and updating the controller function

1. Open your Terminal window and type the following command:

```
php artisan make:controller API/BuilderController --api
```

Note that the `--api` flag creates four methods for us inside the `BuilderController` class:

- `index()` = GET
- `store()` = POST
- `show($id)` = GET
- `update(Request $request, $id)` = PUT
- `destroy($id)` = POST

2. Open `project/app/Http/Controllers/API/BuilderController.php` and add the `App\Builder` code right after the Controller import.

3. Now, let's add the content for each method.
   Open `project/app/Http/Controllers/API/BuilderController.php` and replace the content with the following code:

```php
<?php
namespace App\Http\Controllers\API;
use Illuminate\Http\Request;
use App\Http\Controllers\Controller;
use App\Builder;
class BuilderController extends Controller
{
    /**
     * Display a listing of the resource.
     *
```

```
 * @return \Illuminate\Http\Response
 *
 * @SWG\Get(
 * path="/api/builders",
 * tags={"Builders"}
 * summary="List Builders",
 * @SWG\Response(
 * response=200,
 * description="Success: List all Builders",
 * @SWG\Schema(ref="#/definitions/Builder")
 * ),
 * @SWG\Response(
 * response="404",
 * description="Not Found"
 * )
 * ),
 */
public function index()
{
    $listBuilder = Builder::all();
    return $listBuilder;

}
```

4. Now, let's add the code for the `store/create` method. Add the following code right after the `index()` function:

```
/**
 * Store a newly created resource in storage.
 *
 * @param \Illuminate\Http\Request $request
 * @return \Illuminate\Http\Response
 *
 * @SWG\Post(
 * path="/api/builders",
 * tags={"Builders"},
 * summary="Create Builder",
 * @SWG\Parameter(
 *          name="body",
 *          in="body",
 *          required=true,
 *          @SWG\Schema(ref="#/definitions/Builder"),
 *          description="Json format",
 *      ),
 * @SWG\Response(
 * response=201,
 * description="Success: A Newly Created Builder",
 * @SWG\Schema(ref="#/definitions/Builder")
```

```
* ),
* @SWG\Response(
* response="422",
* description="Missing mandatory field"
* ),
* @SWG\Response(
* response="404",
* description="Not Found"
* ),
* @SWG\Response(
*              response="405",
*              description="Invalid HTTP Method
* )
* ),
*/
public function store(Request $request)
{
    $createBuilder = Builder::create($request->all());
    return $createBuilder;
}
```

Now, let's add the code for the get by `id` method. Add the following code right after the `store()` function:

```
/**
* Display the specified resource.
*
* @param int $id* @return \Illuminate\Http\Response
*
* @SWG\Get(
* path="/api/builders/{id}",
* tags={"Builders"},
* summary="Get Builder by Id",
* @SWG\Parameter(
* name="id",
* in="path",
* required=true,
* type="integer",
* description="Display the specified Builder by id.",
*          ),
* @SWG\Response(
* response=200,
* description="Success: Return the Builder",
* @SWG\Schema(ref="#/definitions/Builder")
* ),
* @SWG\Response(
* response="404",
* description="Not Found"
```

```
 *  ),
 *  @SWG\Response(
     *              response="405",
     *              description="Invalid HTTP Method"
     *  )
 *  )
 */
public function show($id)
{
    $showBuilderById = Builder::with('Bike')->findOrFail($id);
    return $showBuilderById;
}
```

Let's add the code for the update method. Add the following code right after the show() function:

```
/**
 * Update the specified resource in storage.
 *
 * @param \Illuminate\Http\Request $request
 * @param int $id
 * @return \Illuminate\Http\Response
 *
 * @SWG\Put(
 * path="/api/builders/{id}",
 * tags={"Builders"},
 * summary="Update Builder",
 * @SWG\Parameter(
 * name="id",
 * in="path",
 * required=true,
 * type="integer",
 * description="Update the specified Builder by id.",
 *         ),
 * @SWG\Parameter(
 *          name="body",
 *          in="body",
 *          required=true,
 *          @SWG\Schema(ref="#/definitions/Builder"),
 *          description="Json format",
 *          ),
 * @SWG\Response(
 * response=200,
 * description="Success: Return the Builder updated",
 * @SWG\Schema(ref="#/definitions/Builder")
 * ),
 * @SWG\Response(
 * response="422",
```

```
 * description="Missing mandatory field"
 * ),
 * @SWG\Response(
 * response="404",
 * description="Not Found"
 * ),
 * @SWG\Response(
 *                 response="405",
 *                 description="Invalid HTTP Method"
 *      )
 * ),
 */
public function update(Request $request, $id)
{
    $updateBuilderById = Builder::findOrFail($id);
    $updateBuilderById->update($request->all());
    return $updateBuilderById;
}
```

Now, let's add the code for the delete method. Add the following code right after the update() function:

```
/**
 * Remove the specified resource from storage.
 *
 * @param int $id
 * @return \Illuminate\Http\Response
 *
 * @SWG\Delete(
 * path="/api/builders/{id}",
 * tags={"Builders"},
 * summary="Delete Builder",
 * description="Delete the specified Builder by id",
 * @SWG\Parameter(
 * description="Builder id to delete",
 * in="path",
 * name="id",
 * required=true,
 * type="integer",
 * format="int64"
 * ),
 * @SWG\Response(
 * response=404,
 * description="Not found"
 * ),
 * @SWG\Response(
 *                 response="405",
 *                 description="Invalid HTTP Method"
```

```
  *  ),
  *  @SWG\Response(
  *  response=204,
  *  description="Success: successful deleted"
  *  ),
  *  )
  */
  public function destroy($id)
  {
      $deleteBikeById = Bike::find($id)->delete();
      return response()->json([], 204);
      }
}
```

Note that in the `index()` function, we are using the `all()` method to list all Bikes and using the associated `::with()` method just on the `show($id)` function.

We have already added the Swagger definitions to the controller, but don't worry: later in this chapter, we will discuss this in detail.

The model association query to list bikes and show bike details, is a simple API decision. As you can see, we are returning the bike list without all associations and just returning the associations on the get bike by id. It doesn't make sense to return every association on every request, so on the Bike list, we just show the bike's details and when we click on details, we will see the complete information with all model association. So don't worry about this now, as later on in the `chapter 10`, *Frontend views with Bootstrap 4 and NgBootstrap*, we will see how to do this.

1. Open your Terminal window and type the following command:

   php artisan make:controller API/ItemController --api

   Open `project/app/Http/Controllers/API/ItemController.php` and add the following code right after the Controller import: `use App\Item;`.

2. Now, let's add the content for each method.
   Open `project/app/Http/Controllers/API/ItemController.php` and add the following code for each one:

   ```php
   <?php
   namespace App\Http\Controllers\API;
   use Illuminate\Http\Request;
   use App\Http\Controllers\Controller;
   use App\Item;
   class ItemController extends Controller
   ```

```
{
    /**
    * Display a listing of the resource.
    *
    * @return \Illuminate\Http\Response
    *
    * @SWG\Get(
    * path="/api/items",
    * tags={"Items"},
    * summary="List Items",
    * @SWG\Response(
    * response=200,
    * description="Success: List all Items",
    * @SWG\Schema(ref="#/definitions/Item")
    * ),
    * @SWG\Response(
    * response="404",
    * description="Not Found"
    * )
    * ),
    */
    public function index()
    {
        $listItems = Item::all();
        return $listItems;
    }
    /**
    * Store a newly created resource in storage.
    *
    * @param \Illuminate\Http\Request $request
    * @return \Illuminate\Http\Response
    *
    * @SWG\Post(
    * path="/api/items",
    * tags={"Items"},
    * summary="Create Item",
    * @SWG\Parameter(
    *           name="body",
    *           in="body",
    *           required=true,
    *           @SWG\Schema(ref="#/definitions/Item"),
    *           description="Json format",
    *       ),
    * @SWG\Response(
    * response=201,
    * description="Success: A Newly Created Item",
    * @SWG\Schema(ref="#/definitions/Item")
    * ),
```

```
 * @SWG\Response(
 * response="422",
 * description="Missing mandatory field"
 * ),
 * @SWG\Response(
 * response="404",
 * description="Not Found"
 * )
 * ),
 */
public function store(Request $request)
{
    $createItem = Item::create($request->all());
    return $createItem;
}
/**
 * Display the specified resource.
 *
 * @param int $id
 * @return \Illuminate\Http\Response
 *
 * @SWG\Get(
 * path="/api/items/{id}",
 * tags={"Items"},
 * summary="Get Item by Id",
 * @SWG\Parameter(
 * name="id",
 * in="path",
 * required=true,
 * type="integer",
 * description="Display the specified Item by id.",
 *          ),
 * @SWG\Response(
 * response=200,
 * description="Success: Return the Item",
 * @SWG\Schema(ref="#/definitions/Item")
 * ),
 * @SWG\Response(
 * response="404",
 * description="Not Found"
 * )
 * ),
 */
public function show($id)
{
    $showItemById = Item::with('Bike')->findOrFail($id);
    return $showItemById;
}
```

```
/**
 * Update the specified resource in storage.
 *
 * @param \Illuminate\Http\Request $request
 * @param int $id
 * @return \Illuminate\Http\Response
 *
 * @SWG\Put(
 * path="/api/items/{id}",
 * tags={"Items"},
 * summary="Update Item",
 * @SWG\Parameter(
 * name="id",
 * in="path",
 * required=true,
 * type="integer",
 * description="Update the specified Item by id.",
 *          ),
 * @SWG\Parameter(
 *              name="body",
 *              in="body",
 *              required=true,
 *              @SWG\Schema(ref="#/definitions/Item"),
 *              description="Json format",
 *          ),
 * @SWG\Response(
 * response=200,
 * description="Success: Return the Item updated",
 * @SWG\Schema(ref="#/definitions/Item")
 * ),
 * @SWG\Response(
 * response="422",
 * description="Missing mandatory field"
 * ),
 * @SWG\Response(
 * response="404",
 * description="Not Found"
 * )
 * ),
 */
public function update(Request $request, $id)
{
    $updateItemById = Item::findOrFail($id);
    $updateItemById->update($request->all());
    return $updateItemById;
}
/**
 * Remove the specified resource from storage.
```

```
 *
 * @param int $id
 * @return \Illuminate\Http\Response
 *
 * @SWG\Delete(
 * path="/api/items/{id}",
 * tags={"Items"},
 * summary="Delete Item",
 * description="Delete the specified Item by id",
 * @SWG\Parameter(
 * description="Item id to delete",
 * in="path",
 * name="id",
 * required=true,
 * type="integer",
 * format="int64"
 * ),
 * @SWG\Response(
 * response=404,
 * description="Not found"
 * ),
 * @SWG\Response(
 * response=204,
 * description="Success: successful deleted"
 * ),
 * )
 */
public function destroy($id)
{
    $deleteItemById = Item::findOrFail($id)->delete();
    return response()->json([], 204);
}
}
```

3. Open your Terminal window and type the following command:

```
php artisan make:controller API/BikeController --api
```

Open `project/app/Http/Controllers/API/BikeController.php` and add the following code right after the Controller import:

```
use App\Bike;
```

4. Now, let's add the content for each method.
   Open `project/app/Http/Controllers/API/BikeController.php` and add
   the following code for each one:

```php
<?php
namespace App\Http\Controllers\API;
use Illuminate\Http\Request;
use App\Http\Controllers\Controller;
use App\Bike;
class BikeController extends Controller
{
    /**
     * Display a listing of the resource.
     ** @return \Illuminate\Http\Response
     *
     * @SWG\Get(
     * path="/api/bikes",
     * tags={"Bikes"},
     * summary="List Bikes",
     * @SWG\Response(
     * response=200,
     * description="Success: List all Bikes",
     * @SWG\Schema(ref="#/definitions/Bike")
     * ),
     * @SWG\Response(
     * response="404",
     * description="Not Found"
     * )
     * ),
     */
    public function index()
    {
        $listBikes = Bike::all();
        return $listBikes;
    }
    /**
     * Store a newly created resource in storage.
     *
     * @param \Illuminate\Http\Request $request
     * @return \Illuminate\Http\Response
     *
     * @SWG\Post(
     * path="/api/bikes",
     * tags={"Bikes"},
     * summary="Create Bike",
     * @SWG\Parameter(
     *          name="body",
```

```
*                in="body",
*                required=true,
*                @SWG\Schema(ref="#/definitions/Bike"),
*                description="Json format",
*            ),
* @SWG\Response(
* response=201,
* description="Success: A Newly Created Bike",
* @SWG\Schema(ref="#/definitions/Bike")
* ),
* @SWG\Response(
* response="422",
* description="Missing mandatory field"
* ),
* @SWG\Response(
* response="404",
* description="Not Found"
* )
* ),
*/
public function store(Request $request)
{
    $createBike = Bike::create($request->all());
    return $createBike;
}
/**
* Display the specified resource.
*
* @param int $id
* @return \Illuminate\Http\Response
*
* @SWG\Get(
* path="/api/bikes/{id}",
* tags={"Bikes"},
* summary="Get Bike by Id",
* @SWG\Parameter(
* name="id",
* in="path",
* required=true,
* type="integer",
* description="Display the specified bike by id.",
*        ),
* @SWG\Response(
* response=200,
* description="Success: Return the Bike",
* @SWG\Schema(ref="#/definitions/Bike")
* ),
* @SWG\Response(
```

```
 * response="404",
 * description="Not Found"
 * )
 * ),
 */
public function show($id)
{
    $showBikeById = Bike::with(['items', 'builder',
'garages'])-
    >findOrFail($id);
    return $showBikeById;
}
/**
 * Update the specified resource in storage.
 *
 * @param \Illuminate\Http\Request $request
 * @param int $id
 * @return \Illuminate\Http\Response
 *
 * @SWG\Put(
 * path="/api/bikes/{id}",
 * tags={"Bikes"},
 * summary="Update Bike",
 * @SWG\Parameter(
 * name="id",
 * in="path",
 * required=true,
 * type="integer",
 * description="Update the specified bike by id.",
 *         ),
 * @SWG\Parameter(
 *           name="body",
 *           in="body",
 *           required=true,
 *           @SWG\Schema(ref="#/definitions/Bike"),
 *           description="Json format",
 *         ),
 * @SWG\Response(
 * response=200,
 * description="Success: Return the Bike updated",
 * @SWG\Schema(ref="#/definitions/Bike")
 * ),
 * @SWG\Response(
 * response="422",
 * description="Missing mandatory field"
 * ),
 * @SWG\Response(
 * response="404",
```

```
 * description="Not Found"
 * )
 * ),
 */
public function update(Request $request, $id)
{
    $updateBikeById = Bike::findOrFail($id);
    $updateBikeById->update($request->all());
    return $updateBikeById;
}
/**
 * Remove the specified resource from storage.
 *
 * @param int $id* @return \Illuminate\Http\Response
 *
 * @SWG\Delete(
 * path="/api/bikes/{id}",
 * tags={"Bikes"},
 * summary="Delete bike",
 * description="Delete the specified bike by id",
 * @SWG\Parameter(
 * description="Bike id to delete",
 * in="path",
 * name="id",
 * required=true,
 * type="integer",
 * format="int64"
 * ),
 * @SWG\Response(
 * response=404,
 * description="Not found"
 * ),
 * @SWG\Response(
 * response=204,
 * description="Success: successful deleted"
 * ),
 * )
 */
public function destroy($id)
{
    $deleteBikeById = Bike::find($id)->delete();
    return response()->json([], 204);
}
}
```

Open your Terminal window and type the following command:

```
php artisan make:controller API/RatingController --api
```

5. Open `project/app/Http/Controllers/API/RatingController.php` and add the following code right after the Controller import:

```
use App\Rating;
```

6. Now, let's add the content for each method.
   Open `project/app/Http/Controllers/API/RatingController.php` and add the following code for each one:

```php
<?php
namespace App\Http\Controllers\API;
use Illuminate\Http\Request;
use App\Http\Controllers\Controller;
use App\Bike;
use App\Rating;
use App\Http\Resources\RatingResource;
class RatingController extends Controller
{
    /**
     * Store a newly created resource in storage.
     *
     * @param \Illuminate\Http\Request $request
     * @return \Illuminate\Http\Response
     *
     * @SWG\Post(
     * path="/api/bikes/{bike_id}/ratings",
     * tags={"Ratings"},
     * summary="rating a Bike",
     * @SWG\Parameter(
     * in="path",
     * name="id",
     * required=true,
     * type="integer",
     * format="int64",
     *          description="Bike Id"
     *      ),
     * @SWG\Parameter(
     *          name="body",
     *          in="body",
     *          required=true,
     *          @SWG\Schema(ref="#/definitions/Rating"),
     *          description="Json format",
     *      ),
     * @SWG\Response(
     * response=201,
     * description="Success: A Newly Created Rating",
     * @SWG\Schema(ref="#/definitions/Rating")
```

```
 *  ),
 *  @SWG\Response(
 *  response=401,
 *  description="Refused: Unauthenticated"
 *  ),
 *  @SWG\Response(
 *  response="422",
 *  description="Missing mandatory field"
 *  ),
 *  @SWG\Response(
 *  response="404",
 *  description="Not Found"
 *  ),
 *  @SWG\Response(
 *          response="405",
 *      description="Invalid HTTP Method"
 *  ),
 *  security={
 *          { "api_key":{} }
 *  }
 *  ),
 */
public function store(Request $request, Bike $bike)
{
    $rating = Rating::firstOrCreate(
        [
            'user_id' => $request->user()->id,
            'bike_id' => $bike->id,
        ],
        ['rating' => $request->rating]
    );
    return new RatingResource($rating);
}
}
```

You should be finding some strange things in the rating controller code. Among them, we have some new error codes, `422`, `405`, and a security tag in the Swagger documentation, plus a new import called **rating resource**.

This may sound strange, but do not panic; we'll look at this in detail in the following sections.

Creating the API routes

Now, it is time to create some API routes and check what we have built so far. We are using the new feature of `apiResource`.

Open `project/routes/api.php` and add the following code:

```
Route::apiResources([
    'bikes' => 'API\BikeController',
    'builders' => 'API\BuilderController',
    'items' => 'API\ItemController',
    'bikes/{bike}/ratings' => 'API\RatingController'
]);
```

At this moment, we already have the necessary code for our API, so we need to make some small adjustments and explain some more things.

Generating Swagger UI documentation

As you can see from the previous examples, we have already added the documentation of our API through the Swagger definitions to our recently created controllers. This is the same code we used in the previous example. Let's generate the documentation on the Swagger UI.

Open your Terminal window and type the following command:

```
php artisan 15-swagger:generate
```

As you can note on the previous Swagger definitions on error messages, we have some new HTTP errors, such as 422.

This means that if the user tries to input some data with one or more missing required fields, our API must return an HTTP error code. This will be 422. So, let's see how we can implement some validation and verify some common API HTTP codes.

Summary

We have come to the end of part one of our chapter, where we created a robust and scalable RESTful foundation for our API. We learned how to create controllers, routes, and how to deal with Eloquent relationships.

We still have a lot of work ahead, as we need to deal with error messages, resources, and token-based authentication. In the next chapter, we will see how to accomplish this.

6
Creating a RESTful API Using Laravel - Part 2

In this chapter, we will continue to build our API. We still have a long way to go in Laravel.

We will learn how to use some features that are very common in every web application, such as authentication and the customization of API errors.

Remember, we are creating a RESTful API and, unlike traditional applications such as MVC, our error model is extremely varied and always returned when we used the JSON format.

In this chapter, you will learn how to build a solid RESTful API by doing the following:

- Dealing with request validation and error messages
- Using token-based authentication
- Dealing with Laravel resources

Dealing with request validation and error messages

The Laravel framework offers us many ways to show error messages, and, by default, Laravel's **base controller class** uses a `ValidatesRequests` trait that provides methods to validate the incoming HTTP request, including many default rules such as required, email format, date format, string, and much more.

 You can read more about the possible validation rules at `https://laravel.com/docs/5.6/validation#available-validation-rules`.

It is pretty simple to use request validation, as we can see in the following code block:

```
$validatedData = $request->validate([
'field name' => 'validation rule, can be more than one',
'field name' => 'validation rule',
'field name' => 'validation rule',
...
]);
```

For example, let's see how we can validate the incoming request to the `bikes` endpoint using the HTTP `POST` method to `localhost:8081/api/bikes`.

The validation code will look as follows:

```
$validatedData = $request->validate([
'make' => 'required',
'model' => 'required',
'year'=> 'required',
'mods'=> 'required'
]);
```

The previous operation failed because we purposely didn't send a required file in our imaginary request. However, the return message has some interesting things:

- HTTP status code: `422`

- The following JSON response error message:

```
{
    "message": "The given data was invalid.",
    "errors": {
    "": [
    "The field is required."
    ]}
}
```

Pretty simple, right? Laravel performs all the validations behind the scenes and gives us an elaborate error message.

But what if we want to take control over all the message fields? The answer is that we can do this using manual validation with a validator instance using the validator facade. This is what we'll be looking at in the following sections.

HTTP status code

Before we go further in implementing the validator, let's take a break and review some HTTP status code. As we saw previously, we have a 422 HTTP status code named **Unprocessable entity**.

The following table shows the most common and useful error codes:

Code	Name	Description
200	OK	Everything's all right!
201	Created	Resource was created successfully.
202	Accepted	The request has been accepted for further processing, which will be completed later.
204	OK	Resource was deleted successfully.
302	Redirect	A common redirect response; you can GET the representation at the URI in the location response header.
304	Not Modified	There is no new data to return.
400	Bad Request	Client error.
401	Unauthorized	You are not logged in, for example, you're not using a valid access token.
403	Forbidden	You are authenticated but do not have access to what you are trying to do.
404	Not found	The resource you are requesting does not exist.
405	Method not allowed	The request type is not allowed, for example, /bikes is a resource and POST /bikes is a valid action, but PUT /bikes is not.
409	Conflict	Resource already exists.
422	Unprocessable entity	Validation failed. The request and the format is valid, however, the request was unable to process. For instance, this occurs when sent data does not pass validation tests.
500	Server error	An error occured on the server and it was not the consumer's fault.

> You can read more about status codes at `http://www.restapitutorial.com/httpstatuscodes.html`.

Implementing the Controllers validation

Well, we have gone through a lot of theory, so now it is time to write some code. Let's implement the `Validator` on API controllers:

1. Open `project/app/Http/Controllers/API/BikeController.php` and add the following code right after the use App\Bike statement:

   ```
   use Validator;
   ```

2. Now, add the following code inside the `store (Request $request)` method:

```
$validator = Validator::make($request->all(), [
    'make' => 'required',
    'model' => 'required',
    'year'=> 'required',
    'mods'=> 'required',
    'builder_id' => 'required'
]);
if ($validator->fails()) {
    return response()->json($validator->errors(), 422);
}
```

Note that, in the previous code, we are using the response JSON format and set the errors and status code as parameters of the `json()` method.

3. We will do the same for the `update (Request request, request, id)` method using the same code block from *step 2*.

4. Open `project/app/Http/Controllers/API/BuilderController.php` and add the following code right after the use App\Builder statement:

```
use Validator;
```

5. Now, add the following code inside the `store (Request $request)` method:

```
$validator = Validator::make($request->all(),
    ['name' => 'required',
    'description' => 'required',
    'location'=> 'required'
]);
if ($validator->fails()) {
    return response()->json($validator->errors(), 422);
}
```

6. We will do the same for the `update (Request request, request, id)` method using the same code block from *step 5*.

7. Open `project/app/Http/Controllers/API/ItemController.php` and add the following code right after the use App\Item statement:

```
use Validator;
```

8. Now, add the following code inside the `store (Request $request)` method:

```
$validator = Validator::make($request->all(), [
    'type' => 'required',
```

```
            'name' => 'required',
            'company'=> 'required',
            'bike_id'=> 'required'
    ]);
    if ($validator->fails()) {
        return response()->json($validator->errors(), 422);
    }
```

9. We will do the same for the `update(Request request,request,id)` method using the same code block from *step 7*.

All the validation boilerplate code was placed in the `store()` and `update()` methods, so it is time to write some error handlers.

Adding custom error handling

By default, Laravel has a very powerful error handling engine, but it is totally dedicated to the MVC development pattern, as we mentioned previously. In the next few lines, we'll see how we can change this default behavior and add some specific error handling to our API:

1. Open `project/app/Exceptions/Handler.php` and add the following code inside the `render($request, Exception, $exception)` function:

```
// This will replace our 404 response from the MVC to a JSON
response.
if ($exception instanceof ModelNotFoundException
    && $request->wantsJson() // Enable header Accept:
    application/json to see the proper error msg
) {
    return response()->json(['error' => 'Resource not found'],
404);
}
if ($exception instanceof MethodNotAllowedHttpException) {
    return response()->json(['error' => 'Method Not Allowed'],
405);
}
if ($exception instanceof UnauthorizedHttpException) {
    return response()->json(['error' => 'Token not provided'],
401);
}
// JWT Auth related errors
if ($exception instanceof JWTException) {
    return response()->json(['error' => $exception], 500);
}
if ($exception instanceof TokenExpiredException) {
```

```
            return response()->json(['error' => 'token_expired'],
            $exception->getStatusCode());
    } else if ($exception instanceof TokenInvalidException) {
            return response()->json(['error' => 'token_invalid'],
            $exception->getStatusCode());
    }
    return parent::render($request, $exception);
```

In the previous code, besides mapping the main errors of our API, we still need to add some custom errors for operations involving authentication with JWT. Don't worry; in the next section, we will see how to use JWT to protect some routes for our API.

2. Now, let's add the following code to the top of the file, after the `ExceptionHandler` import:

```
use Illuminate\Database\Eloquent\ModelNotFoundException as
ModelNotFoundException;
use
Symfony\Component\HttpKernel\Exception\UnauthorizedHttpException as
UnauthorizedHttpException;
use Tymon\JWTAuth\Exceptions\JWTException as JWTException;
use Tymon\JWTAuth\Exceptions\TokenExpiredException as
TokenExpiredException;
use Tymon\JWTAuth\Exceptions\TokenInvalidException as
TokenInvalidException;
```

Now, we will be able to see the proper message instead of the default error page from Laravel.

Note that we keep the default Laravel error page and just add custom handling. It is very important that we send the `header: accept: application / json`. In this way, Laravel can identify that it should send the response in JSON format instead of sending the standard error page.

3. Let's take a brief test and check what happens when we try to access a protected URL. Open a Terminal window and type the following code:

```
curl -X GET "http://localhost:8081/api/bikes/3" -H "accept:
application/json" -H "X-CSRF-TOKEN: "
```

The result will be a JSON with the following content:

```
{"message":"Unauthenticated."}
```

4. Now, let's try another error and see what happens when we try to send a POST method. Type the following code in Terminal:

```
curl -X POST "http://localhost:8081/api/bikes/3" -H "accept:
application/json" -H "X-CSRF-TOKEN: "
```

The result will be a JSON with the following content:

```
{"error":"Method Not Allowed"}
```

Checking API URLs with the Swagger UI

After all of this boilerplate code, it is time to test the API and see all the work we have done in this chapter come to life:

1. Open Terminal and type the following command:

```
php artisan l5-swagger:generate
```

Don't forget to go into the php-fpm containers bash with the following command: docker-compose exec php-fpm bash.

2. Open your default browser and go
   to `http://localhost:8081/api/documentation`.

We will see the following result with all the APIs documented properly:

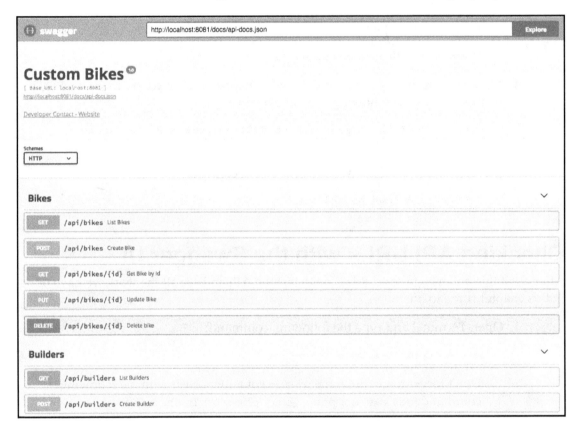

Let's check some operations.

Get all records

Let's see how we can retrieve a list of bikes from our API using the GET method on the Swagger UI:

1. Click on **GET /api/bikes** to open the panel.
2. Click on the **try it out** button.
3. Click on the **execute** button.

We will see something similar to the following screenshot:

```
Request URL

http://localhost:8081/api/bikes

Server response

Code        Details

200
            Response body

            [
              {
                "id": 1,
                "make": "Harley Davidson",
                "model": "XL1200 Nightster",
                "year": "2009",
                "mods": "Nobis vero sint non eius. Laboriosam sed odit hic quia doloribus. Numquam laboriosam numquam quas quis.",
                "picture": "https://placeimg.com/640/480/nature",
                "builder_id": 1,
```

GET request

Get record by ID

Let's see how we can get a list of bikes from our API:

1. Click on **GET /api/bikes/{id}** to open the panel.
2. Click on the **try it out** button.
3. Type 3 inside the ID input box.
4. Click on the **execute** button.

Will see something similar to the following screenshot:

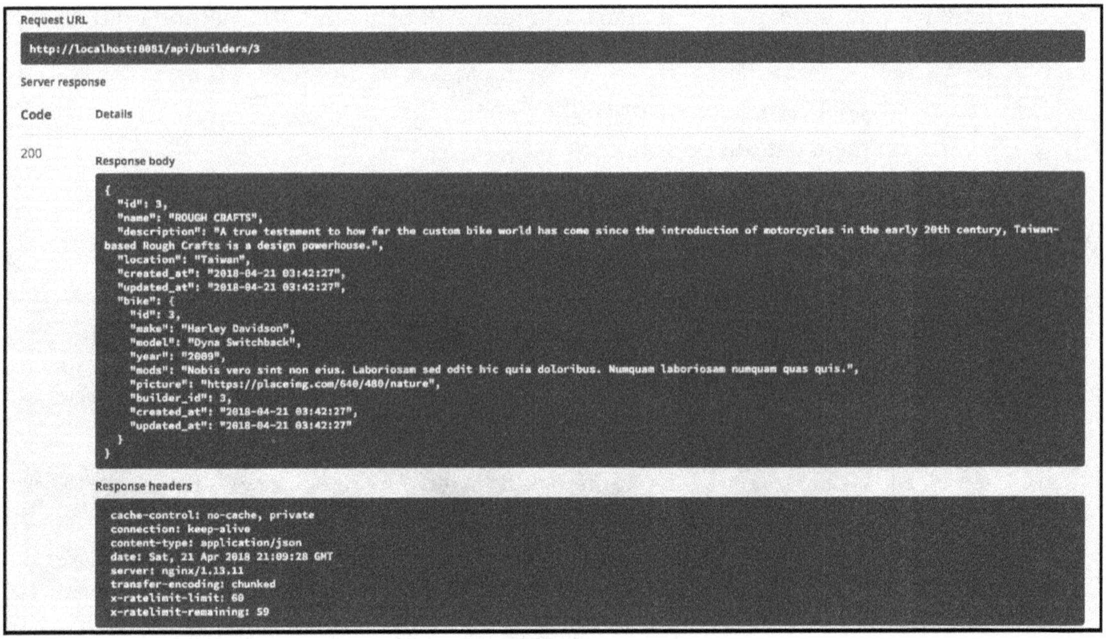

GET by ID request

Checking API response errors

Now, it is time to check some error messages:

1. Click on **PUT /api/bikes/{id}** to open the panel.
2. Click on the **try it out** button.
3. Type 1 inside the ID input box.
4. Replace the `Example Value` placeholder with the following code:

```
{
  "make": "Yamaha",
  "model": "V-Star",
  "year": "2001",
  "mods": "New exhaust system and Grips",
  "picture": "http://www.sample.com/my.bike.jpg"
}
```

5. Click on the **execute** button.

We will see something similar to the following screenshot:

```
Request URL

http://localhost:8081/api/bikes/1

Server response

Code            Details

422             Error: Unprocessable Entity

                Response body

                {
                  "builder_id": [
                    "The builder id field is required."
                  ]
                }

                Response headers

                cache-control: no-cache, private
                connection: keep-alive
                content-type: application/json
                date: Sat, 21 Apr 2018 21:17:22 GMT
                server: nginx/1.13.11
                transfer-encoding: chunked
                x-ratelimit-limit: 60
                x-ratelimit-remaining: 59
```

Update failed with error message

As we can observe, everything happened as expected.

Token-based authentication

Let's understand a bit more about API authentication with Laravel. Even though Laravel is an MVC framework, we can use the token-based authentication feature. Even Laravel itself has a library called Passport.

Laravel Passport is a library that works with the OAuth2 standard. This pattern determines a way to perform application authentication for a web application (API) through tokens, while JWT focuses on authenticating users through tokens.

Laravel Passport is a much bigger layer of abstraction than simple JWT, and it is primarily designed to be fully fledged and easy to set up and use as an OAuth2 server.

An alternative to this is the use of libraries such as `tymon/jwt-auth`.

In fact, Laravel Passport uses JWT for authentication, but that's just an implementation detail. `tymon/jwt-auth` is closer to a simple token-based authentication, though it is still pretty powerful and useful.

For the type of API we are building, JWT is the ideal method for our implementation.

You can read more about `jwt-auth` at `https://github.com/tymondesigns/jwt-auth`.

Installing tymon-jwt-auth

Let's learn how to install and configure `tymon/jwt-auth`.

The installation process is pretty simple, but, as the `tymon/jwt-auth` library is in constant development, we should take some care related what the version we will use:

1. Open the `project/composer.json` file and add the following line of code, right after Laravel/Tinker:

   ```
   "tymon/jwt-auth": "1.0.*"
   ```

2. Now, it is time to publish the vendor package. Still in your Terminal window and inside the Tinker console, type the following command:

   ```
   php artisan vendor:publish --
   provider="Tymon\JWTAuth\Providers\LaravelServiceProvider"
   ```

Note that we are using Laravel 5.6 and `jwt-auth` 1.0, so we don't need to perform any additional actions to load JWT providers. The `jwt-auth` documents sometimes look like a mess and are very confusing, but don't worry, just follow our steps and you will be safe from mismatching documentation.

3. Let's generate the secret. Still in the Terminal window, type the following command:

   ```
   php artisan jwt:secret
   ```

4. The previous command will generate a secret key on your `.env` file, and will look something like the following line:

   ```
   JWT_SECRET=McR1It4Bw9G8jU1b4XJhDMeZs4Q5Zwear
   ```

At this point, we have successfully installed `jwt-auth`, but we need to take some more steps to make our API secure.

Updating the User model

Now, we need to update the `User` model so that we can start to protect the API endpoints with user authentication.

First, we need to implement the `Tymon\JWTAuth\Contracts\JWTSubject` contract on our `User` model, which requires two methods: `getJWTIdentifier()` and `getJWTCustomClaims()`.

Open `project/User.php` and replace its content with the following code:

```php
<?php
namespace App;
use Illuminate\Notifications\Notifiable;
use Illuminate\Foundation\Auth\User as Authenticatable;
use Tymon\JWTAuth\Contracts\JWTSubject;
/**
 * @SWG\Definition(
 * definition="User",
 * required={"name", "email", "password"},
 * @SWG\Property(
 * property="name",
 * type="string",
 * description="User name",
 * example="John Conor"
 * ),
 * @SWG\Property(
 * property="email",
 * type="string",
 * description="Email Address",
 * example="john.conor@terminator.com"
 * ),
 * @SWG\Property(
 * property="password",
 * type="string",
 * description="A very secure password",
 * example="123456"
 * ),
 * )
 */
class User extends Authenticatable implements JWTSubject
{
    use Notifiable;
    /**
     * The attributes that are mass assignable.
     *
     * @var array
```

```
    */
    protected  $fillable = [
        'name', 'email', 'password',
    ];
    /**
     * The attributes that should be hidden for arrays.
     *
     * @var array
     */
    protected  $hidden = [
        'password', 'remember_token',
    ];
    /**
     * Get JSON WEB TOKEN methods.
     *
     * @var array
     */
    public  function  getJWTIdentifier()
    {
        return  $this->getKey();
    }
    public  function  getJWTCustomClaims()
    {
        return [];
    }
    /**
     * Relationship.
     *
     * @var string
     */
    public  function  bikes()
    {
        return  $this->hasMany(App\Bike);
    }
}
```

Setting up the auth guard

Now, let's make some adjustments to the `config.auth.php` file in order to protect some routes:

1. Open `project/config/auth.php` and replace the API driver with the following code:

```
        'defaults' => [                'guard'  =>  'api',
```

```
                    'passwords'  =>  'users',
        ],
        'guards'  => [
                        'web'  => [
                                'driver'  =>  'session',
                                'provider'  =>  'users',
                ],
        'api'  => [
                        'driver'  =>  'jwt',
                        'provider'  =>  'users',
                ],
        ],
```

2. Note that we replaced the default Laravel authentication drivers with `api` and `jwt`.

Creating the authController

For our application, we will use only one controller to contain all our operations of registration and login, which are register, login, and logout.

Later in this book, you will understand why we are using all operations within a single controller instead of creating a controller for each action:

1. Open your Terminal window and type the following command:

```
php artisan make:controller API/AuthController
```

2. Open `project/app/Http/Controllers/API/AuthController.php` and replace its content with the following code:

```php
<?php
namespace App\Http\Controllers\API;
use  Illuminate\Http\Request;
use  App\Http\Controllers\Controller;
use  App\User;
use  Validator;
class  AuthController  extends  Controller
{
    /**
     * Register a new user.
     *
     * @param \Illuminate\Http\Request $request
     * @return \Illuminate\Http\Response
     *
```

```
 * @SWG\Post(
 * path="/api/register",
 * tags={"Users"},
 * summary="Create new User",
 * @SWG\Parameter(
 * name="body",
 * in="body",
 * required=true,
 * @SWG\Schema(ref="#/definitions/User"),
 * description="Json format",
 * ),
 * @SWG\Response(
 * response=201,
 * description="Success: A Newly Created User",
 * @SWG\Schema(ref="#/definitions/User")
 * ),
 * @SWG\Response(
 * response=200,
 * description="Success: operation Successfully"
 * ),
 * @SWG\Response(
 * response=401,
 * description="Refused: Unauthenticated"
 * ),
 * @SWG\Response(
 * response="422",
 * description="Missing mandatory field"
 * ),
 * @SWG\Response(
 * response="404",
 * description="Not Found"
 * )
 * ),
 */
public function register(Request $request)
{
    $validator = Validator::make($request->all(), [
        'email' =>
'required|string|email|max:255|unique:users',
        'name' => 'required',
        'password'=> 'required'
    ]);
    if ($validator->fails()) {
        return  response()->json($validator->errors(), 422);
        }
    $user = User::create([
    'name' => $request->name,
    'email' => $request->email,
```

```
        'password' => bcrypt($request->password),
        ]);
        $token = auth()->login($user);
        return  response()->json([
            'access_token' => $token,
            'token_type' => 'bearer',
            'expires_in' => auth()->factory()->getTTL() * 60
        ], 201);
    }
/**
 * Log in a user.
 *
 * @param \Illuminate\Http\Request $request
 * @return \Illuminate\Http\Response
 *
 * @SWG\Post(
 * path="/api/login",
 * tags={"Users"},
 * summary="loggin an user",
 * @SWG\Parameter(
 * name="body",
 * in="body",
 * required=true,
 * @SWG\Schema(ref="#/definitions/User"),
 * description="Json format",
 * ),
 * @SWG\Response(
 * response=200,
 * description="Success: operation Successfully"
 * ),
 * @SWG\Response(
 * response=401,
 * description="Refused: Unauthenticated"
 * ),
 * @SWG\Response(
 * response="422",
 * description="Missing mandatory field"
 * ),
 * @SWG\Response(
 * response="404",
 * description="Not Found"
 * )
 * ),
 */
public  function  login(Request  $request)
{
    $validator = Validator::make($request->all(), [
        'email' => 'required|string|email|max:255',
```

```
                              'password'=> 'required'
                    ]);
                    if ($validator->fails()) {
                        return  response()->json($validator->errors(), 422);
                        }
                    $credentials = $request->only(['email', 'password']);
                    if (!$token = auth()->attempt($credentials)) {
                        return  response()->json(['error' => 'Invalid
                        Credentials'], 400);
                    }
                    $current_user = $request->email;
                        return  response()->json([
                        'access_token' => $token,
                        'token_type' => 'bearer',
                        'current_user' => $current_user,
                        'expires_in' => auth()->factory()->getTTL() * 60
                        ], 200);
                        }
    /**
    * Register a new user.
    *
    * @param \Illuminate\Http\Request $request
    * @return \Illuminate\Http\Response
    *
    * @SWG\Post(
    * path="/api/logout",
    * tags={"Users"},
    * summary="logout an user",
    * @SWG\Parameter(
    * name="body",
    * in="body",
    * required=true,
    * @SWG\Schema(ref="#/definitions/User"),
    * description="Json format",
    * ),
    * @SWG\Response(
    * response=200,
    * description="Success: operation Successfully"
    * ),
    * @SWG\Response(
    * response=401,
    * description="Refused: Unauthenticated"
    * ),
    * @SWG\Response(
    * response="422",
    * description="Missing mandatory field"
    * ),
    * @SWG\Response(
```

```
 *  response="404",
 *  description="Not Found"
 *  ),
 *  @SWG\Response(
 *  response="405",
 *  description="Invalid input"
 *  ),
 *  security={
 *  { "api_key":{} }
 *  }
 *  ),
 */
public  function  logout(Request  $request){
    auth()->logout(true); // Force token to blacklist
    return  response()->json(['success' => 'Logged out
    Successfully.'], 200); }
}
```

There's almost nothing new in the previous code—we just returned a JSON response in the `register`, `login`, and `logout` functions, as we can see in the previous lines.

3. In the `register()` function:

```
$token = auth()->login($user);
        return  response()->json([
                'access_token' => $token,
                'token_type' => 'bearer',
                'expires_in' => auth()->factory()->getTTL() * 60
], 201);
```

After we created a `user`, we returned a HTTP status code of `201` with an `access_token` and an expiry date.

4. In the `login()` function:

```
$current_user = $request->email;
        return  response()->json([
                'access_token' => $token,
                'token_type' => 'bearer',
                'current_user' => $current_user,
                'expires_in' => auth()->factory()->getTTL() * 60
], 200);
```

Here, in the `login()` function, we returned the current user based on the user's email address, an `access_token`, and the expiry date.

5. In the `logout()` function:

```
auth()->logout(true); // Force token to blacklist
    return  response()->json(['success' => 'Logged out
    Successfully.'], 200);
```

Note that the `true` parameter inside the `logout()` function tells `jwt-auth` to invalidate the token forever.

Creating user routes

Now, it's time to create the new routes for the registration, login, and logout operations and also protect some routes in our API, as discussed at the beginning of this chapter. Our users can interact with partial content of the application, but, to have access to all of its content, it is necessary to create a user and log in to the application.

Open `project/routes/api.php` and replace its content with the following code:

```php
<?php
use  Illuminate\Http\Request;
use  App\Bike;
use  App\Http\Resources\BikesResource;

/*
|--------------------------------------------------------------------------
| API Routes
|--------------------------------------------------------------------------
|
| Here is where you can register API routes for your application. These
| routes are loaded by the RouteServiceProvider within a group whic
| is assigned the "api" middleware group. Enjoy building your API!
|
*/

// Register Routes
Route::post('register', 'API\AuthController@register');
Route::post('login', 'API\AuthController@login');
Route::post('logout', 'API\AuthController@logout');

Route::apiResources([

    'bikes' => 'API\BikeController',

    'builders' => 'API\BuilderController',
```

```
    'items' => 'API\ItemController',

    'bikes/{bike}/ratings' => 'API\RatingController'

]);

Route::middleware('jwt.auth')->get('me', function(Request $request){
    return auth()->user();
});
```

The last step is to protect the endpoint; we do this in the `project/routes/api.php` file or directly inside the controllers function. We will do this in the controllers function.

Protecting API routes

It is extremely simple to protect our routes using the application controllers. All we have to do is edit the `Controller` files and add the following code.

Open `project/Http/Controllers/API/BikeController.php` and add the following code right before the `GET` method:

```
/**
 * Protect update and delete methods, only for authenticated users.
 *
 * @return Unauthorized
 */
public  function  __construct()
{
        $this->middleware('auth:api')->except(['index']);
}
```

The previous code means that we are using the `auth:api` middleware to protect all bikers routes except for the `index()` method. So, our users can see the bike list, but, to see the bike's details and post a bike, they must be logged in. Later, in the `Chapter09`, *Creating Services and User Authentication*, on Angular, we will look at token-based authentication in detail.

Creating and logging in a User

Now, it is time to check the user routes. As we don't have a user interface, we will be using a Chrome extension called Restlet Client. It is free and very powerful.

You can read more about it and download it at `https://restlet.com/modules/client`:

1. Open the Restlet extension and fill in the following fields, as shown in the following screenshot:

Register endpoint

2. The result will be the following response:

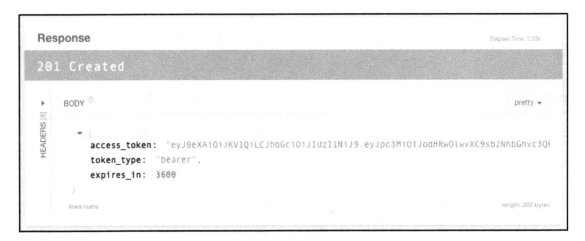

Created response

3. Now, let's log in with the newly created user. Fill in fields as shown in the following screenshot:

User login

The result will be the following response:

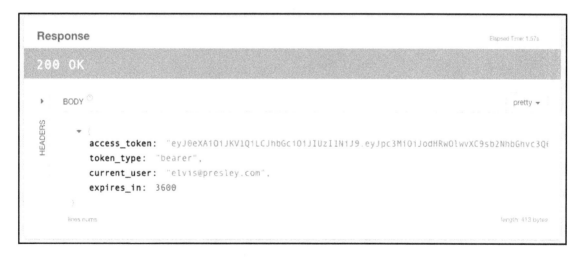

User logged response

Well, our API authentication is ready and good to go. Later, in the `chapter 09`, *Creating Services and User Authentication*, on Angular, we will look at the authentication process in detail.

Dealing with Laravel resources

In some previous versions of Laravel, it was possible to use a feature called Fractal, to dealing with JSON web API, but with this new version of Laravel we have the **Resources** feature, a very powerful tool to dealing with JSON web API.

In this section, we'll see how we can use the Resources feature, so that we can get the most out of our API. A Resource class is a way to transform data from one format to another.

When dealing with resources and transforming them into responses for the client, we basically have two types: an item and a collection. An item resource, as you might have guessed, is basically a one-to-one representation of our model, whereas a collection is the representation of many items. Collections may also have metadata and other navigation information, as we will see later in this section.

Creating BikesResource

So, let's create our first resource:

1. Open your Terminal window and type the following command:

   ```
   php artisan make:resource BikesResource
   ```

   The previous command will generate the following file:

   `App\Http\Resource\BikesResource.php`.

2. Open `App\Http\Resource\BikesResource.php` and add the following code:

   ```php
   <?php
   namespace App\Http\Resources;
   use Illuminate\Http\Resources\Json\JsonResource;
   use App\Builder;
   class BikesResource extends JsonResource
   {
       /**
       * Transform the resource into an array.
       *
       * @param \Illuminate\Http\Request $request
       * @return array
       */
       public function toArray($request)
       {
           return [
               'id' => $this->id,
   ```

```
                'make' => $this->make,
                'model' => $this->model,
                'year' => $this->year,
                'mods' => $this->mods,
                'picture' => $this->picture,
                'garages' => $this->garages,
                'items' => $this->items,
                'builder' => $this->builder,
                'user' => $this->user,
                'ratings' => $this->ratings,
                'average_rating' => $this->ratings->avg('rating'),
                // Casting objects to string, to avoid receive
create_at              and update_at as object
                'created_at' => (string) $this->created_at,
                'updated_at' => (string) $this->updated_at
            ];
        }
    }
```

Note that we are including all relationships in the `bike` model in our Array function.

Creating BuildersResource

Now, let's create `BuildersResource` using the `make` command:

1. Open your Terminal window and type the following command:

   php artisan make:resource BuildersResource

2. The previous command will generate the following file:

   `App\Http\Resource\BuildersResource.php`.

3. Open `App\Http\Resource\BuildersResource.php` and add the following code:

```php
<?php
namespace App\Http\Resources;
use Illuminate\Http\Resources\Json\JsonResource;
class BuildersResource extends JsonResource
{
    /**
     * Transform the resource into an array.
     *
     * @param \Illuminate\Http\Request $request
     * @return array
```

```
    */
    public function toArray($request)
    {
        return [
            'id' => $this->id,
            'name' => $this->name,
            'description' => $this->description,
            'location' => $this->location,
            'bike' => $this->bike,
            // Casting objects to string, to avoid receive
create_at                and update_at as object
            'created_at' => (string) $this->created_at,
            'updated_at' => (string) $this->updated_at,
        ];
    }
}
```

Creating ItemsResource

Now, let's create `ItemsResource` using the `make` command:

1. Open your Terminal window and type the following command:

   php artisan make:resource ItemsResource

2. The previous command will generate the following file:
   `App\Http\Resource\ItemsResource.php`.

3. Open `App\Http\Resource\ItemsResource.php` and add the following code:

```php
<?php
namespace App\Http\Resources;
use Illuminate\Http\Resources\Json\JsonResource;
class ItemsResource extends JsonResource
{
    /**
     * Transform the resource into an array.
     *
     * @param \Illuminate\Http\Request $request
     * @return array
     */
    public function toArray($request)
    {
        return [
            'id' => $this->id,
            'type' => $this->type,
            'name' => $this->name,
```

```
                        'company' => $this->company,
                        'bike_id' => $this->bike_id,
                        // Casting objects to string, to avoid receive
    create_at               and update_at as object
                        'created_at' => (string) $this->created_at,
                        'updated_at' => (string) $this->updated_at
                ];
        }
}
```

Creating ratingResource

Now, let's create a new `Resource`, this time for ratings:

1. Open your Terminal window and type the following command:

   php artisan make:resource ratingResource

2. The previous command will generate the following file:

   `App\Http\Resource\RatingResource.php`.

3. Open `App\Http\Resource\RatingResource.php` and add the following code:

```php
<?php
namespace App\Http\Resources;
use Illuminate\Http\Resources\Json\JsonResource;
use App\Bike;
class RatingResource extends JsonResource
{
    /**
     * Transform the resource into an array.
     *
     * @param \Illuminate\Http\Request $request
     * @return array
     */
    public function toArray($request)
    {
        return [
                'user_id' => $this->user_id,
                'bike_id' => $this->bike_id,
                'rating' => $this->rating,
                'bike' => $this->bike,
                'average_rating' =>
$this->bike->ratings->avg('rating'),
                // Casting objects to string, to avoid receive
```

```
                                     create_at and update_at as object
                                     'created_at' => (string) $this->created_at,
                                     'updated_at' => (string) $this->updated_at
                            ];
                    }
            }
```

Adding resources to controllers

Now, we need to make some minor changes to our controllers in order to use the resource we just created. To avoid any mistakes, we will look at the code for all of our controllers:

1. Edit the `Bike` controller by replacing the content in `App/Http/Controllers/API/BikeController.php` with the following code:

```php
<?php
namespace App\Http\Controllers\API;
use Illuminate\Http\Request;
use App\Http\Controllers\Controller;
use App\Bike;
use Validator;
use App\Http\Resources\BikesResource;
class BikeController extends Controller
{
    /**
     * Protect update and delete methods, only for authenticated
      users.
     *
     * @return Unauthorized
     */
    public function __construct()
    {
        $this->middleware('auth:api')->except(['index']);
    }
    /**
     * Display a listing of the resource.
     *
     * @return \Illuminate\Http\Response
     *
     * @SWG\Get(
     * path="/api/bikes",
     * tags={"Bikes"},
     * summary="List Bikes",
     * @SWG\Response(
     * response=200,
```

```
 * description="Success: List all Bikes",
 * @SWG\Schema(ref="#/definitions/Bike")
 * ),
 * @SWG\Response(
 * response="404",
 * description="Not Found"
 * ),
 * @SWG\Response(
 *          response="405",
 *          description="Invalid HTTP Method"
 * )
 * ),
 */
public function index()
{
    $listBikes = Bike::all();
    return $listBikes;
    // Using Paginate method We explain this later in the book
    // return BikesResource::collection(Bike::with('ratings')-
    >paginate(10));
}
```

Now, let's add the code for the `store`/`create` method. Add the following code right after the `index()` function:

```
/**
 * Store a newly created resource in storage.
 *
 * @param \Illuminate\Http\Request $request
 * @return \Illuminate\Http\Response
 *
 * @SWG\Post(
 * path="/api/bikes",
 * tags={"Bikes"},
 * summary="Create Bike",
 * @SWG\Parameter(
 *          name="body",
 *          in="body",
 *          required=true,
 *          @SWG\Schema(ref="#/definitions/Bike"),
 *          description="Json format",
 *      ),
 * @SWG\Response(
 * response=201,
 * description="Success: A Newly Created Bike",
 * @SWG\Schema(ref="#/definitions/Bike")
```

```
 *   ),
 *   @SWG\Response(
 *   response=401,
 *   description="Refused: Unauthenticated"
 *   ),
 *   @SWG\Response(
 *   response="422",
 *   description="Missing mandatory field"
 *   ),
 *   @SWG\Response(
 *   response="404",
 *   description="Not Found"
 *   ),
 *   @SWG\Response(
 *              response="405",
 *              description="Invalid HTTP Method"
 *        ),
 *        security={
 *             { "api_key":{} }
 *          }
 *   ),
 */
public function store(Request $request)
{
    $validator = Validator::make($request->all(), [
        'make' => 'required',
        'model' => 'required',
        'year'=> 'required',
        'mods'=> 'required',
        'builder_id' => 'required'
        ]);
    if ($validator->fails()) {
        return response()->json($validator->errors(), 422);
    }
    // Creating a record in a different way
    $createBike = Bike::create([
        'user_id' => $request->user()->id,
        'make' => $request->make,
        'model' => $request->model,
        'year' => $request->year,
        'mods' => $request->mods,
        'picture' => $request->picture,
    ]);
    return new BikesResource($createBike);
}
```

Add the following code for the `Get` by `id` method. Add the following code right after the `store()` function:

```
/**
 * Display the specified resource.
 *
 * @param int $id
 * @return \Illuminate\Http\Response
 *
 * @SWG\Get(
 * path="/api/bikes/{id}",
 * tags={"Bikes"},
 * summary="Get Bike by Id",
 * @SWG\Parameter(
 * name="id",
 * in="path",
 * required=true,
 * type="integer",
 * description="Display the specified bike by id.",
 *        ),
 * @SWG\Response(
 * response=200,
 * description="Success: Return the Bike",
 * @SWG\Schema(ref="#/definitions/Bike")
 * ),
 * @SWG\Response(
 * response="404",
 * description="Not Found"
 * ),
 * @SWG\Response(
 *          *          response="405",
 *          *          description="Invalid HTTP Method"
 *       * ),
 * security={
 *        { "api_key":{} }
 *    }
 * ),
 */
public function show(Bike $bike)
{
    return new BikesResource($bike);
}
```

Now, let's add the code for the `update` method. Add the following code right after the `show()` function:

```
/**
 * Update the specified resource in storage.
 *
 * @param \Illuminate\Http\Request $request
 * @param int $id
 * @return \Illuminate\Http\Response
 *
 * @SWG\Put(
 * path="/api/bikes/{id}",
 * tags={"Bikes"},* summary="Update Bike",
 * @SWG\Parameter(
 * name="id",
 * in="path",
 * required=true,
 * type="integer",
 * description="Update the specified bike by id.",
 *         ),
 * @SWG\Parameter(
 *         name="body",
 *         in="body",
 *         required=true,
 *         @SWG\Schema(ref="#/definitions/Bike"),
 *         description="Json format",
 *         ),
 * @SWG\Response(
 * response=200,
 * description="Success: Return the Bike updated",
 * @SWG\Schema(ref="#/definitions/Bike")
 * ),
 * @SWG\Response(
 * response="422",
 * description="Missing mandatory field"
 * ),
 * @SWG\Response(
 * response="404",
 * description="Not Found"
 * ),
 * @SWG\Response(
 *         response="403",
 *         description="Forbidden"
 *     ),
```

```
*  @SWG\Response(
*              response="405",
*              description="Invalid HTTP Method"
*  ),
*  security={
*          { "api_key":{} }
*          }
*  ),
*/
public function update(Request $request, Bike $bike)
{
    // check if currently authenticated user is the bike owner
    if ($request->user()->id !== $bike->user_id) {
        return response()->json(['error' => 'You can only edit your
        own bike.'], 403);
    }

        $bike->update($request->only(['make', 'model', 'year',
        'mods',     'picture']));
    return new BikesResource($bike);
}
```

The last method is to delete all records. Add the following code right after the
update() function:

```
/**
* Remove the specified resource from storage.
*
* @param int $id
* @return \Illuminate\Http\Response
*
* @SWG\Delete(
* path="/api/bikes/{id}",
* tags={"Bikes"},
* summary="Delete bike",
* description="Delete the specified bike by id",
* @SWG\Parameter(
* description="Bike id to delete",
* in="path",
* name="id",
* required=true,
* type="integer",
* format="int64"
* ),
* @SWG\Response(
* response=404,
* description="Not found"
* ),
* @SWG\Response(
```

```
*   response=204,
*   description="Success: successful deleted"
*   ),
*   @SWG\Response(
        *               response="405",
        *               description="Invalid HTTP Method"
        *   ),
        *   security={
        *       { "api_key":{} }
        *       }
*   )
*/
public function destroy($id)
{
    $deleteBikeById = Bike::findOrFail($id)->delete();
    return response()->json([], 204);
    }
}
```

And we will do the same for the `Builders` controller.

2. Edit the `Builder` controller by replacing the content
   in `App/Http/Controllers/API/BuilderController.php` with the following
   code:

```php
<?php
namespace App\Http\Controllers\API;
use Illuminate\Http\Request;
use App\Http\Controllers\Controller;
use App\Builder;
use Validator;
use App\Http\Resources\BuildersResource;
class BuilderController extends Controller
{
    /**
    * Display a listing of the resource.
    *
    * @return \Illuminate\Http\Response
    *
    * @SWG\Get(
    * path="/api/builders",
    * tags={"Builders"},
    * summary="List Builders",
    * @SWG\Response(
    * response=200,
    * description="Success: List all Builders",
    * @SWG\Schema(ref="#/definitions/Builder")
    * ),
```

```
 * @SWG\Response(
 * response="404",
 * description="Not Found"
 * )
 * ),
 */
public function index()
{
    $listBuilder = Builder::all();
    return $listBuilder;
}
```

Now, let's add the code for the `store/create` method. Add the following code right after the `index()` function:

```
/**
 * Store a newly created resource in storage.
 *
 * @param \Illuminate\Http\Request $request
 * @return \Illuminate\Http\Response
 *
 * @SWG\Post(
 * path="/api/builders",
 * tags={"Builders"},
 * summary="Create Builder",
 * @SWG\Parameter(
 *         name="body",
 *         in="body",
 *         required=true,
 *         @SWG\Schema(ref="#/definitions/Builder"),
 *         description="Json format",
 *      ),
 * @SWG\Response(
 * response=201,
 * description="Success: A Newly Created Builder",
 * @SWG\Schema(ref="#/definitions/Builder")
 * ),
 * @SWG\Response(
 * response="422",
 * description="Missing mandatory field"
 * ),
 * @SWG\Response(
 * response="404",
 * description="Not Found"
 * ),
 * @SWG\Response(
 *         response="405",
 *         description="Invalid HTTP Method"
```

```
        *  )
 *  ),
 */
public function store(Request $request)
{
    $validator = Validator::make($request->all(), [
        'name' => 'required',
        'description' => 'required',
        'location'=> 'required'
        ]);
    if ($validator->fails()) {
        return response()->json($validator->errors(), 422);
    }
    $createBuilder = Builder::create($request->all());
        return $createBuilder;
}
```

Let's add the code for the Get by id method. Add the following code right after the store() function:

```
/**
 * Display the specified resource.
 *
 * @param int $id
 * @return \Illuminate\Http\Response
 *
 * @SWG\Get(
 * path="/api/builders/{id}",
 * tags={"Builders"},
 * summary="Get Builder by Id",
 * @SWG\Parameter(
 * name="id",
 * in="path",
 * required=true,
 * type="integer",
 * description="Display the specified Builder by id.",
 *          ),
 * @SWG\Response(
 * response=200,
 * description="Success: Return the Builder",
 * @SWG\Schema(ref="#/definitions/Builder")
 * ),
 * @SWG\Response(
 * response="404",
 * description="Not Found"
 * ),
 * @SWG\Response(
 *              response="405",
```

```
 *                        description="Invalid HTTP Method"
 *  )
 *  ),
 */
public function show(Builder $builder)
{
    // $showBuilderById = Builder::with('Bike')->findOrFail($id);
    // return $showBuilderById;
    return new BuildersResource($builder);
}
```

Now, let's add the code for the update method. Add the following code right after the show() function:

```
/**
 * Update the specified resource in storage.
 *
 * @param \Illuminate\Http\Request $request
 * @param int $id
 * @return \Illuminate\Http\Response
 *
 * @SWG\Put(
 * path="/api/builders/{id}",
 * tags={"Builders"},
 * summary="Update Builder",
 * @SWG\Parameter(
 * name="id",
 * in="path",
 * required=true,
 * type="integer",
 * description="Update the specified Builder by id.",
 *        ),
 * @SWG\Parameter(
 *           name="body",
 *           in="body",
 *           required=true,
 *           @SWG\Schema(ref="#/definitions/Builder"),
 *           description="Json format",
 *        ),
 * @SWG\Response(
 * response=200,
 * description="Success: Return the Builder updated",
 * @SWG\Schema(ref="#/definitions/Builder")
 * ),
 * @SWG\Response(
 * response="422",
 * description="Missing mandatory field"
 * ),
```

```
     *  @SWG\Response(
     *  response="404",
     *  description="Not Found"
     *  ),
     *  @SWG\Response(
         *              response="405",
         *              description="Invalid HTTP Method"
         *  )
     *  ),
     */
    public function update(Request $request, $id)
    {
        $validator = Validator::make($request->all(), [
            'name' => 'required',
            'description' => 'required',
            'location'=> 'required'
            ]);
        if ($validator->fails()) {
            return response()->json($validator->errors(), 422);
        }
        $updateBuilderById = Builder::findOrFail($id);
        $updateBuilderById->update($request->all());
        return $updateBuilderById;
    }
```

The last method is used to delete all records. Add the following code right after the update() function:

```
    /**
     * Remove the specified resource from storage.
     *
     * @param int $id
     * @return \Illuminate\Http\Response
     *
     * @SWG\Delete(
     * path="/api/builders/{id}",
     * tags={"Builders"},
     * summary="Delete Builder",
     * description="Delete the specified Builder by id",
     * @SWG\Parameter(
     * description="Builder id to delete",
     * in="path",
     * name="id",
     * required=true,
     * type="integer",
     * format="int64"
     * ),
     * @SWG\Response(
```

```
*  response=404,
*  description="Not found"
*  ),
*  @SWG\Response(
    *               response="405",
    *               description="Invalid HTTP Method"
    *  ),
*  @SWG\Response(
*  response=204,
*  description="Success: successful deleted"
*  ),
*  )
*/
public function destroy($id)
{
    $deleteBikeById = Bike::find($id)->delete();
    return response()->json([], 204);
    }
}
```

3. In order to edit the `Rating` controller, replace the content
   in `App/Http/Controllers/API/RatingController.php` with the following
   code:

```php
<?php
namespace App\Http\Controllers\API;
use Illuminate\Http\Request;
use App\Http\Controllers\Controller;
use App\Bike;
use App\Rating;
use App\Http\Resources\RatingResource;
class RatingController extends Controller
{
    /**
     * Protect update and delete methods, only for authenticated
users.
     *
     * @return Unauthorized
     */
    public function __construct()
    {
        $this->middleware('auth:api');
    }
    /**
     * Store a newly created resource in storage.
     *
     * @param \Illuminate\Http\Request $request
```

```
 * @return \Illuminate\Http\Response
 *
 * @SWG\Post(
 * path="/api/bikes/{bike_id}/ratings",
 * tags={"Ratings"},
 * summary="rating a Bike",
 * @SWG\Parameter(
 * in="path",
 * name="id",
 * required=true,
 * type="integer",
 * format="int64",
 *      description="Bike Id"
 *    ),
 * @SWG\Parameter(
 *      name="body",
 *      in="body",
 *      required=true,
 *      @SWG\Schema(ref="#/definitions/Rating"),
 *      description="Json format",
 *      ),
 * @SWG\Response(
 * response=201,
 * description="Success: A Newly Created Rating",
 * @SWG\Schema(ref="#/definitions/Rating")
 * ),
 * @SWG\Response(
 * response=401,
 * description="Refused: Unauthenticated"
 * ),
 * @SWG\Response(
 * response="422",
 * description="Missing mandatory field"
 * ),
 * @SWG\Response(
 * response="404",
 * description="Not Found"
 * ),
 * @SWG\Response(
 *    *      response="405",
 *    *   description="Invalid HTTP Method"
 *    * ),
 * security={
 *      { "api_key":{} }
 * }
 * ),
 */
public function store(Request $request, Bike $bike)
```

```
    {
        $rating = Rating::firstOrCreate(
        [
        'user_id' => $request->user()->id,
        'bike_id' => $bike->id,
        ],
        ['rating' => $request->rating]
        );
        return new RatingResource($rating);
    }
}
```

Well done! Now, we have the necessary code to go ahead with our API JSON. In the next few chapters, you will understand in greater detail what we have accomplished so far. We already have our API ready.

Summary

We have come to the end of one more chapter. We saw how to build token-based authentication, how to protect endpoints only for logged-in users, and how to deal with custom error messages.

We also learned how to use Laravel resources to return a JSON API format.

We are in the middle of our journey, yet we need to build all of the interface and implement the Angular frontend application so that we can have a pleasant visual result for our application.

In the next chapter, we will see how to integrate Angular as well as some more tools into our application.

7
Progressive Web Applications with the Angular CLI

As we mentioned in `Chapter 3`, *Understanding the Core Concepts of Angular 6*, Angular is one of the main frameworks for developing modern web applications based on JavaScript.

In `Chapter 6`, *Creating a RESTful API Using Laravel Framework-2*, we completed the backend API using Laravel resources, eloquent relationships, and token-based authentication. Now, we have everything we need to connect the frontend application to the backend; before we do that, let's look at what we will learn in this chapter.

In this chapter, we will see some changes that occurred in the `angular-cli.json` file, which now provides improved support for multiple applications.

We will also look at how to use `ng add` to create a **Progressive Web Application (PWA)**, and how we can organize our project as modules.

In this chapter, we will cover the following:

- Starting a web application with the Angular CLI
- Building the baseline for a PWA
- Creating boilerplate components

Starting a web application with the Angular CLI

When we started writing this chapter, the Angular framework had launched its newest version: version 6. In previous chapters, we have already commented on some of the novelties that are present in this version.

The new version is more focused on development tools (such as the Angular CLI) than the evolution of the framework itself. We can cite the new functions of the Angular CLI with commands such as `ng update` and `ng add`, which are very useful for updating packages and adding new ones.

The first thing that we need to do is update the Angular CLI on the machine; open your Terminal window and type the following command:

```
npm install -g @angular/cli
```

The preceding command will install Angular CLI 6.0.0 on your machine globally.

Preparing the baseline code

Now, we need to prepare our baseline code, a process very similar to that of previous chapters. Follow these steps:

1. Copy all of the content from the `chapter-05` folder.
2. Rename the folder to `chapter-07`.
3. Delete the `storage-db` folder.

   Now, let's make some changes to the `docker-compose.yml` file, to fit a new database and server containers.

4. Open `docker-compose.yml` and replace the contents with the following:

```yaml
version: "3.1"
services:
    mysql:
      image: mysql:5.7
      container_name: chapter-07-mysql
      working_dir:     /application
      volumes:
        - .:/application
        - ./storage-db:/var/lib/mysql
      environment:
        - MYSQL_ROOT_PASSWORD=123456
        - MYSQL_DATABASE=chapter-06
        - MYSQL_USER=chapter-07
        - MYSQL_PASSWORD=123456
      ports:
        - "8083:3306"
    webserver:
      image: nginx:alpine
```

```
container_name: chapter-07-webserver
working_dir: /application
volumes:
   - .:/application-
   ./phpdocker/nginx/nginx.conf:/etc/nginx/conf.d/default.conf
ports:
   - "8081:80"
php-fpm:
   build: phpdocker/php-fpm
   container_name: chapter-07-php-fpm
   working_dir: /application
   volumes:
      - ./Server:/application
      - ./phpdocker/php-fpm/php-ini-overrides.ini:
         /etc/php/7.2/fpm/conf.d/99-overrides.ini
```

Note that we changed the container names, the database, and the MySQL user:

- container_name: chapter-07-mysql

- container_name: chapter-07-webserver

- container_name: chapter-07-php-fpm

- MYSQL_DATABASE=chapter-07

- MYSQL_USER=chapter-07

Another important point to pay attention to is the configuration of the php-fpm container volume, which we are now naming as Server instead of project on previous chapters, according to the following highlighted code:

```
php-fpm:
        build: phpdocker/php-fpm
        container_name: chapter-07-php-fpm
        working_dir: /application
        volumes:
        - ./Server:/application
        - ./phpdocker/php-fpm/php-ini-
overrides.ini:/etc/php/7.2/fpm/conf.d/99-overrides.ini
```

5. Open chapter-07 in vs.code and rename the project folder to Server.

As you saw in the previous chapters, the Laravel framework has a well-defined way of using its views; this is due to the MVC standard upon which Laravel is built.

In addition, Laravel uses a JavaScript framework called Vue.js, which can be found in the ./Server/resources/assets/js folder.

In order to not mix things up, we will create our frontend application in a folder called `Client`, at the same level as the newly named `Server` folder.

6. Create a new folder called `Client` at the root of the `chapter-07` folder.

At the end of these changes, you should see the same project structure as the following screenshot:

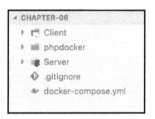

Application structure

This is the best way to keep your application uncoupled from your API. With this method, we have some advantages:

- The frontend code is isolated from the rest of the application; we can host it in a static web service, such as an **Amazon Web Services** (**AWS**) bucket, or any other web server.
- Application deployments can be done separately, so that the API evolves independently of the frontend application, and vice versa.

Add the changes that we made to the Git source control. Open your Terminal window and type the following command:

```
git add .
git commit -m "Initial commit chapter 07"
```

Scaffolding a web application with the Angular CLI

Let's start building our frontend application with the new version of Angular, using the Angular CLI:

1. Open your Terminal window at the root project and type the following command:

```
ng new Client --style=scss --routing
```

2. The previous command will create all of the boilerplate code that we need, this time using the SCSS syntax for style sheets and the `--routing` flag to create application routes.

3. At the end of the previous command, our application will have the following structure:

New application structure

4. One of the changes that version 6 of Angular and the Angular CLI brings is the `angular.json` file, which was previously named `angular-cli.json`. Its structure is very different, as you can see in the following screenshot:

```
 1   {
 2       "$schema": "./node_modules/@angular/cli/lib/config/schema.json",
 3       "version": 1,
 4       "newProjectRoot": "projects",
 5       "projects": {
 6 ⊞       "Client": {⋯
101       },
102 ⊞     "Client-e2e": {⋯
123       }
124     },
125     "defaultProject": "Client"
126   }
```

Angular JSON file

5. As for the application files, we have almost the same code organization and files that we had before, as you can see in the following screenshot:

New Angular app structure

In the previous screenshot, note that we now have a file called `browserlist`; it is used to add browser-specific prefixes to CSS-generated code.

Creating the directory structure

To facilitate our development, we will create some directories in the application so that our project will be ready to be scaled. This means that we can add any modules/features that we want, in an organized way.

This step is very important, because, sometimes, the structure within the project is defined; it is not recommended to change it.

For this step, we will use a nomenclature of modules or pages. We will use the API definition services that we made in the previous chapter as the baseline:

- A home page, which we will call a `home` page
- A page of motorcycles, which we will call a `bike-list` page
- A bike detail page, which we will call a `bike-details` page
- A builders page, which we will call a `builders-list` page
- A builder details page, which we will call a `builder-details` page
- A register page, which we will call a `register` page
- A login page, which we will call a `login` page

Based on the preceding descriptions, our application will have the following pages, or modules:

- `bike`
- `builder`
- `register`
- `login`
- `home`

We prefer to use a nomenclature of *modules* or *pages* instead of components at this time, not to be confused with the terminology of components proposed by Angular, where everything is based on components.

In the end, this is just a different way of referring to the application structure.

1. Open VS Code, and, inside `Client/src/app`, create a new folder named `pages`.

2. Still in VS Code and inside `Client/src/app`, create a new folder named `layout`.

3. Still in VS Code and inside `Client/src/app`, create a new folder named `shared`.

Let's look at what the folder names mean in the following table:

Folder	Description
pages	Holds all of the application's modules and pages; for example, `pages/bike/bike-component.html` and `pages/builder/builder-component.html`.
layout	Holds all layout components; for example, `layout/nav/nav-component.html`, `layout/footer/footer-component.html`.
shared	Holds shared services, pipes, and so on; for example, a service shared by all application pages or components.

So, at the end of step 3, we will have the following structure:

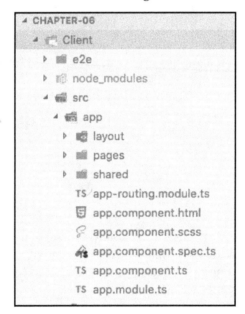

Folder structure

Building the baseline for a PWA

As we discussed earlier, we can now use the new `ng add` command to create a PWA. But, before that, let's take a look at the concept of a PWA.

A PWA is a set of techniques for developing web applications, progressively adding features that were previously only possible in native apps.

The main advantage for the user is that they do not have to download an application before knowing if it will be worth it or not. In addition, we can cite the following advantages:

- **Progressive**: For any user, regardless of browser
- **Responsive**: Made for any device: desktop, tablet, and mobile
- **Connection**: Works even if the user is offline
- **App-like**: The user feels as if they are in a native app
- **Updated**: No need to download application updates; the browser will simply detect and update automatically, if necessary
- **Secure**: Only with HTTPs
- **Engaging**: Through push notifications, the user can be constantly engaged
- **Installable**: You can add an icon on your smartphone's home screen with just one click
- **SEO-friendly**: Search engines can find the contents of applications (which benefits both users and businesses)

 You can read more about progressive web applications at `https://developers.google.com/web/progressive-web-apps/`.

There are still disadvantages to PWA in building native applications, as follows:

- PWAs do not yet have full control over the hardware of the device; Bluetooth, contact lists, and NFC are some examples of features that cannot be accessed by PWA.
- Although Google, Microsoft, and Mozilla are betting high on PWAs, Apple isn't.
- There are still two important features not supported by Safari: push notifications and offline operation. But Apple is already considering implementing PWAs, even though it may not have much of a choice.

For all of the negatives, it is only a matter of time – thinking about it, the Angular team already provides us with support for creating PWAs using only the Angular CLI.

Adding PWA features using ng add

Now, let's look at how we can do this.

Open your Terminal window inside of the `chapter-06/Client` folder and type the following command:

```
ng add @angular/pwa
```

The previous command will generate an output similar to the following screenshot:

```
Installing packages for tooling via npm.
+ @angular/pwa@0.6.0
added 2 packages in 40.873s
Installed packages for tooling via npm.
CREATE ngsw-config.json (392 bytes)
CREATE src/assets/icons/icon-128x128.png (1253 bytes)
CREATE src/assets/icons/icon-144x144.png (1394 bytes)
CREATE src/assets/icons/icon-152x152.png (1427 bytes)
CREATE src/assets/icons/icon-192x192.png (1790 bytes)
CREATE src/assets/icons/icon-384x384.png (3557 bytes)
CREATE src/assets/icons/icon-512x512.png (5008 bytes)
CREATE src/assets/icons/icon-72x72.png (792 bytes)
CREATE src/assets/icons/icon-96x96.png (958 bytes)
CREATE src/manifest.json (1069 bytes)
UPDATE angular.json (3598 bytes)
UPDATE package.json (1381 bytes)
UPDATE src/app/app.module.ts (605 bytes)
UPDATE src/index.html (384 bytes)
added 1 package in 42.137s
```

Angular PWA output

Understanding the key files in PWA

Let's check some important changes made in our application files. The previous command will add two new files at the root folder.

The `manifest.json` file is used to set up the:

- Theme color
- Application name
- Default display mode
- Icon configuration and size

Also, it is possible to set up description tags, related applications, and the platform.

A `ngsw-config.json` file (also known as a service worker configuration), used to setup assetsGroup, dataGroups, navigationUrls and cache.

Inside `src/assets` was created a new folder called `icons`; this icon will be shown as an application bookmark on your mobile phone screen.

And the following files was updated:

- `angular.json`.
- `package.json` adding: `@angular/pwa` and `@angular/service-worker`.
- `app.module.ts` registers the service-worker in production. This means that we can see the service-worker in action by using the production command; later in this chapter, we will see how to use it.
- `index.html` adds the `manifest.json` file and the theme color in the `<head>` tag.

PWA in action

As we mentioned in step 4, the Angular engine applies the service work in the application only in production mode; that is, only when we use the `ng build` command.

So, let's look at how this works in practice. But first, let's see if everything has happened as expected, with the creation of the application and the installation of `@angular/pwa`:

1. Open your Terminal window in the `./Client` folder, and type the following command:

   npm start

   Remember that the `npm start` command is the same as `ng server`; you can check all of the `npm` aliases on the `scripts` tag inside of `package.json`. There, we have the following aliases:

   ```
   "scripts": {
           "ng": "ng",
           "start": "ng serve",
           "build": "ng build",
           "test": "ng test",
           "lint": "ng lint",
           "e2e": "ng e2e"
       }
   ```

At the end of the previous command, we can see the following message as the output:

```
** Angular Live Development Server is listening on localhost: 4200,
open your browser on http://localhost:4200/ **
```

This is followed by an output similar to the following:

```
Hash: fae81311f4e8496e26e1
Time: 33005ms
chunk {main} main.js, main.js.map (main) 13.5 kB [initial] [rendered]
chunk {polyfills} polyfills.js, polyfills.js.map (polyfills) 226 kB [initial] [rendered]
chunk {runtime} runtime.js, runtime.js.map (runtime) 5.4 kB [entry] [rendered]
chunk {styles} styles.js, styles.js.map (styles) 16 kB [initial] [rendered]
chunk {vendor} vendor.js, vendor.js.map (vendor) 3.64 MB [initial] [rendered]
ℹ ⌜wdm⌟: Compiled successfully.
```

Angular dev server output

2. Open your default browser and navigate to `http://localhost:4200/`.

    Now, you can see the welcome screen:

Angular welcome screen

Let's check the `manifest.json` file. Almost all new browsers have a web inspector, where we can debug any website or web application. For the next check, we will use the Chrome browser, but you can use your default or favorite browser.

3. In your browser, click **Open** to open the web inspector.
4. If you are in Chrome, click on the **Application** menu tab.
5. Click on **manifest** on the left-hand menu, and you should see a panel similar to the following screenshot:

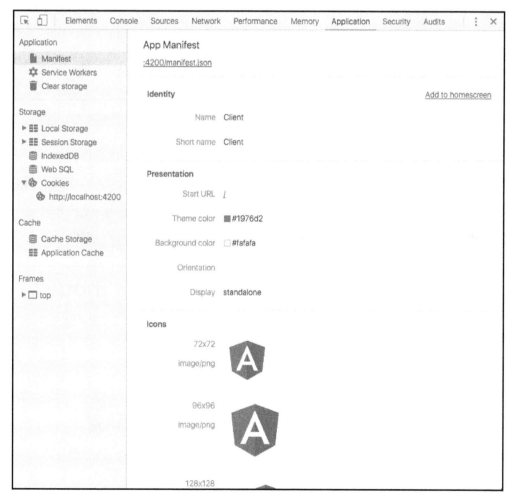

Web inspector

As you can see in the previous screenshot, everything looks as expected; our `manifest.json` file is available, with all of the configurations we saw earlier.

Note the **Add to homescreen** link at the right-hand side of the **Identity** heading; this means that we can add this application on a mobile phone homescreen or a browser application's tab.

6. However, if you click on this link, you will see a console error, as shown in the following screenshot:

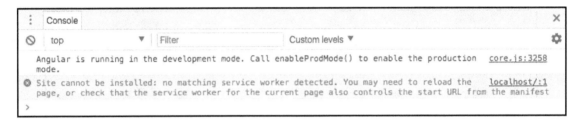

Service worker console error

This means that we don't have a service worker, and it's true. Remember that Angular will only inject the **Service Workers** in production, and we are using `ng server` behind the scenes.

Also, if you click on the service work right-hand side menu, you will see an empty panel.

Running the application in production mode

Now, it's time to check out our application in production mode, to understand how a service works:

1. Go back to your Terminal window and stop the Angular server with the following command:

   ```
   control + c
   ```

2. Still in the Terminal, type the `build` command:

   ```
   ng build --prod
   ```

   Note that the preceding `npm build` alias command doesn't make use of the `--prod` flag. So, you need to use the `ng build --prod` command, or update the `npm build` command with the `--prod` flag.

At the end of the previous command, we can see another folder inside the `Client` directory, called `dist`.

Angular service – workers in action

Now, it's time to start the application generated inside the `./Client/dist/Client` folder, to see the service work in action. Don't worry about this path for now; later in the book, we will change it:

1. Open your Terminal window inside the `./Client/dist/Client` folder, and type the following command:

```
http-server -p 8080
```

Remember that we installed the HTTP server in the previous chapter; if you haven't done so, go to `https://www.npmjs.com/package/http-server` and follow the installation process.

2. Open your browser at `http://localhost:4200/`.

3. In the browser, open the web inspector panel and click on the **Application** tab menu.

   You will see the following:

Web inspector application panel

Now, we have the service worker properly configured and running in our application.

4. Go back to your browser and click on the **Manifest** menu in the right-hand side menu.

5. Now, click on the **add to homescreen** link.

Congratulations! You have added our application to your apps panel. If you are in Chrome, you will see the following:

Application icon

So, if you click on the Angular icon, you will be redirected to `http://localhost:8080/`.

At this moment, we already have the basis for our PWA.

Don't worry about the application name; we are using `Client`, but in the real world, you can choose your own name.

Debugging a progressive web application

Now, we are going to present a very useful tool for debugging progressive web applications. It is an extension to the Chrome navigator, called the Lighthouse:

 You can get more information about Lighthouse at `https://chrome.google.com/webstore/detail/lighthouse/blipmdconlkpinefehnmjammfjpmpbjk/related?hl=us-EN`.

1. Open the Chrome browser and click on the right-hand side **Lighthouse** extension, as shown in the following screenshot:

Lighthouse extension

2. Click on the **Generate report** button.

After the report generation, you will see a result similar to the following screenshot:

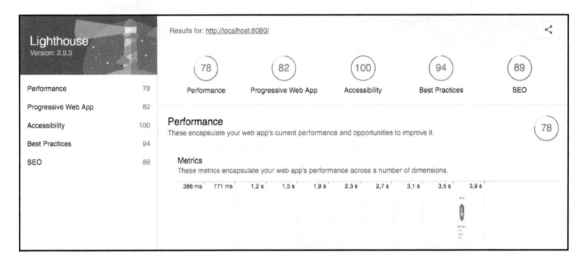

Lighthouse report

The Lighthouse will analyze five primary items:

- Performance
- PWA
- Accessibility
- Best practices
- **Search engine optimization (SEO)**

Note that we have a high score level in each category, even without any content; let's focus on the SEO category for now.

Let's look at how we can improve SEO.

3. Click on **SEO** in the menu on the left-hand side; you will see the following screenshot:

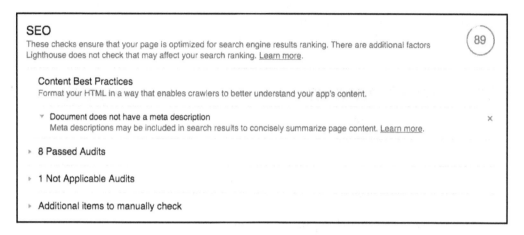

The preceding warning tells us that our application doesn't have a meta description tag on `index.html`. So, let's fix it.

Open `./Client/src/index.html` and add the following code right after the viewport meta tag:

```
<metaname="description" content="Hands-On Full-Stack Web
Development with Angular 6 and Laravel 5">
```

If we check again, we will see the following report:

Note that we have a 100% score for **SEO**

This way, we can locate all of the problems in our application and correct them properly.

We now have everything we need to prepare our application to consume our API, but we still have a lot of work left to build the frontend application.

In the next steps, we will look at how to add our components using the Angular CLI.

Creating boilerplate Angular components

As we saw previously, our application has some pages for registration, login, and the visualization of the motorcycles list, builders list, and motorcycle voting scheme. At this point, we are going to create all of the necessary code to compose these features.

Creating the home module and component

In the next lines, we will create the home module and component:

1. Open your Terminal window in ./Client/src/app and type the following command:

    ```
    ng generate module pages/home --routing
    ```

    As we saw previously, the preceding command will generate three new files:

    - src/app/pages/home/home-routing.module.ts
    - src/app/pages/home/home.modules.spec.ts
    - src/app/pages/home/home.module.ts

    Now, we just need to generate the home component.

2. Still in the Terminal, type the following command:

    ```
    ng g c pages/home
    ```

    At the end of the previous command, you will see the following structure in the pages folder:

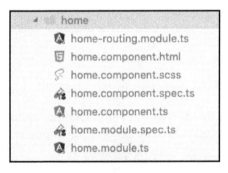

Home module structure

Note that we created a complete module/folder, as we explained previously. Now, we can call the new folder `home`. We need to import the newly created `home` module into our main project; let's look at how we can do that.

3. Open `src/app/app.modules.ts` and add the following lines of code:

```
// Application modules
import { HomeModule } from './pages/home/home.module';
@NgModule({
    declarations: [
    AppComponent
    ],
imports: [
    BrowserModule,
    AppRoutingModule,
    HomeModule,
    ServiceWorkerModule.register('/ngsw-worker.js', { enabled:
environment.production })
    ],
providers: [],
bootstrap: [AppComponent]
})
export class AppModule { }
```

Creating the bikes module and component

Now, it's time to create another module and component; let's look at how to do it:

1. Still in your Terminal window, in `./Client/src/app`, type the following command:

```
ng generate module pages/bikes --routing
```

As we saw previously, the preceding command will generate three new files:

- `src/app/pages/bikes/bikes-routing.module.ts`
- `src/app/pages/bikes/bikes.modules.spec.ts`
- `src/app/pages/bikes/bikes.module.ts`

Now, we just need to generate the `bike` component.

2. Type the following command:

```
ng g c pages/bikes
```

At the end of the previous command, you will see the following structure in the pages folder:

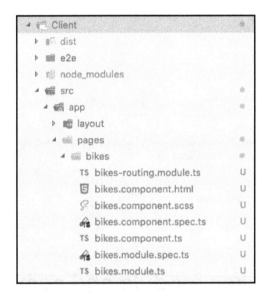

Bike module structure

Now, we can call the new folder `bikes` (as the Bikes module). We need to import the newly created `bikes` module into our main project; let's see how we can do that.

3. Open `src/app/app.modules.ts` and add the following lines of code:

```
// Application modules
import { BikesModule } from './pages/bikes/bikes.module';
@NgModule({
    declarations: [
    AppComponent
    ],
imports: [
    BrowserModule,
    AppRoutingModule,
    HomeModule,
    BikesModule,
```

```
      ServiceWorkerModule.register('/ngsw-worker.js', { enabled:
environment.production })
   ],
providers: [],
   bootstrap: [AppComponent]
})
export class AppModule { }
```

Note that we are injecting the newly created `BikesModule` as a dependent of `app.module`.

Now, it is time to perform the same action for the Builders, Login, and Register pages.

Creating the builders module and component

It is time to create the `builders` module, using the Angular CLI. Let's look at how we can do that:

1. Open your Terminal window and type the following command:

   ng generate module pages/builders --routing

   As you saw previously, the preceding command will generate three new files:

   - `src/app/pages/builders/builders-routing.module.ts`
   - `src/app/pages/builders/builders.modules.spec.ts`
   - `src/app/pages/builders/builders.module.ts`

2. Still in your Terminal window, type the following command to generate the component:

   ng g c pages/builders

3. Add the newly created module to the app modules; open `src/app/app.modules.ts` and add the following lines of code:

```
// Application modules
import { BikesModule } from './pages/bikes/bikes.module';
import { BuildersModule } from './pages/builders/builders.module';
@NgModule({
   declarations: [
   AppComponent
   ],
imports: [
   BrowserModule,
   AppRoutingModule,
```

```
        HomeModule,
    BikesModule,
    BuildersModule,
    ServiceWorkerModule.register('/ngsw-worker.js', { enabled:
environment.production })
    ],
providers: [],
    bootstrap: [AppComponent]
})
export class AppModule { }
```

Preparing Auth routes – login, register, and logout components

Now, we can create the Auth routes, including `Login` and `Register`; again, we will use the power of the Angular CLI to create a new module and components:

1. Open your Terminal window and type the following command:

   ng generate module pages/auth --routing

2. Still in your Terminal window, type the following command to generate the component:

   ng g c pages/auth/login

3. Add the newly created module to the app modules; open `src/app/auth/auth.modules.ts` and add the following lines of code:

   ```
   import { LoginComponent } from  './login/login.component';

   @NgModule({

   imports: [

   CommonModule,

   AuthRoutingModule

   ],
   declarations: [LoginComponent]

   })
   ```

Pay attention; this time, we added `LoginComponent` to `auth.module.ts`, and didn't add it to `app.module.ts`.

Now, it is time to create the `register` component inside of `auth.module`.

4. Open your Terminal window and type the following command:

```
ng g c pages/auth/register
```

5. Add the newly created module to the app modules; open `src/app/auth/auth.modules.ts` and add the following lines of code:

```
import { RegisterComponent } from  './register/register.component';

@NgModule({

imports: [

CommonModule,

AuthRoutingModule

],

declarations: [LoginComponent, RegisterComponent]

})
```

6. Open your Terminal window and type the following command:

```
ng g c pages/auth/logout
```

7. Add the newly created module to the app modules; open `src/app/auth/auth.modules.ts` and add the following lines of code:

```
import { LogoutComponent } from  './logout/logout.component';

@NgModule({

imports: [

CommonModule,
AuthRoutingModule

],

declarations: [LoginComponent, RegisterComponent,
```

```
        LogoutComponent]

   })
```

At this point, our authentication module is complete; that is, we have all of the components that we will use – `register`, `login`, and `logout`. But we still need to inject our new module into the main application module.

8. Open the app modules, open `src/app/app.modules.ts`, and add the following lines of code:

```
// Application modules
import { BikesModule } from './pages/bikes/bikes.module';
import { BuildersModule } from './pages/builders/builders.module';
import { AuthModule } from './pages/auth/auth.module';
@NgModule({
    declarations: [
    AppComponent
    ],
imports: [
    BrowserModule,
    AppRoutingModule,
    BikesModule,
    BuildersModule,
    AuthModule,
    ServiceWorkerModule.register('/ngsw-worker.js', { enabled:
environment.production })
    ],
    providers: [],
    bootstrap: [AppComponent]
    })
export class AppModule { }
```

At the end of this step, you will have the following structure:

Application modules structure

Creating a layout component

For the last step of this section, we will create a layout component for the main navigation of our app. Note that, this time, we will only create the component itself, without the module and route.

Still in your Terminal window, type the following command:

```
ng g c layout/nav
```

The preceding command will generate the following structure:

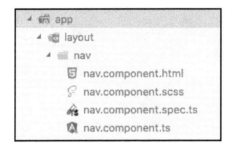

Layout folder structure

Summary

Congratulations; you just finished one more chapter, and you now have a solid frontend application, prepared to receive all of the features it needs.

In this chapter, we created a progressive web application with Angular, using the advanced techniques of code organization. You also learned how to create modules and components using the Angular CLI.

In the next chapter, we will learn how to create the components and routes of our application.

8
Dealing with the Angular Router and Components

We have come to one of the most important parts of **Single Page Applications** (**SPAs**): the use of routes. As you saw in Chapter 3, *Understanding the Core Concepts of Angular 6*, the Angular framework provides a powerful tool for dealing with application routing: @angular/router dependency.

In the next few sections, you'll learn how to use some of these features, such as child-views, and how to create master detail pages. In addition, we will start building the application's visual field, filling in the templates with HTML markup.

In this chapter, we will cover the following topics:

- Preparing the baseline code
- Adding components to the application
- Dealing with Angular routes
- Configuring child routes for detail pages
- Building frontend views

Preparing the baseline code

Now, we need to prepare our baseline code, a process very similar to that under previous chapters. Let's follow these steps:

1. Copy all of the content from the chapter-08 folder.

2. Rename the folder to chapter-08.

3. Delete the storage-db folder.

Now, let's make some changes to the `docker-compose.yml` file, to fit a new database and server containers.

4. Open `docker-compose.yml` and replace the contents with the following code:

```
version: "3.1"
services:
    mysql:
      image: mysql:5.7
      container_name: chapter-08-mysql
      working_dir: /application
      volumes:
        - .:/application
        - ./storage-db:/var/lib/mysql
      environment:
        - MYSQL_ROOT_PASSWORD=123456
        - MYSQL_DATABASE=chapter-08
        - MYSQL_USER=chapter-08
        - MYSQL_PASSWORD=123456
      ports:
        - "8083:3306"
    webserver:
      image: nginx:alpine
      container_name: chapter-08-webserver
      working_dir: /application
      volumes:
        - .:/application
        - ./phpdocker/nginx/nginx.conf:/etc/nginx/conf.d/default
          .conf
      ports:
        - "8081:80"
    php-fpm:
      build: phpdocker/php-fpm
      container_name: chapter-08-php-fpm
      working_dir: /application
      volumes:
        - ./Server:/application
        - ./phpdocker/php-fpm/php-ini-
          overrides.ini:/etc/php/7.2/fpm/conf.d/99-overrides.ini
```

Note that we changed the container names, the database, and the MySQL user:

- container_name: chapter-08-mysql
- container_name: chapter-08-webserver
- container_name: chapter-08-php-fpm
- MYSQL_DATABASE=chapter-08
- MYSQL_USER=chapter-08

5. Add the changes that we made to the Git source control. Open your Terminal window and type the following command:

```
git add .
git commit -m "Initial commit chapter 08"
```

Adding components to our application

Now, we are going to continue to add some more components to our application. We must remember that, in the application summary, we defined a page for the bikes list that refers to the api/bikes endpoint of our API; also, we will have a bike details page that refers to the api/bikes/id   endpoint, containing the details of the selected bike. And, we will do the same to the api/builders endpoint.

So, let's start creating the components:

1. Open your Terminal window inside ./Client/src/app, and type the following command:

```
ng g c pages/bikes/bike-detail
```

At the end of the previous command, you will see the following structure, inside the `bikes` modules:

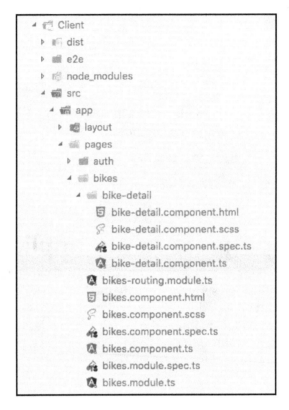

Bikes module structure

The preceding command will create a root `bikes` folder to store every module related to the `bikes` endpoint; this pattern allows us to have a modular application, where each new feature (for example, `bikes-detail` or `bike-list`) will be organized in the same way.

For example, we can add a new inventory module that will be created inside its own module (`inventory.module.ts`) and stored inside the `bikes` module directory.

Consider this a good practice, and keep your modules and components organized in this way; avoid grouping more than one component in the root of the same folder. This prevents your code from turning into spaghetti code.

2. Open your Terminal window inside `./Client/src/app`, and type the following command:

```
ng g c pages/builders/builder-detail
```

Now, you will see the following result for the `builders` module:

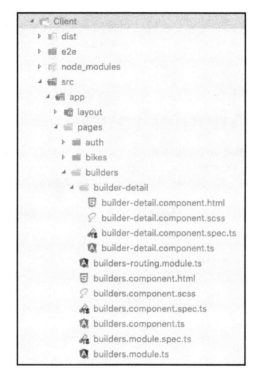

Builders folder structure

Note that the `builders` module (at `./Client/src/app/pages/builders/builders.module.ts`) was updated with the new Builder-detail component added to the declarations property, as you can see in the following highlighted code:

```
import { NgModule } from '@angular/core';
import { CommonModule } from '@angular/common';
import { BuildersRoutingModule } from './builders-routing.module';
import { BuildersComponent } from './builders.component';
import { BuilderDetailComponent } from './builder-detail/builder-detail.component';
@NgModule({
```

```
    imports: [
        CommonModule,
        BuildersRoutingModule
    ],
    declarations: [BuildersComponent, BuilderDetailComponent]
    })
export class BuildersModule { }
```

The best part of this is that the Angular CLI is clever enough to add the newly created component to the module it belongs to. The same was done when we created the `bike-detail` component.

Dealing with Angular routes

At this point, we will continue with the development of our sample application. In the previous chapter, we created some Angular components for the frontend application, but before we write the contents of each one of them, we are going to create some routes.

Before we dive into the code, it's important for you to understand how the Angular router works.

When you click on a link or go to a URL (for example, `http://localhost:4200/bikes`), the Angular router:

1. Checks the browser URL.
2. Finds which router state corresponds to the URL.
3. Applies route guards, if they were defined in the router state.
4. Activates the respective Angular component to display the page.

Also, each route can contain the following properties:

- **path**: String; the path to match the URL
- **patchMatch**: String; how to match the URL
- **component**: Class reference; component to activate when the route is activated
- **redirectTo**: String; URL to redirect to when this route is activated
- **data**: Static data to assign to the route
- **resolve**: Dynamic data to resolve and merge with the data, when resolved
- **children**: Child routes

In the next sections, we will see two methods for creating routes for our application, one of them using children routes.

You can read more about routes in the official documentation at `https://angular.io/guide/router`.

Creating authentication routes

Let's take a look at the current folder structure of our authentication module:

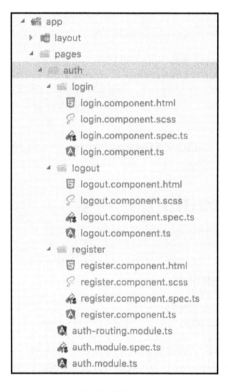

Auth module folder structure

In the preceding screenshot, note that we created only one route file inside the root of the `auth` folder; we did not include any route files in any of the other folders/modules inside the `auth` folder, such as `login`, `register`, and `logout`. This is because we will use the `auth-routing.module.ts` file to create all of the routes related to authentication.

Now, we will create the authentication routes:

1. Open the `auth-routing.module.ts` file inside the `./Client/src/app/pages/auth` directory, and add the following block of code right after `Router import`:

```
// Auth Routes Imports
import { RegisterComponent } from
'./register/register.component';
import { LoginComponent } from  './login/login.component';
import { LogoutComponent } from  './logout/logout.component';
```

2. Now, add the following code inside the `routes` constant:

```
const  routes:  Routes  = [
        { path:  'register', component:  RegisterComponent },
        { path:  'login', component:  LoginComponent },
        { path:  'logout', component:  LogoutComponent }
];
```

Now, let's work on the other routes for the application, starting with the `home` module.

Creating home routing

Now, we will create the `home` routes, as follows:

1. Open `./Client/src/app/pages/home/home-routing.module.ts` and `import` the component:

```
// Home Routes Imports
import { HomeComponent } from  './home.component';
```

2. Open `./Client/src/app/pages/home/home-routing.module.ts` and add the following route object inside the `routes` constant:

```
const  routes:  Routes  = [
        { path: "  '', component:  HomeComponent }
];
```

As our home page is very simple, it contains only one route; later on, in other modules, you will see more complex routes.

Configuring child routes for details pages

We will use another approach to create the builders and bikes routes in Angular. We will use child routes, also called nested views.

When you are using multiple children, it is pretty important to be careful with the route object order.

When the router receives a URL, it follows the contents in order, starting with the first element of the array; if it finds a match to the complete URL, it stops and instantiates the corresponding component(s).

In the next sections, you will see how to implement a well-known UI pattern called **master detail page**. We will make another component to help us organize the folder structure.

Adding builders child routes

Let's create the child routes for the following views in our frontend application:

- `builders-list`
- `builders-detail`

1. Open `./Client/src/app/pages/builders/builders-routing.module.ts` and import the component:

```
imports
import { BuilderDetailComponent } from './builder-detail/builder-detail.component';
import { BuilderListComponent } from './builder-list/builder-list.component';
```

2. Still in `./Client/src/app/pages/builders/builders-routing.module.ts,` add the following `routes` object inside the `routes` constant:

```
const routes: Routes = [
{
    path: 'builders',
    children: [
    {
    path: '',
component: BuilderListComponent
},
    {
```

```
        path: ':id',
        component: BuilderDetailComponent
      }
    ]
  }
];
```

In the preceding code snippet, you will notice two things that are different: one is that we are using a `children` route array property, and the other is a new component, called `BuilderListComponent`. So, let's create this new component.

3. Inside `./Client/src/app`, type the following command:

ng g c pages/builders/builder-list

You will see the following structure in the `builders` module:

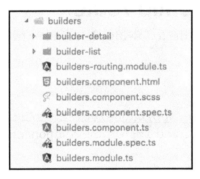

Builders module with builder-list module

Adding bikers child routes

Let's create the child routes for the following views in our frontend application:

- `bike-list`
- `bike-detail`

Now we will import the components at the top of file:

1. Open `./Client/src/app/pages/bikes/bikes-routing.module.ts` and `import` the component:

```
// Bikes Routes Imports
 import { BikeDetailComponent } from  './bike-detail/bike-
detail.component';
 import { BikeListComponent } from  './bike-list/bike-
list.component';
```

2. Still in ./Client/src/app/pages/bikes/bikes-routing.module.ts, add the following route object inside the `routes` constant:

```
const  routes:  Routes  = [
  { path:  'bikes',
    children: [
    {
      path:  "''",
      component:  BikeListComponent
    },{
      path:  ':id',
      component:  BikeDetailComponent
    }]
  }
];
```

Now, it is time to create the new `BikeListComponent`, as we did previously, with `Builders`.

3. Inside ./Client/src/app, type the following command:

ng g c pages/bikes/bike-list

You will see the following structure in the `bikes` module:

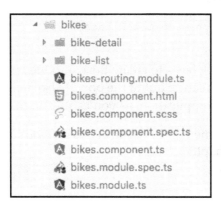

Bikes module with bike-list module

Refactoring app.component.html

As we discussed previously, let's now make our views a little more attractive.

Let's add our navigation component. For now, we will not put content in this file; we'll do that later on.

Open `./Client/src/app/app.component.html` and replace the code with the following:

```
<app-nav></app-nav>
<router-outlet></router-outlet>
    <footer  class="footer">
    <div  class="pl-3">
        <span  class="text-muted">2018 &copy; All Rights
        Reserved</span>
    </div>
    </footer>
```

Note that the preceding code doesn't have any content right now – just a simple markup for footer notes. In the next section, you will see how to add something more interesting.

Building frontend views

Most of the components that we create with Angular receive an HTML template, as you saw in previous chapters:

```
@Component({
        selector:  'app-nav',
        templateUrl:  './nav.component.html',
        styleUrls: ['./nav.component.scss']
})
```

This ability that the framework has – to create the component connected to its respective view – is fantastic. It has that feature out of the box. It also includes a style sheet totally independent of the rest of the application, as you can see in the previous code.

In the next step, we will add the HTML necessary to give our application a pleasant look, as we suggested in previous chapters.

Creating the navigation component

Open `./Client/src/app/layout/nav/nav.component.html` and replace the paragraph with the `nav works` string with the following code:

```
<header>
<nav class="navbar navbar-expand-md navbar-dark fixed-top bg-dark">
<a class="navbar-brand" [routerLink]="['/']" (click)="setTitle('Custom
Bikes Garage')">Custom Bikes Garage</a>
    <button class="navbar-toggler" type="button" data-toggle="collapse"
data-target="#navbarCollapse" aria-controls="navbarCollapse"
    aria-expanded="false" aria-label="Toggle navigation">
        <span class="navbar-toggler-icon"></span>
    </button>
    <div class="collapse navbar-collapse" id="navbarCollapse">
    <ul class="navbar-nav ml-auto">
    <li class="nav-item">
    <a class="nav-link" [routerLink]="['/bikes']"
    routerLinkActive="active" (click)="setTitle('Bikes')">Bikes</a>
    </li>
    <li class="nav-item">
    <a class="nav-link" [routerLink]="['/builders']"
            routerLinkActive="active"
        (click)="setTitle('Builders')">Builders</a>
    </li>
    <li class="nav-item">
    <a class="nav-link" [routerLink]="['/login']"
     routerLinkActive="active" (click)="setTitle('Login')">Login</a>
    </li>
    <li class="nav-item">
    <a class="nav-link" [routerLink]="['/register']"
     routerLinkActive="active"
        (click)="setTitle('Register')">Register</a>
    </li>
    <li class="nav-item">
    <a class="nav-link" [routerLink]="['/logout']"
     routerLinkActive="active">Logout</a>
    </li>
    </ul>
    </div>
</nav></header>
```

There are two important things about the preceding code:

- We are using the `routerLink` property; later in this chapter, you will see how to use it.
- We are setting the title page with the `<title>` tag, using the `Title` service, a built-in service from Angular. As we are building an SPA, we need to use this resource to give a title to our views; without it, all of the pages in our application will have the same client name. Remember, the `Title` tag was set when we first created the application with the Angular CLI, and it will receive the application name that we defined.

Let's update the `<title>` tag, as follows:

1. Open `./Client/src/app/layout/nav/nav.component.ts` and add the following code:

```
import { Component, OnInit } from '@angular/core';
import { Title } from '@angular/platform-browser';
@Component({
    selector: 'app-nav',
        templateUrl: './nav.component.html',
        styleUrls: ['./nav.component.scss']
    })
    export class NavComponent implements OnInit {
    public constructor(private titleTagService: Title ) { }
    public setTitle( pageTitle: string) {
    this.titleTagService.setTitle( pageTitle );
    }
    ngOnInit() {
    }
}
```

2. Open `./Client/src/app/app.module.ts` and add the `Title` import to the top of the file:

```
import { BrowserModule, Title } from '@angular/platform-browser';
```

3. Now, add the `Title` provider to the `@ngModules` provider:

```
providers: [
Title
],
```

So, if we check the browser at the same URL again (`http://localhost:4200/`), we can see a list of links, and we can navigate through them. The result will be similar to the following screenshot:

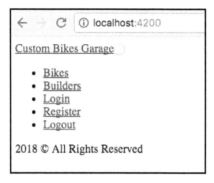

Navigation links

Don't worry about the class names in our markup; later on in the book, we will add some style sheets, including some Bootstrap components.

Creating the home view and template

Open `./Client/src/app/pages/home/home.component.html` and replace the paragraph with the `home works` string with the following code:

```html
<main role="main">
<div class="jumbotron">
<div class="container text-center">
<h1 class="display-3 ">Custom Bikes Garage</h1>
<p>Motorcycle builders and road lovers</p>
<p>
<a class="btn btn-primary btn-lg"
[routerLink]="['/register']"role="button">Register</a>
</p>
</div>
</div>
<div class="container">
<div class="row">
<div class="col-md-4">
<h2>Heading</h2>
<p>Donec id elit non mi porta gravida at eget metus. Fusce dapibus, tellus
ac cursus commodo, tortor mauris condimentum
nibh, ut fermentum massa justo sit amet risus. Etiam porta sem malesuada
magna mollis euismod. Donec sed odio dui.
```

```
</p>
<p>
<a class="btn btn-secondary" href="#" role="button">View details
&raquo;</a>
</p>
</div>
<div class="col-md-4">
<h2>Heading</h2>
<p>Donec id elit non mi porta gravida at eget metus. Fusce dapibus, tellus
ac cursus commodo, tortor mauris condimentum
nibh, ut fermentum massa justo sit amet risus. Etiam porta sem malesuada
magna mollis euismod. Donec sed odio dui.
</p>
<p>
<a class="btn btn-secondary" href="#" role="button">View details
&raquo;</a>
</p>
</div>
<div class="col-md-4">
<h2>Heading</h2>
<p>Donec sed odio dui. Cras justo odio, dapibus ac facilisis in, egestas
eget quam. Vestibulum id ligula porta felis euismod
semper. Fusce dapibus, tellus ac cursus commodo, tortor mauris condimentum
nibh, ut fermentum massa justo sit amet
risus.</p>
<p>
<a class="btn btn-secondary" href="#" role="button">View details
&raquo;</a>
</p>
</div>
</div>
</div>
</main>
```

Creating the bikes router-outlet

Open `./Client/src/app/pages/bikes/bikes.component.html` and replace the
paragraph with the `bikes works` string with the following code:

```
<router-outlet></router-outlet>
```

Creating the bike-list view and template

Open ./Client/src/app/pages/bikes/bike-list/bike-list.component.html and replace the paragraph with the bike-list works string with the following code:

```html
<main role="main">
<div class="py-5 bg-light">
<div class="container">
<form>
<div class="form-group row">
<label for="search" class="col-sm-2 col-form-label">Bike List</label>
<div class="col-sm-8">
<input type="text" class="form-control" id="search"placeholder="Search">
</div>
<div class="col-sm-2">
<div class="dropdown">
<button class="btn btn-outline-primary dropdown-toggle btn-block"
type="button" id="dropdownMenuButton" data-toggle="dropdown" aria-
haspopup="true" aria-expanded="false">
Filter
</button>
<div class="dropdown-menu" aria-labelledby="dropdownMenuButton">
<a class="dropdown-item" href="#">Action</a>
</div>
</div>
</div>
</div>
</form>
<div class="row">
<div class="col-md-4">
<div class="card mb-4 box-shadow">
<img class="card-img-top"
src="https://dummyimage.com/640x480/717171/fff.jpg&text=placeholder-image"
alt="Card image cap">
<div class="card-body">
<p>Model | year</p>
<p class="card-text">This is a wider card with supporting text below as a
natural lead-in to additional content. This content is a little bit
longer.</p>
<div class="d-flex justify-content-between align-items-center">
    <div class="btn-group">
    <button routerLink="/bikes/1" type="button" class="btn btn-sm
      btn-    outline-primary">View</button>
    <button type="button" class="btn btn-sm btn-outline-
        primary">Vote</button>
</div>
<small class="text-muted">4 ratings</small>
```

```
      </div>
    </div>
  </div>
</div>
<div class="col-md-4">
  <div class="card mb-4 box-shadow">
    <img class="card-img-
top"src="https://dummyimage.com/640x480/717171/fff.jpg&text=placeholder-ima
ge" alt="Card image cap">
    <div class="card-body">
      <p>Model | year</p>
      <p class="card-text">This is a wider card with supporting text below as a
natural lead-in to additional content. This content is
a little bit longer.</p>
      <div class="d-flex justify-content-between align-items-center">
        <div class="btn-group">
          <button routerLink="/bikes/2" type="button" class="btn btn-sm btn-outline-
primary">View</button>
          <button type="button" class="btn btn-sm btn-outline-primary">Vote</button>
        </div>
        <small class="text-muted">9 ratings</small>
      </div>
    </div>
  </div>
</div>
<div class="col-md-4">
  <div class="card mb-4 box-shadow">
    <img class="card-img-top"
src="https://dummyimage.com/640x480/717171/fff.jpg&text=placeholder-image"
alt="Card image cap">
    <div class="card-body">
      <p>Model | year</p>
      <p class="card-text">This is a wider card with supporting text below as a
natural lead-in to additional content. This content is
a little bit longer.</p>
      <div class="d-flex justify-content-between align-items-center">
        <div class="btn-group">
          <button routerLink="/bikes/3" type="button" class="btn btn-sm btnoutline-
primary">View</button>
          <button type="button" class="btn btn-sm btn-outline-primary">Vote</button>
        </div>
        <small class="text-muted">5 ratings</small>
      </div>
    </div>
  </div>
</div>
</div>
</div>
```

```
</div>
</main>
```

Creating the bike-detail view and template

Open ./Client/src/app/pages/bikes/bike-detail/bike-
detail.component.html and replace the paragraph with the bike-detail works string
with the following code:

```
<main role="main">
<div class="py-5">
<div class="container">
<div class="row">
<div class="col-md-4">
    <img class="card-img-top"
    src="https://dummyimage.com/340x280/717171/fff.jpg&text=placeholder-
    image" alt="Card image cap">
</div>
<div class="col-md-8">
<div class="card">
<div class="card-body">
    <h5 class="card-title">Card title | Year | Ratings</h5>
    <p class="card-text">Some quick example text to build on the card
     title and make up the bulk of the card's content.</p>
</div>
    <div class="card-header">
        Builder Name
    </div>
<div class="card-header">
    Featured items
</div>
<ul class="list-group list-group-flush">
    <li class="list-group-item">Cras justo odio</li>
    <li class="list-group-item">Dapibus ac facilisis in</li><li
        class="list-group-item">Vestibulum at eros</li>
</ul>
    <div class="card-body">
        <a href="#" class="card-link">Vote</a>
    </div>
</div>
</div>
</div>
</div>
</div>
</main>
```

Creating the builders router-outlet

Open `./Client/src/app/pages/builders/builders.component.html` and replace the paragraph with the `builders` works string with the following code:

```
<router-outlet></router-outlet>
```

Creating the builder-list view and template

Open `./Client/src/app/pages/builders/builder-list/builder-list.component.html` and replace the paragraph with the following code:

```html
<main role="main">
<div class="py-5 bg-light">
<div class="container">
<div class="card-deck mb-3 text-center">
<div class="card mb-4 box-shadow">
<div class="card-header">
<h4 class="my-0 font-weight-normal">Builder Name</h4>
</div>
<div class="card-body">
    <p class="mt-3 mb-4">
    Lorem ipsum dolor sit amet consectetur, adipisicing elit. Quam
     aspernatur sit cum necessitatibus.
    </p>
    <button routerLink="/builders/1" type="button" class="btn btn-lg
btn-block btn-outline-primary">View Bikes</button>
</div>
<div class="card-footer text-muted">
City/State
</div>
</div>
<div class="card mb-4 box-shadow">
<div class="card-header">
    <h4 class="my-0 font-weight-normal">Builder Name</h4>
</div>
<div class="card-body">
    <p class="mt-3 mb-4">
    Lorem ipsum dolor sit amet consectetur, adipisicing elit. Quam
     aspernatur sit cum necessitatibus.
</p>
    <button routerLink="/builders/2" type="button" class="btn btn-lg
     btn-block btn-outline-primary">View Bikes</button>
</div>
<div class="card-footer text-muted">
City/State
```

```
    </div>
    </div>
    <div class="card mb-4 box-shadow">
    <div class="card-header">
        <h4 class="my-0 font-weight-normal">Builder Name</h4>
    </div>
    <div class="card-body">
        <p class="mt-3 mb-4">
        Lorem ipsum dolor sit amet consectetur, adipisicing elit. Quam
         aspernatur sit cum necessitatibus.
    </p>
        <button routerLink="/builders/3" type="button" class="btn btn-lg
         btn-block btn-outline-primary">View Bikes</button>
    </div>
    <div class="card-footer text-muted">
    City/State
    </div>
    </div>
    </div>
    </div>
    </div>
    </div>
    </main>
```

Creating the builder-detail view and template

Open `./Client/src/app/pages/builders/builder-detail/builder-detail.component.html` and replace the paragraph with `builder-detail` works string with the following code:

```
<main role="main">
<div class="py-5">
<div class="container">
<div class="row">
<div class="col-md-12">
<div class="card">
<div class="card-body">
    <h5 class="card-title">Builder Name</h5>
    <p class="card-text">Some quick example text to build on the card
title and make up the bulk of the card's content.</p>
</div>
<div class="card-header">
    Featured Bikes
</div>
    <ul class="list-group list-group-flush">
    <li class="list-group-item">Cras justo odio</li>
    <li class="list-group-item">Dapibus ac facilisis in</li>
```

```
    <li class="list-group-item">Vestibulum at eros</li>
    </ul>
</div>
</div>
</div>
</div>
</div>
</main>
```

Creating the login view and template

Open `./Client/src/app/pages/auth/login/login.component.html` and replace the paragraph with the `login` works string with the following code:

```
<main role="main">
<div class="container">
<form class="form-signin">
<div class="text-center mb-4">
    <h1 class="h3 mt-3 mb-3 font-weight-normal">Welcome</h1>
    <p>Motorcycle builders and road lovers</p>
    <hr>
</div>
<div class="form-group">
    <label for="email">Email address</label>
    <input type="email" class="form-control" id="email"
     ariadescribedby="emailHelp" placeholder="Enter email">
</div>
    <div class="form-group">
    <label for="password">Password</label>
    <input type="password" class="form-control" id="password"
        placeholder="Password">
</div>
    <button class="btn btn-lg btn-primary btn-block mt-5"
        type="submit">Login</button>
</form>
</div>
</main>
```

Creating the register view and template

Open `./Client/src/app/pages/auth/register/register.component.html` and replace the paragraph with the `register` works string with the following code:

```
<main role="main">
<div class="container">
<form class="form-signin">
<div class="text-center mb-4">
<h1 class="h3 mt-3 mb-3 font-weight-normal">Welcome</h1>
<p>Motorcycle builders and road lovers</p>
<hr>
</div>
<div class="form-group">
<label for="name">Name</label><input type="name" class="form-control"
id="name" aria-describedby="nameHelp" placeholder="Enter your name">
</div>
<div class="form-group">
    <label for="email">Email address</label>
    <input type="email" class="form-control" id="email" aria-
    describedby="emailHelp" placeholder="Enter email">
</div>
<div class="form-group">
    <label for="password">Password</label>
    <input type="password" class="form-control" id="password"
     placeholder="Password">
</div>
    <button class="btn btn-lg btn-primary btn-block mt-5"
    type="submit">Register</button>
</form>
</div>
</main>
```

We now have the necessary code in our templates. However, we have not applied any style sheets yet. Don't worry about it at the moment; in the next sections, you'll see some more important points in the application, before we apply our style sheet. Let's take a look at what we have so far.

Testing routes and views

Let's start the application in development mode and check some URLs, to see the results of our routes and templates:

1. Open your Terminal window inside the `./Client` folder and type the following command:

   npm start

2. Open your default browser, and go to `http://localhost:4200/bikes/1`.

   You will see a result very similar to the following screenshot:

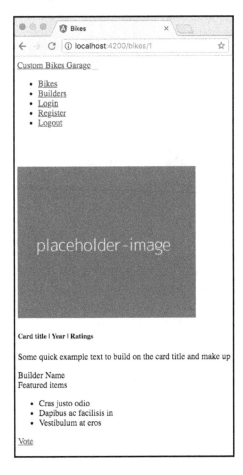

Bike detail page

Summary

You have come to the end of another chapter. In this chapter, you learned how to create additional components in modules, such as the `bikes` module. You added some routes using the Angular router, and learned how to use child routes. In addition, you learned how to create a navigation component and update the `<title>` tag of your pages, using an Angular default service.

Creating Services and User Authentication

9

In this chapter, we have a lot of work ahead of us. We will create many new things and refactor some things too. This is a great way to learn things in a regular and progressive way.

We will do a deep dive into the operation and use of the HTTP module of Angular, known as `HttpClient`.

In addition, we will see how to use interceptors and handle errors.

The new version of Angular provides extremely useful tools for creating modern web applications, and in this chapter we will use many of these resources.

In this chapter, we will cover the following topics:

- Dealing with models and classes
- Using the new `HttpModule` and `HttpModuleClient` to deal with XHR requests
- Dealing with the `HttpErrorHandler` service
- How to use authorization headers
- How to protect application routes with route guards

Preparing the baseline code

Now, we need to prepare our baseline code, a process very similar to what we did in the previous chapter. Let's follow these steps:

1. Copy all the content from the `chapter-08` folder.
2. Rename the folder to `chapter-09`.
3. Delete the `storage-db` folder.

   Now, let's make some changes to the `docker-compose.yml` file so that it can fit a new database and server containers.

4. Open `docker-compose.yml` and replace its content with the following code:

```
version: "3.1"
services:
    mysql:
      image: mysql:5.7
      container_name: chapter-09-mysql
      working_dir: /application
      volumes:
        - .:/application
        - ./storage-db:/var/lib/mysql
      environment:
        - MYSQL_ROOT_PASSWORD=123456
        - MYSQL_DATABASE=chapter-09
        - MYSQL_USER=chapter-09
        - MYSQL_PASSWORD=123456
      ports:
        - "8083:3306"
    webserver:
      image: nginx:alpine
      container_name: chapter-09-webserver
      working_dir: /application
      volumes:
        - .:/application
        -./phpdocker/nginx/nginx.conf:/etc/nginx/conf.d/default
        .conf
      ports:
        - "8081:80"
    php-fpm:
      build: phpdocker/php-fpm
      container_name: chapter-09-php-fpm
      working_dir: /application
      volumes:
```

```
    - ./Server:/application
    - ./phpdocker/php-fpm/php-ini-
      overrides.ini:/etc/php/7.2/fpm/conf.d/99-overrides.ini
```

Note that we changed the container names, database, and MySQL user:

- `container_name: chapter-09-mysql`
- `container_name: chapter-09-webserver`
- `container_name: chapter-09-php-fpm`
- `MYSQL_DATABASE=chapter-09`
- `MYSQL_USER=chapter-09`

5. Add the changes we made to Git source control. Open your Terminal window and type the following command:

```
git add .
git commit -m "Initial commit chapter 09"
```

Dealing with models and classes

Considered good practice by the community of Angular developers (and we consider it essential) is the creation of classes to use them as models. These are also known as **domain models**.

We believe that creating classes to store our models in is a very important resource for creating large-scale applications or even small apps. This helps you keep your code organized.

Imagine if our project is much larger—if all the data was stored inside the plain objects, it would be hard for a new developer to find out where the data is stored.

This is also a good reason to use classes to store our model information.

Creating the User class model

Let's start by creating the class to store our user information. By convention, we will name this file `user.ts`:

1. Open your Terminal window.

2. Go to `./Client/src/app` and type the following command:

   ```
   ng g class pages/auth/user
   ```

3. The previous command will create a new file in `./app/pages/auth/auth.ts`. Open this file and add the following code:

   ```
   export  class  User {
           name?:   string;
           email?:  string;
           password?:  string;
           constructor() {}
   }
   ```

Creating the builders class model

Now, let's create the model for the builder and understand the operation of classes as models a little better. Before that, we will observe the return of the API when we make a GET to the `api/builders/1` endpoint, as we can see in the following screenshot:

Builder-detail JSON result

In the previous screenshot, we have already included the bike information on the builders detail request. Let's see how we can do this using the `builders` class:

1. Still in your Terminal, type the following command:

```
ng g class pages/builders/builder
```

2. The previous command will create a new file in `./app/pages/builders/builder.ts`. Open this file and add the following code:

```
import { Bike } from '../bikes/bike';

export class Builder {
    id: number;
    name: string;
    description: string;
    location: string;
    bike?: Bike;
```

```
        constructor() {}
    }
```

Note that, in the previous code, we added an optional `bike` property and set its type to `Bike` model.

Creating the Bike class model

Now, it's time to create the bike model class, but first let's check the JSON format that we have on the bike's detail endpoint, `api/bikes/2`, as we can see in the following screenshot:

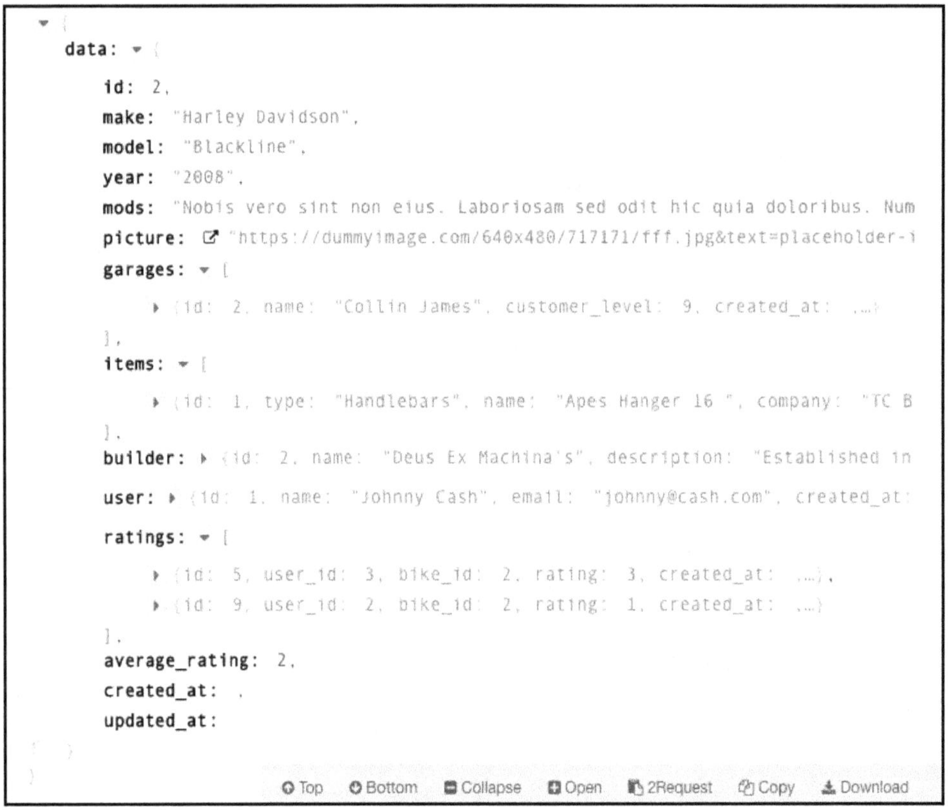

bike-detail JSON result

Here, we can note that the `bike-detail` result points to `garages`, `items`, `builder`, `user`, and `ratings`. For the sample application we are building, we will just use the builder and user model. Don't worry about the others; the example we are going to use here is enough for understanding the model domain:

1. Still in your Terminal, type the following command:

    ng g class pages/bikes/bike

2. The previous command will create a new file in `./app/pages/bikes/bike.ts`. Open this file and add the following code:

```
import { User } from  './../auth/user';
import { Builder } from  '../builders/builder';

export  class  Bike {
        id:  number;
        make:  string;
        model:  string;
        year:  string;
        mods:  string;
        picture:  string;
        user_id:  number;
        builder_id:  number;
        average_rating?: number;
        user?:  User;
        builder?:  Builder;
        items?:  any;
        ratings?:  any;

        constructor() {}
}
```

Note that, in the previous code, we are using all properties from the previous screenshot, including `items` and `ratings`, as optional properties with type `any`, as we didn't create models for these properties.

Using the new HttpClient to deal with XHR requests

The vast majority of web applications nowadays use `XMLHttpRequest` (XHR) requests, and applications made with Angular are no different. For that, we have the `HTTPClient` module that replaced the old HTTP module in previous versions.

In this session, we will understand how to use XHR requests inside our Angular services.

It is highly recommended that you use Angular services to handle requests of this type so that the code of the component is more organized and easy to maintain.

You can read more about XHR requests at `https://developer.mozilla.org/en-US/docs/Web/API/XMLHttpRequest`.

Creating the auth service

Let's create the file that will store the necessary code for our authentication module:

1. Still in your Terminal, type the following command:

    ```
    ng g service pages/auth/_services/auth
    ```

    The previous command will create a new folder and file in `./app/pages/auth/_services/auth.service.ts`. Now, let's add some pieces of code.

2. Open `./app/pages/auth/_services/auth.service.ts` and add the following imports to the top of the file:

    ```
    import { HttpClient, HttpParams, HttpErrorResponse } from
    '@angular/common/http';
    import { HttpHeaders } from  '@angular/common/http';
    import { Router } from  '@angular/router';
    import { Observable, throwError } from  'rxjs';
    import { catchError, map, tap } from  'rxjs/operators';

    // App imports
    import { environment } from
    './../../../environments/environment';
    import { User } from  './user';
    ```

    Now, we will use `HttpHeaders` to set the content type of our XHR requests.

3. Add the following code right after the import files:

    ```
    // Setup headers
    const httpOptions  = {
    ```

```
headers: new  HttpHeaders({
        'Content-Type': 'application/json'
    })
};
```

The previous code sample will add a new header to our requests using
`HttpHeaders`.

4. Inside the `AuthService` class, add the following code:

```
public  currentUser:  User;
private  readonly  apiUrl  =  environment.apiUrl;
private  registerUrl  =  this.apiUrl  +  '/register';
private  loginUrl  =  this.apiUrl  +  '/login';
```

You must be asking yourself why `currentUser` is `public` and the others are
`private`, right?

Well, the `currentUser` property is `public` because we will access it in other
files, as we will see later in this section. Therefore, the other properties will not be
available outside the `AuthService`.

5. Now, let's create our `constructor` function. Inside the `constructor` function,
    add the following code:

private http: HttpClient, private router: Router

6. The `constructor` class will look like the following code:

```
constructor(
        private  http:  HttpClient,
        private  router:  Router) {}
```

Note here that we are using the `HttpClient` and `Router` module, so it is time to write our
functions to see this module in practice.

Creating the Register function

Let's create the `Register` function. After the `constructor` function, let's add the
following code:

```
onRegister(user: User): Observable<User> {
        const request  =  JSON.stringify(
                { name: user.name, email: user.email, password:
```

```
        user.password }
    );
    return  this.http.post(this.registerUrl, request,
    httpOptions)
    .pipe(
        map((response:  User) => {
            // Receive jwt token in the response
            const  token: string  =
            response['access_token'];
            // If we have a token, proceed
            if (token) {
                    this.setToken(token);
                    this.getUser().subscribe();
            }
            return  response;
        }),
    catchError(error  =>  this.handleError(error))
    );
}
```

Note that we are using the `pipe()`, `map()`, and `catchError()` functions from the **Reactive Extensions Library for JavaScript (RxJS)** that's included in Angular.

Before using the RxJS library, it was very common in AngularJS applications to use a library called Lodash to manipulate the results.

 You can read more about the RxJS library in the official documentation link `https://rxjs-dev.firebaseapp.com/api`.

We are using the `pipe()` function which allows us to chain other functions, and this is pretty interesting when we are working with observables. Inside the `pipe()` function, this is exactly what we're doing with the `map()` and `catchError()` functions.

In addition, we are using three more local functions called `setToken()`, `getUser()`, and `handleError()`, which we will look at later.

Keep in mind that function names are extremely important. Try to use self-explanatory names like we did in `setToken` and `getUser`.

Creating the Login function

The `Login` function follows almost the same structure as the `Register` function. The difference here is that we are just sending the email address and password to the server.

Add the following code right after the `onRegister()` function:

```
onLogin(user: User): Observable<User> {
        const request =  JSON.stringify(
                { email: user.email, password: user.password }
        );
        return  this.http.post(this.registerUrl, request,
        httpOptions)
        .pipe(
                map((response:  User) => {
                        // Receive jwt token in the response
                        const  token: string  =
                        response['access_token'];
                        // If we have a token, proceed
                        if (token) {
                                this.setToken(token);
                                this.getUser().subscribe();
                        }
                        return  response;
                }),
        catchError(error  =>  this.handleError(error))
        );
}
```

Note that we are saving the user token using the `setToken()` function and getting the user's details using the `getUser()` function. We will see this in detail later in this section.

Creating the Logout function

For the Logout function, we will use a different approach. Instead of using the `map()` operator, we will use the `tap()` operator.

Add the following code right after the `onLogin()` function:

```
onLogout():  Observable<User> {
        return  this.http.post(this.apiUrl  +  '/logout',
        httpOptions).pipe(
                tap(
                        () => {
                                localStorage.removeItem('token');
                                this.router.navigate(['/']);
                        }
                )
        );
}
```

In the previous code, we just remove the token from `localStorage` and redirect the user to the home page. Now, it is time to create the local functions to deal with data.

Creating the setToken and getToken functions

We are almost at the end of our authentication service, but we still need to create some helper functions that we will use in other application blocks.

Let's create the functions to handle the user token. Recreating call from our backend with Laravel that we are using the `jwt-auth` library to authenticate our users.

In this example, we are using `localStorage` to store the user's token. So, let's create two very simple functions to write and retrieve this token.

Right after the `logout()` function, add the following block of code:

```
setToken(token:  string):  void {
      return  localStorage.setItem('token', token );
}

getToken():  string {
      return  localStorage.getItem('token');
}
```

Creating the getUser function

Now, we will see how to get the information of the logged-in user. Remember that our API has an endpoint that gives us the information of the logged-in user based on the authentication token.

Let's see how we can do this in a simple way.

Add the following code right after the `getToken()` function:

```
getUser():  Observable<User> {
      return  this.http.get(this.apiUrl  +  '/me').pipe(
            tap(
                  (user: User) => {
                        this.currentUser  =  user;
                  }
            )
      );
}
```

The previous code receives the user's information from the API and applies this to the `currentUser` property.

Creating the isAuthenticated function

Now, we will create just one more function. This function will help us to identify if the user is logged in.

Add the following code right after the `getUser()` function:

```
isAuthenticated(): boolean {
// get the token
const token: string = this.getToken();
if (token) {
    return true;
}
return false;
}
```

Now, we can use this information anywhere we want just by using the `AuthService.currentUser` and `AuthService.isAuthenticated` methods.

Creating the handleError function

You should have noticed that the `login()` and `register()` functions have a `catchError` function that points to another function called the `handleError`. At this moment in time, we are going to create this function, which is in charge of showing the possible errors that our request may have.

Add the following code right after the `getUser()` function:

```
private  handleError(error:  HttpErrorResponse) {
    if (error.error  instanceof  ErrorEvent) {
        // A client-side error.
        console.error('An error occurred:',
        error.error.message);
    } else {
        // The backend error.
        return  throwError(error);
    }
    // return a custom error message
    return  throwError('Ohps something wrong happen here; please try
again later.');
}
```

We are logging the error messages to the browser console, just for this example.

Creating the bikes service

Now, we are going to create the service to hold all bike operations. Remember, for both bikes and builders, our service must have methods for listing, details, creation, updating, and deletion:

1. Still in your Terminal, type the following command:

   ng g service pages/bikes/_services/bike

   The previous command will create a new folder and file in `./app/pages/bikes/_services/bike.service.ts`. Now, let's add some pieces of code.

2. Open `./app/pages/bikes/_services/bike.service.ts` and add the following imports to the top of the file:

   ```
   import { Injectable } from '@angular/core';
   import { HttpClient, HttpParams, HttpErrorResponse } from
   '@angular/common/http';
   import { HttpHeaders } from '@angular/common/http';
   import { Observable, throwError } from 'rxjs';
   import { catchError } from 'rxjs/operators';

   // App import
   import { environment } from
   '../../../../environments/environment';
   import { Bike } from '../bike';
   ```

3. Inside the `bikesService` class, add the following properties:

   ```
   private readonly apiUrl = environment.apiUrl;
   private bikesUrl = this.apiUrl + '/bikes';
   ```

4. Now, let's create our `constructor` function. Inside the `constructor` function, add the following code:

   ```
   constructor(private http: HttpClient) {}
   ```

Now, we are ready to create the functions of our bike service.

Creating CRUD functions

As we mentioned earlier, **CRUD** stands for Create, Read, Update, and Delete. We will add the code for the operations all at once, and then we will make the necessary comments.

Add the following blocks of code right after the constructor() function:

```
/** GET bikes from bikes endpoint */
getBikes ():  Observable<Bike[]> {
      return  this.http.get<Bike[]>(this.bikesUrl)
      .pipe(
            catchError(error  =>  this.handleError(error))
      );
}

/** GET bike detail from bike-detail endpoint */
getBikeDetail (id:  number):  Observable<Bike[]> {
      return  this.http.get<Bike[]>(this.bikesUrl  +  `/${id}`)
      .pipe(
            catchError(error  =>  this.handleError(error))
      );
}

/** POST bike to bikes endpoint */
addBike (bike:  Bike):  Observable<Bike> {
      return  this.http.post<Bike>(this.bikesUrl, bike)
      .pipe(
            catchError(error  =>  this.handleError(error))
      );
}

/** PUT bike to bikes endpoint */
updateBike (bike:  Bike, id:  number):  Observable<Bike> {
      return  this.http.put<Bike>(this.bikesUrl  +  `/${id}`,
bike)
      .pipe(
            catchError(error  =>  this.handleError(error))
      );
}

/** DELETE bike bike endpoint */
deleteBike (id:  number):  Observable<Bike[]> {
      return  this.http.delete<Bike[]>(this.bikesUrl  +
`/${id}`)
      .pipe(
            catchError(error  =>  this.handleError(error))
      );
}
```

```
/** Vote on bike */
voteOnBike (vote:  any, bike:  number):  Observable<any> {
        const  rating  =  vote;
        return  this.http.post(this.bikesUrl  +
`/${bike}/ratings`, {rating})
        .pipe(
                catchError(error  =>  this.handleError(error))
        );
}
```

The previous code does not have anything particularly different from what we used in our authentication service, except for the use of the template string:

```
this.bikesUrl  +  `/${id}`
this.bikesUrl  +  `/${bike}/ratings`, {rating}
```

These are represented by back-tick (` `) characters, instead of single or double quotes marks, and an expression beginning with a dollar sign.

Creating the voteOnBike function

Our service still has one more function, which we will use to send the user's votes for a specific bike. Remember, whenever you need to use the HTTPClient module, do this within a service. This is considered good practice in Angular development.

Add the following code right after the deleteBike() function:

```
/** Vote on bike */
voteOnBike (vote:  number, bike:  number):  Observable<any> {
        const  rating  =  vote;
        return  this.http.post(this.bikesUrl  +
        `/${bike}/ratings`, {rating})
        .pipe(
                catchError(error  =>  this.handleError(error))
        );
}
```

Creating the handleError function

Now, let's add the error handling for the bikes service. Add the following code, right after the voteOnBike() function:

```
/** Error handler */
private  handleError(error:  HttpErrorResponse) {
        if (error.error  instanceof  ErrorEvent) {
```

```
                    // A client-side error.
                    console.error('An error occurred:',
        error.error.message);
        } else {
                    // The backend error.
                    return   throwError(error);
        }
        // return a custom error message
        return   throwError('Something bad happened; please try
        again later.');
    }
```

As we can see, the `handleError()` function on the bike service is the same as the authentication service, and will be the same on the builders service. Whenever you need to write the same code more than once, it is highly recommended that you use a service for this, thereby avoiding the repetition of code.

Later, we will create a service to solve this problem, but for now we will create the service of builders.

Creating the builders service

Now, we will create the `builder` service with the `Create`, `Read`, `Update`, and `Delete` methods:

1. Still in your Terminal, type the following command:

   ng g service pages/builders/_services/builder

   The previous command will create a new folder and file in `./app/pages/builders/_services/builder.service.ts`. Now, let's add some pieces of code.

2. Open `./app/pages/builders/_services/builder.service.ts` and replace its code with the following block:

   ```
   import { Injectable } from  '@angular/core';

       import { HttpClient, HttpParams, HttpErrorResponse } from
       '@angular/common/http';
       import { HttpHeaders } from  '@angular/common/http';
       import { Observable, throwError } from  'rxjs';
       import { catchError } from  'rxjs/operators';

       // App import
   ```

```
import { environment } from
'../../../../environments/environment';
import { Builder } from '../builder';
@Injectable({
        providedIn: 'root'
})

export  class  BuildersService {
        private  readonly  apiUrl  =  environment.apiUrl;
        private  buildersUrl  =  this.apiUrl  +
  '/builders';
        constructor(private  http:  HttpClient) { }

        /** GET builders from builders endpoint */
        getBuilders ():  Observable<Builder[]> {
                return  this.http.get<Builder[]>
(this.buildersUrl)
                        .pipe(
                                catchError(error  =>
 this.handleError(error))
                        );
        }

        /** GET builder detail from builder-detail endpoint
   */
        getBuilderDetail (id:  number):
  Observable<Builder[]> {
                return  this.http.get<Builder[]>(this.buildersUrl
 +
  `/${id}`)
                        .pipe(
                                catchError(error  =>
 this.handleError(error))
                        );
        }

        /** POST builder to builders endpoint */
        addBuilder (builder:  Builder):
  Observable<Builder>
        {
                        return  this.http.post<Builder>
      (this.buildersUrl, builder)
                                .pipe(
                                        catchError(error  =>
      this.handleError(error))
                                );
        }
```

```
        /** PUT builder to builders endpoint */
        updateBuilder (builder: Builder, id: number):
Observable<Builder> {
            return this.http.put<Builder>
(this.buildersUrl + `/${id}`, builder)
                .pipe(
                        catchError(error =>
this.handleError(error))
                    );
        }

        /** DELETE builder builder endpoint */
        deleteBuilder (id: number): Observable<Builder[]>
{
            return this.http.delete<Builder[]>
(this.buildersUrl + `/${id}`)
                .pipe(
                        catchError(error =>
this.handleError(error))
                    );
        }

        /** Error handler */
        private handleError(error: HttpErrorResponse) {
            if (error.error instanceof ErrorEvent) {
                // A client-side error.
                console.error('An error occurred:',
error.error.message);
            } else {
                // The backend error.
                return throwError(error);
            }
            // return a custom error message
            return throwError('Something bad happened;
please try again later.');
        }
    }
```

The previous code is pretty much the same as the bike service, and we can note that the last function is the `handleError()` function, so it is time to learn how to create an error service.

Dealing with the HttpErrorHandler service

As mentioned previously, it is not a good practice to repeat code in a modern web application, so we can use many resources to avoid this practice. In Angular development, we can use a shared service to handle the application errors in just one place.

Creating a handler error service

As mentioned earlier in this chapter, let's create our error handler service:

1. Open your Terminal window inside `./Client/src/app` and type the following command:

   ```
   ng g service pages/shared/_services/httpHandleError
   ```

   The previous command will create a new folder called `_services` inside the `pages/shared` folder for a simple reason: we will share this service between all services that we created inside the `bikes`, `builders`, and `auth` modules. The previous command also created a file called `http-handle-error.service.ts`.

2. Open `./Client/src/app/shared/_services/http-handle-error.service.ts` and add the following imports:

   ```
   import { HttpErrorResponse } from '@angular/common/http';
   import { Observable, of } from 'rxjs';
   ```

3. Let's create an Angular `type` for our error. Add the following code right after the imports:

   ```
   export type HandleError =
       <T> (operation?: string, result?: T) => (error:
   HttpErrorResponse) => Observable<T>;
   ```

   The previous code creates a new `Type` called `HandleError`, and we will use it in the following lines.

Remember that Angular has many types such as array, void, any many more. We already saw this in Chapter 3, *Understanding the Core Concepts of Angular 6.*

4. Let's add the error function. Add the following block of code right after the `constructor()` function:

```
/** Pass the service name to map errors */
    createHandleError  = (serviceName  =  '') => <T>
           (operation  =  'operation', result  = {} as  T) =>
    this.handleError(serviceName, operation, result)
    handleError<T> (serviceName  =  '', operation  =
'operation', result  = {} as  T) {
           return (response:  HttpErrorResponse):
           Observable<T> => {
                  // Optionally send the error to a third
part
                  error logging service
                  console.error(response);
                  // Show a simple alert if error
                  const  message  = (response.error
                  instanceof  ErrorEvent) ?
                  response.error.message  :
                  `server returned code ${response.status}
                  with body "${response.error.error}"`;
                  // We are using alert just for example, on
                  real world avoid this pratice
                  alert(message);
                  // Keep running and returning a safe
result.
                  return  of( result );
           };
       }
```

The previous code creates a function called `handleError` that receive three parameters—`serviceName`, `operation`, and `result`—and returns an observable type called `HandleError`.

We are also using the basic built-in JavaScript function to show an alert to the user if we have an error, and a `console.log()` function with all the HTTP response.

Nowadays, it is very common to use a payed logging service to monitor web applications and issue silent errors to the user.

Some private services for this, as is the case are Rollbar, TrackJS, Bugsnag, and Sentry. All of them offer a powerful API for tracking errors in production mode and sent then to a dashboard panel easy to use, without alarm the application users or search for application logs.

 We also recommend, for beta and alpha applications, a free account from bugsnag at `https://www.bugsnag.com/platforms/javascript/`.

Importing HttpErrorHandler into app.module.ts

Now, we need to add our service to the central module of our application. Remember that we are using a directory called `shared`; the appropriate place to put our service is directly in the `app.module.ts` file:

1. Open the `./Client/src/app/app.module.ts` file and add following code right after the `NavComponent` import:

   ```
   import { HttpErrorHandler } from './shared/_services/http-handle-
   error.service';
   ```

2. Still on `./Client/src/app/app.module.ts`, add the `HttpErrorHandler` property to the `providers` array after the `Title` property:

   ```
   providers: [
           Title,
           HttpErrorHandler,
       ],
   ```

At the end of this step, we have the following directory structure in our app:

Shared services folder

Refactoring the builders service

Now that we have created the error handling service, we need to refactor our builders and bikes services to use the new error handling.

Open `./app/pages/builders/_services/builder.service.ts` and replace its content with the following code:

```
import { Injectable } from '@angular/core';
import { HttpClient, HttpParams, HttpErrorResponse } from
'@angular/common/http';
import { HttpHeaders } from '@angular/common/http';
import { Observable, throwError } from 'rxjs';
import { catchError } from 'rxjs/operators';
// App import
import { environment } from
'../../../../environments/environment';
import { Builder } from '../builder';
import { HttpErrorHandler, HandleError } from
'../../../shared/_services/http-handle-error.service';
```

```
@Injectable({
    providedIn: 'root'
})

export class BuildersService {
    private readonly apiUrl = environment.apiUrl;
    private buildersUrl = this.apiUrl +
    '/builders';
    private handleError: HandleError;

    constructor(
        private http: HttpClient,
        httpErrorHandler: HttpErrorHandler ) {
        this.handleError =
httpErrorHandler.createHandleError('BuildersService');
    }
    /** GET builders from builders endpoint */
    getBuilders (): Observable<Builder[]> {
        return this.http.get<Builder[]>
    (this.buildersUrl)
            .pipe(
    catchError(this.handleError('getBuilders', []))
            );
    }

    /** GET builder detail from builder-detail endpoint
     */
    getBuilderDetail (id: number):
    Observable<Builder[]> {
        return this.http.get<Builder[]>
    (this.buildersUrl + `/${id}`)
            .pipe(
    catchError(this.handleError('getBuilderDetail', []))
            );
    }

    /** POST builder to builders endpoint */
    addBuilder (builder: Builder): Observable<Builder> {
        return this.http.post<Builder>
    (this.buildersUrl, builder)
            .pipe(
    catchError(this.handleError('addBuilder', builder))
            );
    }

    /** PUT builder to builders endpoint */
    updateBuilder (builder: Builder, id: number):
    Observable<Builder> {
```

```
                   return  this.http.put<Builder>(this.buildersUrl
       +  `/${id}`, builder).pipe(
          catchError(this.handleError('updateBuilder', builder))
                          );
          }

          /** DELETE builder builder endpoint */
          deleteBuilder (id:  number):  Observable<Builder[]> {
                 return  this.http.delete<Builder[]>
          (this.buildersUrl  +  `/${id}`)
                          .pipe(
                   catchError(this.handleError('deleteBuilder'))
                          );
          }
     }
```

In the previous code, we replaced our local error function to use the new error service. We added a new property called `handleError` and created a new handler named `BuildersService` with the following code:

```
this.handleError = httpErrorHandler.createHandleError ('BuildersService');
```

Each handler received the `serviceName` as `getBuilders`, `getBuilderDetail`, `addBuilder`, `updateBuilder`, and `deleteBuilder`.

Now, we will do the same for the bikes service.

Refactoring the bikes service

Now, let's add the new error handling to the bikes service.

Open `./app/pages/bikes/_services/bike.service.ts` and replace its contents with the following code:

```
     import { Injectable } from  '@angular/core';
        import { HttpClient, HttpParams, HttpErrorResponse } from
     '@angular/common/http';
        import { HttpHeaders } from  '@angular/common/http';
        import { Observable, throwError } from  'rxjs';
        import { catchError } from  'rxjs/operators';
        // App import
        import { environment } from
     '../../../../environments/environment';
        import { Bike } from  '../bike';
        import { HttpErrorHandler, HandleError } from
     '../../../shared/_services/http-handle-error.service';
```

```
@Injectable({
    providedIn: 'root'
})

export  class  BikesService {
    private  readonly  apiUrl  =  environment.apiUrl;
    private  bikesUrl  =  this.apiUrl  +  '/bikes';
    private  handleError:  HandleError;
    constructor(
            private  http:  HttpClient,
            httpErrorHandler:  HttpErrorHandler ) {
            this.handleError  =
    httpErrorHandler.createHandleError('BikesService');
    }

    /** GET bikes from bikes endpoint */
    getBikes ():  Observable<Bike[]> {
            return  this.http.get<Bike[]>(this.bikesUrl)
                    .pipe(
      catchError(this.handleError('getBikes', []))
                    );
    }

    /** GET bike detail from bike-detail endpoint */
    getBikeDetail (id:  number):  Observable<Bike[]> {
            return  this.http.get<Bike[]>(this.bikesUrl  +
    `/${id}`)
                    .pipe(
    catchError(this.handleError('getBikeDetail', []))
                    );
    }

    /** POST bike to bikes endpoint */
    addBike (bike:  Bike):  Observable<Bike> {
            return  this.http.post<Bike>(this.bikesUrl,
    bike)
                    .pipe(
    catchError(this.handleError('addBike', bike))
                    );
    }

    /** PUT bike to bikes endpoint */
    updateBike (bike:  Bike, id:  number):
    Observable<Bike> {
            return  this.http.put<Bike>(this.bikesUrl  +
    `/${id}`, bike)
                    .pipe(
    catchError(this.handleError('updateBike', bike))
```

```
                                );
        }

        /** DELETE bike bike endpoint */
        deleteBike (id:  number):  Observable<Bike[]> {
                return  this.http.delete<Bike[]>(this.bikesUrl
+  `/${id}`)
                        .pipe(
catchError(this.handleError('deleteBike'))
                        );
        }
        /** Vote on bike */
        voteOnBike (vote:  number, bike:  number):
Observable<any> {
                const  rating  =  vote;
                return  this.http.post(this.bikesUrl  +
`/${bike}/ratings`, {rating})
                        .pipe(
  catchError(this.handleError('voteOnBike', []))
                        );
        }
}
```

In the previous code, we did the same as we did in the builders service and added each handler with a `serviceName` as `getBikes`, `getBikeDetail`, `addBike`, `updateBike`, and `deleteBike`.

How to use authorization headers

When we talk about authorization in the header, we are basically talking about making some modifications in the header of the application to send some kind of authorization. In our case, we are specifically talking about an authorization token generated by our API backend.

The best way to do this is by using Angular interceptors. An interceptor, as its name suggests, allows us to simply intercept and configure requests before they are triggered to the server.

This allows us to do a lot of things. An example of this would be to configure a token authentication on any request, or suddenly add custom headers that our application may need, until we handle answers before finishing the request.

When a JWT token is sent to the backend, remember that we are using the `jwt-auth` library on our Laravel API: it is expected to be in the authorization header of the HTTP request.

The most common approach for adding an authorization header to an HTTP request in Angular is creating an interceptor class and having the interceptor make modifications to the requests by attaching a JWT (or other form of access token) as an authorization header with the Bearer scheme, as we explained previously.

Creating an HTTP interceptor

Let's take a look at how to use Angular's `HttpInterceptor` interface to make authenticated HTTP requests.

When we are handling authentication in an Angular app, most of the time, it's generally best to put everything you need in a dedicated service, like we did previously.

Any authentication service should have a few basic methods for allowing users to log in and log out. It should also include a method for retrieving a JSON Web Token and putting it into `localStorage` (like we did previously), on the client, and a way to determine if the user is authenticated or not, in our case, using the `isAuthenticated()` function on `auth.service.ts`.

So, let's create the HTTP interceptor:

1. Open your Terminal window at `./Client/src/app` and type the following command:

   ng g service shared/_services/http-interceptor

   The previous command will generate the following file: `./Client/src/app/shared/_services/app-http-interceptor.service.ts`. Once again, we are creating a file in our `shared` directory, because we can use this service anywhere we want in our application.

2. Open `./Client/src/app/shared/_services/app-http-interceptor.service.ts` and add the following code:

   ```
   import { Injectable, Injector } from '@angular/core';
   import { HttpEvent, HttpHeaders, HttpInterceptor,
   HttpHandler, HttpRequest, HttpErrorResponse, HttpResponse } from
   '@angular/common/http';
   import { Observable } from 'rxjs';
   ```

```
import { catchError, map, tap } from 'rxjs/operators';
import { Router } from '@angular/router';
// App import
import { AuthService } from
'../../pages/auth/_services/auth.service';
@Injectable()
export class AppHttpInterceptorService implements
HttpInterceptor {
constructor(public auth: AuthService, private router:
Router ) { }

intercept(req: HttpRequest<any>, next: HttpHandler):
Observable<HttpEvent<any>> {
        console.log('interceptor running');
        // Get the token from auth service.
        const authToken = this.auth.getToken();
        if (authToken) {
                // Clone the request to add the new header.
                const authReq = req.clone(
                        { headers:
  req.headers.set('Authorization', `Bearer ${authToken}`) }
                );
                console.log('interceptor running with new
headers');
                // send the newly created request
                return next.handle(authReq).pipe(
                        tap((event: HttpEvent<any>) => {
                                if (event instanceof
  HttpResponse) {
                                        // Response wiht
  HttpResponse type
                                        console.log('TAP function',
event);
                                }
                        }, (err: any) => {
                        console.log(err);
                        if (err instanceof
  HttpErrorResponse) {
                                if (err.status === 401) {
  localStorage.removeItem('token');
  this.router.navigate(['/']);
                                }
                        }
                })
                );
        } else {
                console.log('interceptor without changes');
```

```
                                  return   next.handle(req);
                        }
             }
```

3. In the previous code, first we check if we have a token in `localStorage` with the `this.auth.getToken();` function from `AuthService`. So, if we have a token, we add it as a new header using the following:

```
      const  authReq  =  req.clone(
                  { headers: req.headers.set('Authorization', `Bearer
      ${authToken}`)}
                        );
```

4. If the token is invalid, or if the API returned a 401 error, we send the user to the home route using the following:

```
      this.router.navigate(['/']);
```

Adding AppHttpInterceptorService to the main module

Now that we have our interceptor configured and ready to be used, we need to add it into the main application module:

1. Open `./Client/src/app/app.module.ts` and add the following import, right after the `HttpErrorHandler` import:

```
      import { AppHttpInterceptorService } from
      './shared/_services/app-http-interceptor.service';
```

2. Add the following code, inside the `providers` array, right after the HttpErrorHandler property:

```
      {
              provide: HTTP_INTERCEPTORS,
              useClass: AppHttpInterceptorService ,
              multi: true
      }
```

3. At the end of the previous step, our main application module will include the following code:

```
      import { BrowserModule, Title } from  '@angular/platform-
      browser';
```

```
import { NgModule } from  '@angular/core';
import { HttpClientModule, HTTP_INTERCEPTORS } from
'@angular/common/http';
import { AppRoutingModule } from  './app-routing.module';
import { ServiceWorkerModule } from  '@angular/service-
worker';
// Application modules
import { AppComponent } from  './app.component';
import { environment } from  '../environments/environment';
import { HomeModule } from  './pages/home/home.module';
import { BikesModule } from  './pages/bikes/bikes.module';
import { BuildersModule } from
'./pages/builders/builders.module';
import { AuthModule } from  './pages/auth/auth.module';
import { NavComponent } from  './layout/nav/nav.component';
import { HttpErrorHandler } from  './shared/_services/http-
handle-error.service';
import { AppHttpInterceptorService } from
'./shared/_services/app-http-interceptor.service';
@NgModule({
declarations: [
        AppComponent,
        NavComponent
],
imports: [
        BrowserModule,
        AppRoutingModule,
        HttpClientModule,
        HomeModule,
        BikesModule,
        BuildersModule,
        AuthModule,
        ServiceWorkerModule.register('/ngsw-worker.js', {
enabled: environment.production })
],
providers: [
        Title,
        HttpErrorHandler,
        {
        provide: HTTP_INTERCEPTORS,
        useClass: AppHttpInterceptorService ,
        multi: true
        }
],
bootstrap: [AppComponent]
})
export  class  AppModule { }
```

Note that we are separating the Angular imports from application imports. This is a good practice and helps keep your code organized.

Congratulations! Now, we can intercept every request in our application.

How to protect application routes with route guards

In this section, we will talk about another powerful feature of the Angular framework. We call it guards, or even better, route guards.

It is available in the Angular CLI, as we will see in the following lines of code, but first let's understand a bit more about guards.

Protecting routes is a very common task when building modern web applications, as we want to prevent our users from accessing areas that they're not allowed to access, in our case, the bike details. Remember that we define the access to bike details inside `./Server/app/Http/Controllers/API/BikeController.php`:

```
/**
 * Protect update and delete methods, only for authenticated
 users.
 *
 * @return  Unauthorized
 */
public  function  __construct()
{
        $this->middleware('auth:api')->except(['index']);
}
```

The previous code says that only the index route should not be protected.

There are four different guard types we can use to protect our routes:

- `CanActivate`: Choose if a route can be activated
- `CanActivateChild`: Choose if child routes of a route can be activated
- `CanDeactivate`: Choose if a route can be deactivated
- `CanLoad`: Choose if a module can be loaded lazily

In the next example, we will be using the `CanActivate` feature.

Creating the route guard for bike-detail

Guards are implemented as services that need to be provided, so we typically create a guard class using the Angular CLI:

1. Open your Terminal window and type the following command:

   ng g guard pages/auth/_guards/auth

   The previous code will generate the following file:
   `./Client/src/app/pages/auth/_guards/auth.guard.ts`.

2. Open the `./Client/src/app/pages/auth/_guards/auth.guard.ts` file and add the following import after the observable import:

   ```
   import { AuthService } from '../_services/auth.service';
   ```

3. Now, let's add `Router` and `AuthService` inside the `constructor()` function, as shown in the following code:

   ```
   constructor(
           private  router:  Router,
           private  auth:  AuthService) {}
   ```

4. Add the following block of code inside the `canActivate()` function, before the `return` property:

   ```
   if (this.auth.isAuthenticated()) {
   // logged in so return true
         return  true;
   }
   // not logged in so redirect to login page with the return url
   this.router.navigate(['/login'], { queryParams: { returnUrl:
   state.url }});
   ```

In the previous code, we are using the `auth.isAuthenticated()` function from `AuthService` to check if the user is authenticated. This means that, if the user is not authenticated/logged-in, we will redirect them to the login screen.

We are also using the `queryParams` and `returnUrl` functions to send the user back to where they came from.

This means that, if the user clicks to look at the bike's details and they are not logged in to the application, they will be redirected to the login screen. After logging in, the user will be redirected to the details of the bike they intended to look at.

The last step is to add `AuthGuard` to the `bike-detail` route.

5. Open `./Client/src/app/bikes/bikes-routing.module.ts` and add the following import, right after the routes import:

```
import { AuthGuard } from '../auth/_guards/auth.guard';
```

6. Now, add the `canActivate` property right after the `bikeDetailComponent`, as in the following code:

```
{
        path: ':id',
        component: BikeDetailComponent,
        canActivate: [AuthGuard]
}
```

Voilà! Our `bike-detail` route is now protected.

Summary

Now, we are very close to seeing our application in a working state. However, we still need to perform some steps that we will look at in the following chapters.

In the meantime, we have learned some important points for building modern web applications, such as creating services to handle XHR requests, learning how to protect our routes, as well as creating a route interceptor and a service for handling errors.

In the next chapter, we are going to delve deeply into how to use the services we have just created within our components, and we will also apply a visual layer to our application.

10
Frontend Views with Bootstrap 4 and NgBootstrap

In this chapter, we will look at how to include a Bootstrap framework inside a running Angular application using the new `add` feature from the Angular CLI.

The Bootstrap framework is one of the most important UI frameworks, and, with Angular directives/components, we can have all the power of Bootstrap inside our Angular application.

We will also look at how to connect our Angular services with components and how to using the backend API to put it all together. Finally, we will learn how to configure **Cross-Origin Resource Sharing** (**CORS**) on our backend API and how to use it with our Angular client-side application.

In this chapter, we will cover the following topics:

- Installing the Bootstrap CSS framework
- Writing Angular templates with Bootstrap
- How to set up CORS on the Laravel backend
- Connecting Angular services with application components
- Dealing with Angular pipes, forms, and validation

Preparing the baseline code

Now, we need to prepare our baseline code, which is a process that's very similar to what we performed in the previous chapter. Let's follow these steps:

1. Copy all the content from the `chapter-9` folder.
2. Rename the folder `chapter-10`.

3. Delete the `storage-db` folder.

4. Now, let's make some changes to the `docker-compose.yml` file so that we can fit in a new database and server containers. Open `docker-compose.yml` and replace its content with the following code:

```
version: "3.1"
services:
    mysql:
      image: mysql:5.7
      container_name: chapter-10-mysql
      working_dir: /application
      volumes:
        - .:/application
        - ./storage-db:/var/lib/mysql
      environment:
        - MYSQL_ROOT_PASSWORD=123456
        - MYSQL_DATABASE=chapter-10
        - MYSQL_USER=chapter-10
        - MYSQL_PASSWORD=123456
      ports:
        - "8083:3306"
    webserver:
      image: nginx:alpine
      container_name: chapter-10-webserver
      working_dir: /application
      volumes:
        - .:/application
        -./phpdocker/nginx/nginx.conf:/etc/nginx/
          conf.d/default.conf
       ports:
        - "8081:80"
    php-fpm:
      build: phpdocker/php-fpm
      container_name: chapter-10-php-fpm
      working_dir: /application
      volumes:
        - ./Server:/application
        - ./phpdocker/php-fpm/php-ini-
          overrides.ini:/etc/php/7.2/fpm/conf.d/99-overrides.ini
```

Note that we changed the container names, database, and MySQL user:

- `container_name: chapter-10-mysql`
- `container_name: chapter-10-webserver`
- `container_name: chapter-10-php-fpm`

- `MYSQL_DATABASE=chapter-10`
- `MYSQL_USER=chapter-10`

5. Update the `.env` file with the connection string:

```
DB_CONNECTION=mysql
DB_HOST=mysql
DB_PORT=3306
DB_DATABASE=chapter-10
DB_USERNAME=chapter-10
DB_PASSWORD=123456
```

6. Add the changes we made to Git source control. Open your Terminal window and type the following command:

```
git add .
git commit -m "Initial commit chapter 10"
```

7. Now, let's start our Docker containers with the following command:

```
docker-compose up -d
```

Installing the Bootstrap CSS framework

In this section, we will once again use the newest feature that's available in Angular CLI 6: the `add` command. Using this, we will add Bootstrap 4 to our application:

1. Inside the `Client` folder of `chapter-10`, open your Terminal window and type the following command:

```
ng add @ng-bootstrap/schematics
```

2. The previous command will create and update the following files:

```
+ @ng-bootstrap/schematics@2.0.0-alpha.1
added 3 packages in 26.372s
Installed packages for tooling via npm.
UPDATE package.json (1589 bytes)
UPDATE src/app/app.module.ts (1516 bytes)
UPDATE angular.json (3706 bytes)
```

3. In the `package.json` file, we will add the following dependencies:

```
"@ng-bootstrap/schematics": "^2.0.0-alpha.1",
  "@ng-bootstrap/ng-bootstrap": "^2.0.0-alpha.0",
  "bootstrap": "^4.0.0"
```

4. In the `src/app/app.module.ts` file, we will add the following lines:

```
import { NgbModule } from '@ng-bootstrap/ng-bootstrap';

imports: [
        ...
        NgbModule.forRoot()
],
```

5. In the `angular.json` file, we will add the following lines:

```
"styles": [
            "src/styles.scss",
            {
                    "input":
"./node_modules/bootstrap/dist/css/bootstrap.css"
            }
        ],
```

Here, we can see all the power of the Angular CLI in action, because all of these changes were performed automatically.

However, we can see that the `bootstrap.css` file is used in a way that leaves the application frozen, making it difficult to customize the application.

In the next section, we will look at a different way of using Bootstrap for more flexibility.

Removing the Bootstrap CSS import

First, we are going to remove the CSS compiled from Bootstrap that was injected into our `angular.json` file with the installation command of `NgBootstrap`.

Open the `angular.json` file and remove the `input` tag. Only keep the `styles` tag, as shown in the following code:

```
"styles": [
            "src/styles.scss"
        ],
```

Adding Bootstrap SCSS imports

Now, we will use the files installed in the node_modules folder as imports from our main style sheet, which is stored in ./Client/src/style.scss:

1. Open ./Client/src/style.scss and add the following code at the top of the file:

```scss
/*!
 * Bootstrap v4.1.1 (https://getbootstrap.com/)
 * Copyright 2011-2018 The Bootstrap Authors
 * Copyright 2011-2018 Twitter, Inc.
 * Licensed under MIT
 (https://github.com/twbs/bootstrap/blob/master/LICENSE)
 */
@import "../node_modules/bootstrap/scss/functions";
@import "../scss/bootstrap/_variables.scss";
@import "../node_modules/bootstrap/scss/_variables.scss";
@import "../node_modules/bootstrap/scss/mixins";
@import "../node_modules/bootstrap/scss/root";
@import "../node_modules/bootstrap/scss/reboot";
@import "../node_modules/bootstrap/scss/type";
@import "../node_modules/bootstrap/scss/images";
@import "../node_modules/bootstrap/scss/code";
@import "../node_modules/bootstrap/scss/grid";
@import "../node_modules/bootstrap/scss/tables";
@import "../node_modules/bootstrap/scss/forms";
@import "../node_modules/bootstrap/scss/buttons";
@import "../node_modules/bootstrap/scss/transitions";
@import "../node_modules/bootstrap/scss/dropdown";
@import "../node_modules/bootstrap/scss/button-group";
@import "../node_modules/bootstrap/scss/input-group";
@import "../node_modules/bootstrap/scss/custom-forms";
@import "../node_modules/bootstrap/scss/nav";
@import "../node_modules/bootstrap/scss/navbar";
@import "../node_modules/bootstrap/scss/card";
@import "../node_modules/bootstrap/scss/breadcrumb";
@import "../node_modules/bootstrap/scss/pagination";
@import "../node_modules/bootstrap/scss/badge";
@import "../node_modules/bootstrap/scss/jumbotron";
@import "../node_modules/bootstrap/scss/alert";
@import "../node_modules/bootstrap/scss/progress";
@import "../node_modules/bootstrap/scss/media";
@import "../node_modules/bootstrap/scss/list-group";
@import "../node_modules/bootstrap/scss/close";
@import "../node_modules/bootstrap/scss/modal";
@import "../node_modules/bootstrap/scss/tooltip";
```

```
@import "../node_modules/bootstrap/scss/popover";
@import "../node_modules/bootstrap/scss/carousel";
@import "../node_modules/bootstrap/scss/utilities";
@import "../node_modules/bootstrap/scss/print";
```

Note that we keep the Bootstrap comments at the top of the file just to have the Bootstrap version documented in an easy-to-find place.

2. If you want, you can copy the content of the `node_modules/bootstrap/scss/bootstrap.scss` file and just adjust the import paths to `../node_modules/bootstrap/scss`.

Now, our application is compiling the SCSS code directly from the `bootstrap/scss` folder.

Here are some advantages of doing this:

- We can choose which SCSS modules we will import, depending on what components our application uses.
- We reduce SCSS code that will not be used.
- We can easily overwrite the Bootstrap variables.

Overriding Bootstrap variables

In this step, we will see how we can overwrite the `Boostrap` variables in our application:

1. Create a new folder called `scss` at the root of the `Client` folder.
2. Inside the `./Client/scss` folder, add a new folder called `bootstrap`.
3. Inside `./Client/scss/bootstrap`, add a new file called `_variable.scss`.
4. Copy the content from `node_modules/bootstrap/scss/_variables.scss` and paste it into `./Client/scss/bootstrap/_variables.scss`.

Pretty simple; congratulations! We are ready to override Bootstrap variables.

The last step is to import the new `_variables.scss` file into our main `style.scss` file.

5. Open the `./Client/style.scss` file and replace the line `@import "../node_modules/bootstrap/scss/_variables.scss"` with the following:

```
<pre>Error: ENOENT: no such file or directory, open
'/Users/fernandomonteiro/_bitbucket/scss/bootstrap/_variables.scss'
</pre>
```

We also have the option of placing this variable file, using only the variables that we will overwrite, without using the key word `Default`. In this way, the file gets much shorter, since we will not be able to overwrite all the variables in a small project like this. Let's see how we can do that.

6. Let's imagine that we just want to overwrite the `border-radius` of all components and also remove the `box-shadow`. We can only use these variables, so our `_variables.scss` file will have the following appearance:

```scss
// Variables
//
// Removing border-radius and box-shadow from components

$border-radius: 0;
$border-radius-lg: 0;
$border-radius-sm: 0;

$box-shadow-sm: none;
$box-shadow: none;
$box-shadow-lg: none;
```

7. For these changes to take effect, we need to make a small adjustment to `./Client/style.scss` and add the new variable file before the Bootstrap `variables` file, as shown in the following code:

```scss
/*!
 * Bootstrap v4.1.1 (https://getbootstrap.com/)
 * Copyright 2011-2018 The Bootstrap Authors
 * Copyright 2011-2018 Twitter, Inc.
 * Licensed under MIT
(https://github.com/twbs/bootstrap/blob/master/LICENSE)
 */
@import "../node_modules/bootstrap/scss/functions";
@import "../scss/bootstrap/_variables.scss";
@import "../node_modules/bootstrap/scss/_variables.scss";
```

Writing Angular templates with Bootstrap

At this moment in time, our application can already be visualized with the use of Bootstrap CSS, which is what we did in the last section. Recall that, in the previous chapters, we already added the HTML markup to some of our templates.

All of them already contain the Bootstrap classes, and we can already visualize what we have so far in a browser window. Let's check this out:

1. Open your Terminal window inside the `./Client` folder and type the following command:

   npm start

2. Open your default browser and go to `http://localhost:4200/`.

   You will see the following result:

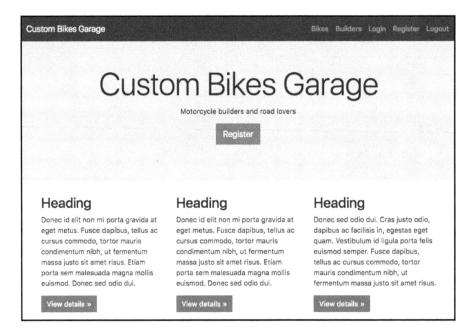

Wow! Now, we have a web application. You will notice that we already have an application that works perfectly.

3. Let's click on the `bikes` link and see what we have so far:

Feel free to browse the rest of the application and check the other pages.

However, all we have at this stage is placeholders, so this is the time to learn how to apply the Angular template syntax in our templates.

Adding template bindings to the navigation component

Now, let's make some changes in our templates so that we can use the Angular syntax:

1. Open `./Client/src/app/layout/nav/nav.component.html` and replace its content with the following code:

```
<header>
<nav class="navbar navbar-expand-md navbar-dark fixed-top bg-dark">
<a class="navbar-brand" [routerLink]="['/']"
(click)="setTitle('Custom Bikes Garage')">Custom
Bikes Garage</a>
<button class="navbar-toggler" type="button" data-toggle="collapse"
data-
target="#navbarCollapse" aria-controls="navbarCollapse" aria-
expanded="false" aria- label="Toggle
navigation">
<span class="navbar-toggler-icon"></span>
</button>
<div class="collapse navbar-collapse" id="navbarCollapse">
<ul class="navbar-nav ml-auto"> <li class="nav-item"> <a
class="nav-link" [routerLink]="['/bikes']"
routerLinkActive="active" (click)="setTitle('Bikes')">Bikes</a>
</li> <li class="nav-item"> <a class="nav-link"
[routerLink]="['/builders']" routerLinkActive="active"
(click)="setTitle('Builders')">Builders</a> </li>
<li *ngIf="!auth.isAuthenticated()" class="nav-item"> <a
class="nav-link" [routerLink]="['/login']"
routerLinkActive="active" (click)="setTitle('Login')">Login</a>
</li>
<li *ngIf="!auth.isAuthenticated()" class="nav-item"> <a
class="nav-link" [routerLink]="['/register']"
routerLinkActive="active"
(click)="setTitle('Register')">Register</a> </li>
  <li *ngIf="auth.isAuthenticated()" class="nav-item">
<div ngbDropdown class="d-inline-block">
<button class="btn btn-secondary" id="dropdownBasic1"
ngbDropdownToggle>{{ auth.currentUser?.name }}</button>
<div ngbDropdownMenu aria-labelledby="dropdownBasic1">
```

```
<button class="dropdown-item" (click)="onLogout();">Logout</button>
</div>
</div>
</li>
</ul>
</div>
</nav>
</header>
```

Note that, in the previous code, we are using the `ngbDropdown` component and also using `auth.isAuthenticated()` to determine if the user is logged in or not. Also note that we included the logout link inside the dropdown.

Now, let's adjust the templates for login and registration.

Adding template bindings to the login page

In Chapter 7, *Progressive Web Applications with Angular-cli*, we already added the HTML markup for all of the app's views/templates, however, we need to add the Angular bindings and models to templates so that everything works correctly:

1. Open `./Client/src/app/auth/login/login.component.html`.

2. Add the following bind function to tag:

   ```
   (ngSubmit)="onSubmit(loginForm)" #loginForm="ngForm"
   ```

   Now, we will add the `ngModel` to the email and password input, while we're still in `./Client/src/app/auth/login/login.component.html`.

3. Add the following code to the `email` input:

   ```
   <input  type="email" [(ngModel)]="user.email" name="email"
   #email="ngModel" class="form-control"  id="email"  aria-
   describedby="emailHelp"  placeholder="Enter email">
   ```

4. Add the following code to the `password` input:

   ```
   <input  type="password" [(ngModel)]="user.password"
   name="password" #password="ngModel" class="form-control"
   id="password"  placeholder="Password">
   ```

Adding template bindings to the register page

Now, let's repeat the same operation on the registration page template:

1. Open `./Client/src/app/auth/register/register.component.html`.

2. Add the following bind function to tag:

   ```
   [formGroup]="registerForm" (ngSubmit)="onSubmit()" class="form-
   signin" novalidate
   ```

   Note the use of `formGroup` attribute. It is part of the Angular reactive forms, but don't worry about this now; later in the book, we will discuss template-driven forms and reactive forms.

   Now, we will add `formControlName` to the `name`, `email`, and `password` inputs, while still
   in `./Client/src/app/auth/register/register.component.html`.

3. Add the following code to the `name` input:

   ```
   <input type="name" formControlName="name" class="form-control"
   id="name" aria-describedby="nameHelp" placeholder="Enter your
   name">
   ```

4. Add the following code to the `email` input:

   ```
   <input type="email" formControlName="email" class="form-control"
   id="email" aria-describedby="emailHelp" placeholder="Enter
   email">
   ```

5. Add the following code to the `password` input:

   ```
   <input formControlName="password" type="password"
   name="password" class="form-control" id="password"
   placeholder="Password">
   ```

Adding template bindings to the bike-detail page

Now, let's make some adjustments to the `bike-detail` page template:

1. Open `./Client/src/app/bikes/bike-detail/bike-detail.component.html`.

2. Replace its content with the following code:

```
<main role="main">
    <div class="py-5">
    <div class="container">
    <div *ngIf="isLoading" class="spinner">
            <div class="double-bounce1"></div>
            <div class="double-bounce2"></div>
    </div>
    <ngb-tabset type="pills" *ngIf="!isLoading">
            <ngb-tab title="Bike Detail">
                    <ng-template ngbTabContent>
                    <br>
                    <div class="row">
                            <div class="col-md-4">
                            <img class="card-img-top" src="{{
bike?.picture }}" alt="Card image cap">
                            </div>
                            <div class="col-md-8">
                            <div class="card">
                                    <div class="card-body">
                                    <h5 class="card-title">{{
bike?.model }} | {{ bike?.year }} | Ratings: {{
bike?.average_rating }}
                                                    <span
*ngIf="userVote">| Your Vote: {{ userVote }}</span>
                                    </h5>
                                    <p class="card-text">{{
bike?.mods }}</p>
                                    </div>
                                    <div *ngIf="bike?.builder"
class="card-header">
                                    <strong>Builder</strong>:
                                    <a
routerLink="/builders/{{bike?.builder['id']}}">{{
bike?.builder['name'] }}</a>
                                    </div>
                                    <div *ngIf="bike?.items"
class="card-header">
                                    <strong>Featured
```

```
items</strong>:
                                               </div>
                                               <ul class="list-group list-
group-flush">
                                               <li *ngFor="let item of
bike?.items" class="list-group-item">
<strong>Type</strong>: {{ item.type }} |
<strong>Name</strong>: {{ item.name }} |
<strong>Company</strong>: {{ item.company }}
                                               </li>
                                               </ul>
                                               <div class="card-body">
                                               <ul class="list-unstyled
list-inline">
                                                        <li class="list-
inline-item">Vote: </li>
                                                        <li class="list-
inline-item">
                                                        <a
(click)="onVote('1')" class="btn btn-outline-secondary">1</a>
                                                        </li>
                                                        <li class="list-
inline-item">
                                                        <a
(click)="onVote('2')" class="btn btn-outline-primary">2</a>
                                                        </li>
                                                        <li class="list-
inline-item">
                                                        <a
(click)="onVote('3')" class="btn btn-outline-success">3</a>
                                                        </li>
                                               </ul>
                                               </div>
                                       </div>
                                       </div>
                               </div>
                               </ng-template>
                       </ngb-tab>
                       <ngb-tab>
                               <ng-template ngbTabTitle
*ngIf="checkBikeOwner()">Edit bike</ng-template>
                               <ng-template ngbTabContent>
                               <br>
                               <form (ngSubmit)="onSubmit(bikeAddForm)"
#bikeAddForm="ngForm" name=bikeAddForm class="bg-light px-4 py-4">
                                       <div class="form-group">
                                       <label for="make">Make</label>
                                       <input type="text"
```

```
[(ngModel)]="bike.make"  name="make" class="form-control" id="make"
placeholder="Enter make">
                                    </div>
                                    <div class="form-group">
                                    <label for="model">Model</label>
                                    <input type="text"
[(ngModel)]="bike.model" name="model" class="form-control"
id="model" placeholder="Enter model">
                                    </div>
                                    <div class="form-group">
                                    <label for="year">Year</label>
                                    <input type="text"
[(ngModel)]="bike.year" name="year" class="form-control" id="year"
placeholder="Enter year, ex: 1990, 2000">
                                    </div>
                                    <div class="form-group">
                                    <label for="mods">Mods</label>
                                    <textarea type="text"
[(ngModel)]="bike.mods" name="mods" class="form-control" id="mods"
placeholder="Enter modifications"></textarea>
                                    </div>
                                    <div class="form-group">
                                    <label
for="picture">Picture</label>
                                    <input type="text"
[(ngModel)]="bike.picture" name="picture" class="form-control"
id="picture" placeholder="Enter picture url">
                                    </div>
                                    <div class="form-group">
                                    <label
for="inputState">Builder</label>
                                    <select
[(ngModel)]="bike.builder.id" name="builder_id" class="form-
control">
                                            <option *ngFor="let builder
of builders"
[(ngValue)]="builder['id']">{{builder['name']}}</option>
                                    </select>
                                    </div>
                                    <button type="submit" class="btn
btn-primary">Submit</button>
                            </form>
                            </ng-template>
                    </ngb-tab>
                    </ngb-tabset>
         </div>
  </div>
  </main>
```

Note that we are using the `*ngIf` directive to hide our bike until the bike object is available. We are also using the click bind function `(click)="onVote('1')"` to vote on the bike, and we're using `*ngFor="let item of bike?.items"` to list the bike items.

We are also using the `ngb-tab`, `ngb-tabset` directive from `NgBootstrap` to create two views on this page: one to show the bike's details, and another to show the edit form so that we can edit the bike's details. Note that we are using a function called `checkBikeOwner()` to make a simple check to see if the user that's logged in is the bike's owner. Otherwise, we hide that tab.

The `(?)` symbol is called the safe navigation operator.

The expected result is what we have in the following screenshot:

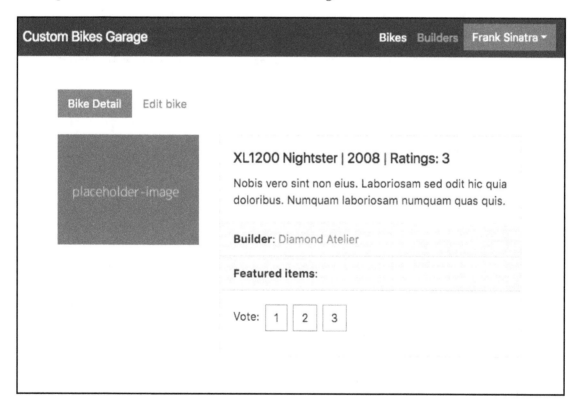

Don't worry about the form for now, as we will look at it in detail at the end of this chapter.

Adding template bindings to the bike-list page

Well, now it is time to create the `bike-list` template bindings:

1. Open `./Client/src/app/bikes/bike-list/bike-list.component.html`.
2. Replace its content with the following code:

```
<main role="main">
  <div class="py-5 bg-light">
    <div class="container">
      <form>
        <div class="form-group row">
          <label for="search" class="col-sm-2 col-form-label">Bike
List</label>
          <div class="col-sm-8">
            <input [(ngModel)]="searchText" [ngModelOptions]="{standalone:
true}" placeholder="buscar" type="text" class="form-control"
              id="search" placeholder="Search">
          </div>
          <div class="col-sm-2">
            <div ngbDropdown class="d-inline-block">
              <button class="btn btn-primary" id="dropdownBasicFilter"
ngbDropdownToggle>Filter</button>
              <div ngbDropdownMenu aria-labelledby="dropdownBasicFilter">
                <button class="dropdown-item">Year</button>
              </div>
            </div>
          </div>
        </div>
      </form>
      <div *ngIf="isLoading" class="spinner">
        <div class="double-bounce1"></div>
        <div class="double-bounce2"></div>
      </div>
      <div class="row">
        <div class="col-md-4" *ngFor="let bike of bikes | bikeSearch:
searchText ">
          <div class="card mb-4 box-shadow">
            <img class="card-img-top" src="{{ bike.picture }}" alt="{{
bike.model }}">
            <div class="card-body">
              <p>{{ bike.model }} | {{ bike.year }}</p>
              <p class="card-text">{{ bike.mods }}</p>
              <a routerLink="/bikes/{{ bike.id }}" class="card-
link">Vote</a>
            </div>
          </div>
```

```
        </div>
      </div>
    </div>
  </div>
</main>
```

Note that we are using the `ngbDropdown`, `ngbDropdownToggle`, and `ngbDropdownMenu` components, and that we are also using `*ngFor="let bike of bikes"` to list all bikes from the `bikes Array` and `*ngIf` to show and hide a loading message.

Now, we can see the power of Angular. With a few changes, our static templates are ready to come to life and interact with our backend. But we still need to write the logic of the components to put everything together.

Before we do that, let's adjust the builder templates.

Adding template bindings to the builder-detail page

Let's add the `builder-detail` pages:

1. Open `./Client/src/app/builders/builder-detail/builder-detail.component.html`.

2. Replace its content with the following code:

```
<main role="main">
  <div class="py-5">
  <div class="container">
  <div *ngIf="isLoading" class="spinner">
    <div class="double-bounce1"></div>
    <div class="double-bounce2"></div>
  </div>
  <ngb-tabset type="pills" *ngIf="!isLoading">
    <ngb-tab title="Bike Detail">
      <ng-template ngbTabContent>
      <br>
      <div class="row">
        <div class="col-md-4">
        <img class="card-img-top" src="{{ bike?.picture }}"
alt="Card image cap">
        </div>
        <div class="col-md-8">
        <div class="card">
```

```
            <div class="card-body">
            <h5 class="card-title">{{ bike?.model }} | {{ bike?.year
}} | Ratings: {{ bike?.average_rating }}
                <span *ngIf="userVote">| Your Vote: {{ userVote
}}</span>
            </h5>
            <p class="card-text">{{ bike?.mods }}</p>
            </div>
            <div *ngIf="bike?.builder" class="card-header">
            <strong>Builder</strong>:
            <a routerLink="/builders/{{bike?.builder['id']}}">{{
bike?.builder['name'] }}</a>
            </div>
            <div *ngIf="bike?.items" class="card-header">
            <strong>Featured items</strong>:
            </div>
            <ul class="list-group list-group-flush">
            <li *ngFor="let item of bike?.items" class="list-group-
item">
                <strong>Type</strong>: {{ item.type }} |
                <strong>Name</strong>: {{ item.name }} |
                <strong>Company</strong>: {{ item.company }}
            </li>
            </ul>
            <div class="card-body">
            <ul class="list-unstyled list-inline">
              <li class="list-inline-item">Vote: </li>
              <li class="list-inline-item">
              <a (click)="onVote('1')" class="btn btn-outline-
secondary">1</a>
              </li>
              <li class="list-inline-item">
              <a (click)="onVote('2')" class="btn btn-outline-
primary">2</a>
              </li>
              <li class="list-inline-item">
              <a (click)="onVote('3')" class="btn btn-outline-
success">3</a>
              </li>
            </ul>
            </div>
          </div>
          </div>
        </div>
        </ng-template>
      </ngb-tab>
      <ngb-tab>
        <ng-template ngbTabTitle *ngIf="checkBikeOwner()">Edit
```

```
bike</ng-template>
      <ng-template ngbTabContent>
      <br>
      <form (ngSubmit)="onSubmit(bikeAddForm)"
#bikeAddForm="ngForm" name=bikeAddForm class="bg-light px-4 py-4">
      <div class="form-group">
      <label for="make">Make</label>
      <input type="text" [(ngModel)]="bike.make"  name="make"
class="form-control" id="make" placeholder="Enter make">
      </div>
      <div class="form-group">
      <label for="model">Model</label>
      <input type="text" [(ngModel)]="bike.model" name="model"
class="form-control" id="model" placeholder="Enter model">
      </div>
      <div class="form-group">
      <label for="year">Year</label>
      <input type="text" [(ngModel)]="bike.year" name="year"
class="form-control" id="year" placeholder="Enter year, ex: 1990,
2000">
      </div>
      <div class="form-group">
      <label for="mods">Mods</label>
      <textarea type="text" [(ngModel)]="bike.mods" name="mods"
class="form-control" id="mods" placeholder="Enter
modifications"></textarea>
      </div>
      <div class="form-group">
      <label for="picture">Picture</label>
      <input type="text" [(ngModel)]="bike.picture"
name="picture" class="form-control" id="picture" placeholder="Enter
picture url">
      </div>
      <div class="form-group">
      <label for="inputState">Builder</label>
      <select [(ngModel)]="bike.builder.id" name="builder_id"
class="form-control">
        <option *ngFor="let builder of builders"
[(ngValue)]="builder['id']">{{builder['name']}}</option>
      </select>
      </div>
      <button type="submit" class="btn btn-
primary">Submit</button>
    </form>
    </ng-template>
  </ngb-tab>
  </ngb-tabset>
  </div>
```

```
            </div>
        </main>
```

In the builders templates, we are using the same technique that we used in the previous templates.

Adding template bindings to the builder-list page

Now, it is time to add the `builder-list` template:

1. Open `./Client/src/app/builders/builder-list/builder-list.component.html`.

2. Replace its content with the following code:

```html
<main  role="main">
    <div  class="py-5 bg-light">
        <div  class="container">
            <div *ngIf="isLoading"  class="spinner">
                <div  class="double-bounce1"></div>
                <div  class="double-bounce2"></div>
            </div>
            <div  class="row">
                <div  class="col-md-4" *ngFor="let
builder of builders">
                    <div  class="card mb-4 box-
shadow">
                        <div  class="card-
header">
                            <h4
class="my-0 font-weight-normal">{{ builder?.name }}</h4>
                            </div>
                            <div  class="card-
body">
                                <p
class="mt-3 mb-4">{{ builder?.description }}</p>
                                <button
routerLink="/builders/{{ builder?.id }}"  type="button"  class="btn
btn-lg btn-block btn-outline-primary">View Bike</button>
                            </div>
                            <div  class="card-
footer text-muted">
                                {{
builder?.location }}
                            </div>
                        </div>
```

```
                                    </div>
                            </div>
                    </div>
            </div>
    </main>
```

Now, we have enough code for our templates to render the contents of our backend. For this, we just need to make some minor adjustments to the backend and write the logic in our components.

Setting up CORS on a Laravel backend

Before proceeding with the necessary changes in our backend, let's talk about a very important and also very common subject in today's modern web applications, known as CORS.

When we use `XMLHttpRequest` or the `Fetch API` to get data from a given server, this call is usually performed from another application, and from somewhere else.

For security reasons, browsers restrict cross-origin HTTP requests.

A simple example to understand how CORS works is this: imagine that a frontend application running in a particular domain, for example, `http://mysimpledomain.com`, sends a request to another application in another domain called `http://myanothersimpledomain.com`.

CORS is a mechanism that uses additional HTTP headers to tell a browser to let a web application run at one origin, `http://mysimpledomain.com`, and have permissions to access selected resources from a server at a different origin, `http://myanothersimpledomain`.

You can read more about CORS at `https://www.w3.org/TR/cors/`.

Setting up Laravel CORS

Laravel has excellent support for using CORS in its applications. Let's see how we can configure it using a library called `barryvdh/laravel-cors`:

1. Open your Terminal window inside the `chapter-10` folder.

2. Type the following command:

   ```
   docker-compose up -d
   ```

3. Now, inside the `php-fpm` container, type the following command:

   ```
   docker-compose exec php-fpm bash
   ```

   This step is very important. If you forget this command, it is very likely that you will find an error, or you may be at risk of using your local composer version to execute the following command.

4. Inside the container's bash, type the following command:

   ```
   composer require barryvdh/laravel-cors
   ```

   Thanks to the newest version of Laravel (5.6), our new library is already ready for use. Let's just make one more little change.

5. Open the `./Server/app/Http/Kernel.php` file and add the following code to the `middlewareGroup` API:

   ```
   protected $middlewareGroups = [

           'web'  => [
                   . . .
           ],
           'api'  => [
                   \Barryvdh\Cors\HandleCors::class,
                   'throttle:60,1',
                   'bindings',
           ],
   ```

It is very important to note that we added `\Barryvdh\Cors\HandleCors :: class` to the first line of dependencies in the API tag. This is very important because we avoid getting errors with status code 0 on our frontend application.

We are ready to go!

Connecting Angular services with application components

Now, we will connect all of the Angular services and templates that we have created during this book. For this, we will create the logic and the functions that we will use inside our components.

Before we begin, let's set the endpoint of our API as a variable in the Angular environment file.

Adding environment configuration

As the name says, this file is used to set up environment variables in our application. The best part about it is that Angular comes with a dev and prod environment that's configured by default and is very simple to use. We can also set a variety of variables.

In this example, we are setting the backend URL using the development file.

Open the `./Client/src/environments/environment.ts` file and add the following URL:

```
export const environment = {
        production: false,
        apiUrl: 'http://localhost:8081/api'
};
```

As you can see, we have another file called `environment.prod.ts` inside the `environments` folder.

Do not worry about this file for now, as we will only use it later in the book.

Creating the navigation methods

Now, it is time to create the navigation behavior inside `nav.component.ts`, so let's see how we can do that:

1. Open `./Client/src/layout/nav/nav.component.ts` and add the following imports, right after the core import:

```
import { Router } from '@angular/router';
import { Title } from '@angular/platform-browser';

// App imports
import { AuthService } from
'../../pages/auth/_services/auth.service';
```

2. Still on `./Client/src/layout/nav/nav.component.ts`, let's create the `constructor()` function:

```
public constructor(
        private titleTagService: Title,
        public auth: AuthService,
        private router: Router ) {}
```

Here, we are using the built-in Angular service called `Title` to update the title tag of the page when navigating between the templates. Remember that our application is a SPA and we do not want to keep the same title in all pages.

In addition, we will use the authentication service to show the name of the user that is logged in to the application, and we will also use the logout function of this service to log the user out. So, let's create this function.

3. Add the following code right after the deconstructor function:

```
public setTitle( pageTitle: string) {
        this.titleTagService.setTitle( pageTitle );
}
```

4. Now, inside the `ngOnInit()` function, add the following code:

```
if (this.auth.getToken()) {
        this.auth.getUser().subscribe();
}
```

5. The last step is to add the `logout()` function, right after the `ngOnInit()` function. Add the following code:

```
onLogout() {
        this.auth.onLogout().subscribe();
}
```

Now, we have our application's navigation ready to use. The expected result is shown in the following screenshot:

Custom Bikes Garage   Bikes   Builders   Login   Register

Navigation view

Creating the bike-detail methods

Let's create the `bike-detail` component:

1. Open `./Client/src/pages/bikes/bike-detail/bike-detail.component.ts` and add the following imports, right after the core import:

```
import { ActivatedRoute } from  '@angular/router';

// App imports
import { Bike } from  '../bike';
import { BikesService } from  '../_services/bikes.service';
import { AuthService } from  '../../auth/_services/auth.service';
import { User } from  './../../auth/user';
```

2. Add the following properties after the `BikeDetailComponent` class declaration:

```
bike:  Bike;
isLoading:  Boolean  =  false;
userVote:  number;
builders: Array<Object> = [
        {id: 1, name: 'Diamond Atelier'},
        {id: 2, name: 'Deus Ex Machina\'s'},
        {id: 3, name: 'Rough Crafts'},
        {id: 4, name: 'Roldand Sands'},
        {id: 5, name: 'Chopper Dave'}
];
```

Note that we are using the `Bike` model as the type of our `bike` property and creating a simple array to hold our builders.

[321]

Note that, in a real-world web application, it is good practice to get a list of builders from the server to avoid becoming hard coded inside the component.

3. Still on `./Client/src/pages/bikes/bike-detail/bike-detail.component.ts`, let's create the `constructor()` function:

```
constructor(
        private  bikeService:  BikesService,
        private  route:  ActivatedRoute,
        private  auth:  AuthService )  {}
```

We will use `ActivatedRoute` to get the bike ID later in this section.

4. Inside the `ngOnInit()` function, add the following code:

```
// Get bike details
this.getBikeDetail();
```

Now, let's create the `getBikeDetail()` function.

5. Add the following code right after the `ngOnInit()` function:

```
getBikeDetail():  void {
        this.isLoading  =  true;
        const  id  =  +this.route.snapshot.paramMap.get('id');
        this.bikeService.getBikeDetail(id)
                .subscribe(bike  => {
                        this.isLoading  =  false;
                        this.bike  =  bike['data'];
        });
}
```

6. Now, let's add the `onVote()` function. Add the following code right after the `getBikeDetail()` function:

```
onVote(rating:  number, id:  number):  void {
        // Check if user already vote on a bike
        if (this.checkUserVote(this.bike.ratings)) {
                alert('you already vote on this bike');
                return;
        }
        // Get bike id
        id  =  +this.route.snapshot.paramMap.get('id');
        // post vote
        this.bikeService.voteOnBike(rating, id)
                .subscribe(
                        (response)  => {
```

```
                                          this.userVote   =
response.data.rating;
                                          // Update the average rating and
rating object on bike
                                          this.bike['average_rating'] =
response.data.average_rating;
                                          // Update ratings array
          this.bike.ratings.push(response.data);
                              }
                      );
     }
```

7. Now, we will create a function that checks if the logged-in user has already voted on the chosen bike. Remember that `RatingController.php` is using the `firstOrCreate` method:

```
        public  function  store(Request $request, Bike $bike)
            {
                $rating =  Rating::firstOrCreate(
                    [
                    'user_id'  => $request->user()->id,
                    'bike_id'  => $bike->id,
                    ],
                    ['rating'  => $request->rating]
                );
                return  new  RatingResource($rating);
            }
```

We will only register the first vote. Thus, we need to show the user a simple message as feedback from the Vote function.

8. Add the following code right after the `onVote()` function:

```
    checkUserVote(ratings:  any[]):  Boolean {
        const  currentUserId  =  this.auth.currentUser.id;
        let  ratingUserId:  number;
        Object.keys(ratings).forEach( (i)  => {
              ratingUserId  =  ratings[i].user_id;
        });
        if ( currentUserId  ===  ratingUserId ) {
              return  true;
        } else {
              return  false;
        }
    }
```

9. The following method uses a submit function to update the `bike` record. Add the following code right after the `checkUserVote()` function:

```
onSubmit(bike) {
        this.isLoading = true;
        const id = +this.route.snapshot.paramMap.get('id');
        this.bikeService.updateBike(id, bike.value)
        .subscribe(response => {
                this.isLoading = false;
                this.bike = response['data'];
        });
}
```

Note that, in this step, we are using the `updateBike` method from `bikeService`.

10. The last method is a simple function to check the bike owner. Remember that the user can only edit their own bike. Add the following code right after the `onSubmit()` function:

```
checkBikeOwner(): Boolean {
        if (this.auth.currentUser.id === this.bike.user.id) {
                return true;
        } else {
                return false;
        }
}
```

In this code, we are using the `authService` to get the `User.id`, which we are comparing with `bike.user.id`.

The expected result for this page when we access the `http://localhost:4200/bikes/3` URL will be similar to the following screenshot:

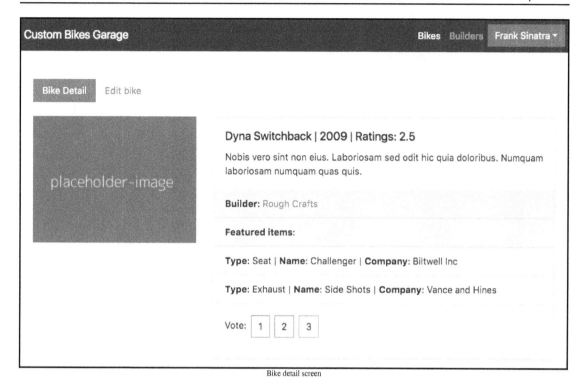

Custom Bikes Garage   Bikes   Builders   Frank Sinatra ▾

Bike Detail   Edit bike

placeholder-image

Dyna Switchback | 2009 | Ratings: 2.5

Nobis vero sint non eius. Laboriosam sed odit hic quia doloribus. Numquam laboriosam numquam quas quis.

Builder: Rough Crafts

Featured items:

Type: Seat | **Name:** Challenger | **Company:** Biltwell Inc

Type: Exhaust | **Name:** Side Shots | **Company:** Vance and Hines

Vote: 1   2   3

Bike detail screen

Note that we can see the **Edit** button on this bike because our application seed already filled the database with some sample information.

So, if we click on the **Edit bike** button, we will see something similar to the following:

Edit bike form

Creating the bike-list methods

Let's create the `bike-list` component:

1. Open `./Client/src/pages/bikes/bike-list/bike-list.component.ts` and add the following imports, right after the core import:

```
import { NgbDropdown } from '@ng-bootstrap/ng-
bootstrap/dropdown/dropdown.module';

// App imports
import { Bike } from '../bike';
import { BikesService } from '../_services/bikes.service';
```

2. Add the following properties after the `bike-list.component` class declaration:

```
// Using Bike Model class
bikes: Bike[];
isLoading: Boolean = false;
public searchText: string;
```

3. Still on `./Client/src/pages/bikes/bike-list/bike-list.component.ts,` let's create the `constructor()` function:

```
constructor(
        private bikeService: BikesService) {}
```

4. Inside the `ngOnInit()` function, add the following code:

```
// Get bike list
this.getBikes();
```

Now, let's create the `this.getBikes()` function.

5. Add the following code right after the `ngOnInit()` function:

```
getBikes(): void {
this.isLoading = true;
this.bikeService.getBikes()
        .subscribe(
        response => this.handleResponse(response),
        error => this.handleError(error));
}
```

Note that, in this code, we are using two functions to deal with success and error responses. It is possible to write everything inside the `subscribe()` function, but a better organization technique is to separate them.

6. Add the following code, right after the `getBikes()` function:

```
protected handleResponse(response: Bike[]) {
        this.isLoading = false,
        this.bikes = response;
}

protected handleError(error: any) {
        this.isLoading = false,
        console.error(error);
}
```

Here, on the protected `handleError` methods, we are just using the `console.log()` to show errors.

The expected result for this page when we access the `http://localhost:4200/bikes` URL will be similar to the following screenshot:

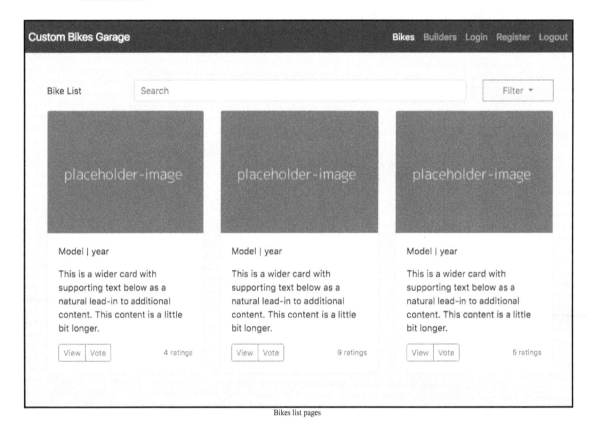

Bikes list pages

Creating the builder-detail methods

Now, it is time to create the `builder-detail` component. Let's see how:

1. Open `./Client/src/pages/builders/builder-detail/builder-detail.component.ts` and add the following imports, right after the core import:

```
import { ActivatedRoute } from '@angular/router';
```

```
// App imports
import { Builder } from './../builder';
import { BuildersService } from '../_services/builders.service';
```

2. Add the following properties after the `builder-detail.component` class declaration:

```
builder: Builder;
isLoading: Boolean = false;
```

3. Still on `./Client/src/pages/builders/builder-detail/builder-detail.component.ts`, let's create the `constructor()` function:

```
constructor(
        private buildersService: BuildersService,
        private route: ActivatedRoute) { }
```

4. Inside the `ngOnInit()` function, add the following code:

```
ngOnInit() {
        // Get builder detail
        this.getBuilderDetail();
}
```

Now, let's create the `this.getBuilderDetail()` function.

5. Add the following code right after the `ngOnInit()` function:

```
getBuilderDetail(): void {
        this.isLoading = true;
        const id = +this.route.snapshot.paramMap.get('id');
        this.buildersService.getBuilderDetail(id)
                .subscribe(builder => {
                this.isLoading = false;
                this.builder = builder['data'];
        });
}
```

The expected result for this page when we access the `http://localhost:4200/builders/4` URL will be similar to the following screenshot:

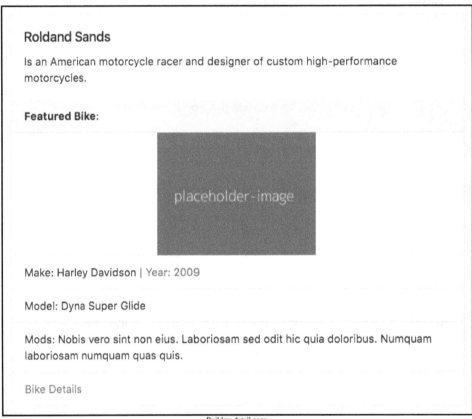

Roldand Sands

Is an American motorcycle racer and designer of custom high-performance motorcycles.

Featured Bike:

Make: Harley Davidson | Year: 2009

Model: Dyna Super Glide

Mods: Nobis vero sint non eius. Laboriosam sed odit hic quia doloribus. Numquam laboriosam numquam quas quis.

Bike Details

Builders detail page

Creating the builder-list methods

Now, let's create the `builder-list` methods to list all builders:

1. Open `./Client/src/pages/builders/builder-list/builder-list.component.ts` and add the following imports, right after the core import:

```
// App imports
import { Builder } from './../builder';
import { BuildersService } from '../_services/builders.service';
```

2. Add the following properties after the `BuilderListComponent` class declaration:

```
// Using Builder Model class
builders: Builder[];
isLoading: Boolean = false;
```

3. Still on `./Client/src/pages/builders/builder-list/builder-list.component.ts`, let's create the `constructor()` function:

```
constructor(private builderService: BuildersService) { }
```

4. Inside the `ngOnInit()` function, add the following code:

```
ngOnInit() {
        // Get builder detail
        this.getBuilders();
}
```

5. Add the following code right after the `ngOnInit()` function:

```
getBuilders(): void {
this.isLoading = true;
this.builderService.getBuilders()
        .subscribe(
        response => this.handleResponse(response),
        error => this.handleError(error));
}
```

Note that, in this code we are using two functions to deal with success and error responses. It is possible to write everything inside the `subscribe()` function, but a better organization technique would be to separate them.

6. Add the following code, right after the `getBuilders()` function:

```
protected handleResponse(response: Builder[]) {
        this.isLoading = false,
        this.builders = response;
}
protected handleError(error: any) {
        this.isLoading = false,
        console.error(error);
}
```

Finally, we have all the components ready to go.

The expected result for this page when we access
the `http://localhost:4200/builders` URL will be similar to the following
screenshot:

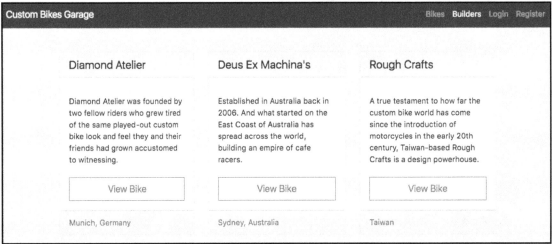

Builders list page

Dealing with Angular pipes, forms, and validation

In this section, we will see how to create a simple search component inside the bike list
page using the new pipe feature. We will also look at how to create Angular forms in two
ways: with template-driven forms, and with reactive forms. Finally, we will show you how
to use form validation with Bootstrap CSS.

Creating a pipe filter

Pipes in Angular are a simple way to filter and transform data, very similar to the old
AngularJS filter.

We have some default pipes in Angular (`DatePipe`, `UpperCasePipe`, `LowerCasePipe`,
`CurrencyPipe`, and `PercentPipe`), and we can also create our own pipes.

To create a custom pipe, we can use the Angular CLI to generate the scaffolding for us. Let's see how it works:

1. Open your Terminal window, and, inside `./Client/src/app`, type the following command:

   ng g pipe pages/bikes/_pipes/bikeSearch

   As always, Angular CLI takes care of creating the file and the appropriate imports.

2. Open `./Client/src/app/pages/bikes/_pipes/bike-search.pipe.ts` and add the following code inside the `BikeSearchPipe` class:

   ```
   transform(items: any, searchText: string): any {
   if (searchText) {
           searchText = searchText.toLowerCase();
           return items.filter((item: any) =>
   item.model.toLowerCase().indexOf(searchText) > -1);
       }
   return items;
       }
   ```

   The previous `transform` function receive two parameters: the list and the search string from the input field on the search box from the bike list page. So, let's see how we can use them inside the `bike-list` template.

3. Open `./Client/src/app/pages/bikes/bike-list/bike-list.component.ts` and add the following properties inside the search input field:

   ```
   <input [(ngModel)]="searchText" [ngModelOptions]="{standalone:
   true}" placeholder="buscar" type="text" class="form-control"
           id="search" placeholder="Search">
   ```

   Now that we already have the search model, let's add the pipe filter on our `*ngFor` loop.

4. Add the following code inside the `*ngFor` property:

   ```
   <div class="col-md-4" *ngFor="let bike of bikes | bikeSearch:
   searchText ">...</div>
   ```

So, when we type the bike model into the search input, we will see the following screenshot:

Search field working

Now, let's see how we can implement the Angular forms.

Intoducing Angular forms

As we all know, forms are an essential part of any modern web application for logging in a a user in to the app, adding products, and sending comments to a blog. Some forms are very simple, but other forms could have an array of fields, and even many steps and pages with tons of input fields.

With Angular, we can implement two types of forms:

- Template-driven forms
- Reactive forms or model-driven forms

Both are equally powerful and belong to the `@angular/forms` library. They are based on the same form control classes. However, they have different philosophies, programming styles, and techniques, and the validation is different too. In the next section, we will see the uniqueness of each technique.

Understanding Angular template-driven forms

Template-driven forms, as we explained previously, are very similar to AngularJS forms and make use of directives such as `ngModel` and perhaps `required`, `minlength`, `maxlength`, and many others. When we are using these form directives, we are letting the template do the work behind the scenes.

Reviewing the login form template and component

A very good example to understand template-driven forms is the login form. Let's see `login.component.html` and `login.component.ts`:

1. Open `./Client/src/app/pages/auth/login/login.component.html` and review the template input tags:

    ```
    [(ngModel)]="user.email"    name="email"
    [(ngModel)]="user.password" name="password"
    ```

    Note that we are using the two-way data binding syntax for `ngModel = [(ngModel)]`. This means that we can set the initial data from the login component class, but we can also update it.

    Remember, Angular's `ngModel` can be used in three different ways:

    - `ngModel`: No binding or value is assigned, and depends on the name attribute
    - `[ngModel]`: One-way data binding syntax
    - `[(ngModel)]`: Two-way data binding syntax

    For the submit button event, we are just using the `(ngSubmit)="onSubmit(loginForm)"` `#loginForm="ngForm"` directive, passing in the `loginForm`.

Now that our `login.component.ts` is intact, the only thing we need is the `onSubmit` function.

2. Now, let's edit the `login.component.ts` by replacing its code with the following:

```
import { Component, OnInit } from '@angular/core';
import { Router, ActivatedRoute } from '@angular/router';

// App imports
import { AuthService } from '../_services/auth.service';
import { User } from '../user';

@Component({
selector: 'app-login',
templateUrl: './login.component.html',
styleUrls: ['./login.component.scss']
})
export class LoginComponent implements OnInit {
        user: User = new User();
        error: any;
        returnUrl: string;

        constructor(
                private authService: AuthService,
                private router: Router,
                private route: ActivatedRoute) { }

        ngOnInit() {
                //  Set the return url
                this.returnUrl =
this.route.snapshot.queryParams['returnUrl'] || '/';
        }

        onSubmit(loginForm): void {
                this.authService.onLogin(this.user).subscribe(
                (response) => {
                        // get return url from route parameters or
default to '/'
                        this.router.navigate([this.returnUrl]);
                },
                (error) => {
                        this.error = error.error;
                }
                );
                // Clear form fields
                loginForm.reset();
```

```
        }

    }
```

Note that we are passing `loginForm` to the `onSubmit(loginForm)` function and using the `authService` to send the data to the endpoint.

Understanding Angular reactive/model-driven forms

One of the differences between reactive/model-driven forms and template-driven forms is the use of directives such as `ngModel`.

The principle behind this is that we transfer the directives responsibly to the `component.ts` code using the forms API. This has much more power and is extremely productive for work, keeping all the logic in the same place, as we will see shortly.

Reviewing the register form template and component

A very good example to understand model-driven forms is the register form. Let's look at `register.component.html` and `register.component.ts`:

1. Open
   `./Client/src/app/pages/auth/register/register.component.html` and review the template input tags:

   ```
   formControlName="name"
   formControlName="email"
   formControlName="password"
   ```

   It is almost the same notation we used on template-driven forms, but a little more clean. Here, we don't need the `name` attribute.

   For the submit button event, we are just using the `[formGroup]="registerForm"  (ngSubmit)="onSubmit()"` attribute and the bind function.

2. Now, let's create the `register.component.ts`. Replace its code with the following:

   ```
   import { Component, OnInit } from '@angular/core';
   import { Router } from '@angular/router';
   import { FormBuilder, FormGroup, Validators } from
   '@angular/forms';
   ```

```
// App imports
import { User } from '../user';
import { AuthService } from '../_services/auth.service';

@Component({
selector: 'app-register',
templateUrl: './register.component.html',
styleUrls: ['./register.component.scss']
})
export class RegisterComponent implements OnInit {

        user: User = new User();
        error: any;
        registerForm: FormGroup;

        constructor(private authService: AuthService, private
router: Router, private fb: FormBuilder) {
                this.createForm();
        }

        ngOnInit() {}

        createForm() {
                this.registerForm = this.fb.group({
                name: [this.user.name,
Validators.compose([Validators.required])],
                email: [this.user.email,
Validators.compose([Validators.required, Validators.email ])],
                password: [this.user.password,
Validators.compose([Validators.required,
Validators.minLength(6)])],
                });
        }

        onSubmit(): void {

this.authService.onRegister(this.registerForm.value).subscribe(
                (response) => {
                        this.router.navigate(['bikes']);
                },
                (response) => {
                        if (response.status === 422) {
                        Object.keys(response.error).map((err) => {
                                this.error =
`${response.error[err]}`;
                        });

                        } else {
```

```
                                    this.error = response.error;
                                    }
                            }
                            );
                    }

            }
```

Note that, in this code, we are dealing with error messages on the submit function. In the following examples, we will look at how to implement form validation on both forms, but for now, let's review some important points.

3. Open `./Client/src/app/pages/auth/register/register.component.ts` ; let's review the `registerComponent` class.

The first difference we can note is the imports of the `FormBuilder`, `FormGroup`, and `Validators` at the top of file:

```
import { FormBuilder, FormGroup, Validators } from
'@angular/forms';
```

We also need to import the `ReactiveFormsModule` inside `auth.module.ts`:

```
import { FormsModule, ReactiveFormsModule } from '@angular/forms';
```

We can create the form using the `FormBuilder` API inside the `createForm()` function:

```
            createForm() {
                    this.registerForm = this.fb.group({
                            name: [this.user.name,
Validators.compose([Validators.required])],
                            email: [this.user.email,
Validators.compose([Validators.required, Validators.email ])],
                            password: [this.user.password,
Validators.compose([Validators.required,
Validators.minLength(6)])],
                    });
            }
```

Here, we are using `Validators` to add form validation directly from the `component.ts` code. Brilliant, right?

Remember that the `fb` variables hold the `FormBuilder` that we placed inside our constructor: private `fb:FormBuilder`. We also set `registerForm` as `FormGroup` inside `RegisterClass`.

Adding frontend form validation

As we know today, it is a good practice to show constant feedback to the end user when we talk about user experience, so it is a good practice to validate your forms before sending them to the backend.

In this section, we will look at how to add form validation to both the login and register forms.

Dealing with form validation on template-driven forms

Open `./Client/src/app/pages/auth/login/login.component.html` and replace the form tag with the following code:

```
<form class="form-signin" (ngSubmit)="onSubmit(loginForm)"
#loginForm="ngForm">
        <div class="text-center mb-4">
                <h1 class="h3 mt-3 mb-3 font-weight-normal">Welcome</h1>
                <p>Motorcycle builders and road lovers</p>
                <hr>
        </div>
        <div class="form-group" [ngClass]="{ 'has-error': !email.valid &&
(email.dirty || email.touched) }">
                <label for="email">Email address</label>
                <input type="email" [(ngModel)]="user.email"  name="email"
#email="ngModel" required class="form-control" id="email" aria-
describedby="emailHelp" placeholder="Enter email">
                <div *ngIf="email.invalid && (email.dirty ||
email.touched)" class="form-feedback">
                        <div *ngIf="email?.errors.required">Email is
required</div>
                        <div *ngIf="email?.errors.email">Email must be a
valid email address</div>
                </div>
        </div>
        <div class="form-group" [ngClass]="{ 'has-error': !password.valid
&& (password.dirty || password.touched) }">
                <label for="password">Password</label>
                <input type="password" [(ngModel)]="user.password"
name="password" #password="ngModel" required minlength="6" class="form-
control" id="password" placeholder="Password">
                <div *ngIf="password.invalid && (password.dirty ||
password.touched)" class="form-feedback">
                        <div *ngIf="password?.errors.required">Password is
required</div>
                        <div *ngIf="password?.errors.minlength">Password
```

```
must be at least 6 characters</div>
                </div>
        </div>
        <div *ngIf="error" class="alert alert-danger" role="alert">
                Ops: {{ error.error }}
        </div>
        <button [disabled]="!loginForm.valid" class="btn btn-lg btn-primary
btn-block mt-5" type="submit">Login</button>
    </form>
```

Let's review the previous code.

Note that we are using the `[ngClass]` that's built into the Angular directive to apply an error class to the `div` form group if the form is invalid:

```
// Email field
    class="form-group" [ngClass]="{ 'has-error': !email.valid &&
(email.dirty || email.touched) }"
    // Password field
    class="form-group" [ngClass]="{ 'has-error': !password.valid &&
(password.dirty || password.touched) }"
```

To show the error message, we will create two new divs right after the input fields:

```
// Email validation
    <div *ngIf="email.invalid && (email.dirty || email.touched)"
class="form-feedback">
            <div *ngIf="email?.errors.required">Email is required</div>
            <div *ngIf="email?.errors.email">Email must be a valid
email address</div>
    </div>
    // Password validation
    <div *ngIf="password.invalid && (password.dirty ||
password.touched)" class="form-feedback">
            <div *ngIf="password?.errors.required">Password is
required</div>
            <div *ngIf="password?.errors.minlength">Password must be at
least 6 characters</div>
    </div>
```

With the help of `ngIf` and the form states (dirty, touched), we can see each error if the input field matches this condition.

The next rule is that the following `div` shows backend errors that may occur:

```
<div *ngIf="error" class="alert alert-danger" role="alert">
        Ops: {{ error.error }}
    </div>
```

Finally, validation is set on the **Submit** button using the `[disabled]` directive:

```
<button [disabled]="!loginForm.valid" class="btn btn-lg btn-primary
btn-block mt-5" type="submit">Login</button>
```

The final result of our form in action will be something like the following:

Login form validation

Dealing with form validation on model-driven forms

Open `./Client/src/app/pages/auth/register/register.component.html` and replace the form tag with the following code:

```
<form [formGroup]="registerForm" (ngSubmit)="onSubmit()" class="form-
register" novalidate>
    <div class="text-center mb-4">
        <h1 class="h3 mt-3 mb-3 font-weight-normal">Welcome</h1>
        <p>Motorcycle builders and road lovers</p>
        <hr>
    </div>
```

```
        <div class="form-group" [ngClass]="{ 'has-error':
!registerForm.get('name').valid && (registerForm.get('name').dirty ||
registerForm.get('name').touched) }">
                <label for="name">Name</label>
                <input type="name" formControlName="name" class="form-
control" id="name" aria-describedby="nameHelp" placeholder="Enter your
name">
                <div class="form-feedback"
                        *ngIf="registerForm.get('name').errors &&
(registerForm.get('name').dirty || registerForm.get('name').touched)">
                        <div
*ngIf="registerForm.get('name').hasError('required')">Name is
required</div>
                </div>
        </div>
        <div class="form-group" [ngClass]="{ 'has-error':
!registerForm.get('email').valid && (registerForm.get('email').dirty ||
registerForm.get('email').touched) }">
                <label for="email">Email address</label>
                <input type="email" formControlName="email" class="form-
control" id="email" aria-describedby="emailHelp" placeholder="Enter email">
                <div class="form-feedback"
                        *ngIf="registerForm.get('email').errors &&
(registerForm.get('email').dirty || registerForm.get('email').touched)">
                        <div
*ngIf="registerForm.get('email').hasError('required')">Email is
required</div>
                        <div
*ngIf="registerForm.get('email').hasError('email')">Email must be a valid
email address</div>
                </div>
        </div>
        <div class="form-group" [ngClass]="{ 'has-error':
!registerForm.get('password').valid && (registerForm.get('password').dirty
|| registerForm.get('password').touched) }">
                <label for="password">Password</label>
                <input type="password" formControlName="password"
class="form-control" id="password" placeholder="Password">
                <div class="form-feedback"
                        *ngIf="registerForm.get('password').errors &&
(registerForm.get('password').dirty ||
registerForm.get('password').touched)">
                        <p
*ngIf="registerForm.get('password').hasError('required')">Password is
required</p>
                        <p
*ngIf="registerForm.get('password').hasError('minlength')">Password must be
6 characters long, we need another
```

```
{{registerForm.get('password').errors['minlength'].requiredLength -
registerForm.get('password').errors['minlength'].actualLength}} characters
</p>
                </div>
        </div>
        <div *ngIf="error" class="alert alert-danger" role="alert">
                Ops: {{ error }}
        </div>
        <button [disabled]="!registerForm.valid" class="btn btn-lg btn-
primary btn-block mt-5" type="submit">Register</button>
    </form>
```

Let's review the previous code.

Note that we are using the `[ngClass]` that's built into Angular to apply an `error` class to the `div` form group if the form is invalid:

```
// Name field
    class="form-group" [ngClass]="{ 'has-error':
!registerForm.get('name').valid && (registerForm.get('name').dirty ||
registerForm.get('name').touched) }"
    // Email field
    class="form-group" [ngClass]="{ 'has-error':
!registerForm.get('email').valid && (registerForm.get('email').dirty ||
registerForm.get('email').touched) }"
    // Password field
    class="form-group" [ngClass]="{ 'has-error':
!registerForm.get('password').valid && (registerForm.get('password').dirty
|| registerForm.get('password').touched) }"
```

Here, you can note that we are using the `registerForm.get()` method to make the input field a little different from the login form.

To show the error message, we will create three new `div` right after the input fields:

```
// Name validation
    <div class="form-feedback"
            *ngIf="registerForm.get('name').errors &&
(registerForm.get('name').dirty || registerForm.get('name').touched)">
            <div
*ngIf="registerForm.get('name').hasError('required')">Name is
required</div>
    </div>

    // Email validation
    <div class="form-feedback"
            *ngIf="registerForm.get('email').errors &&
(registerForm.get('email').dirty || registerForm.get('email').touched)">
```

```
                <div
*ngIf="registerForm.get('email').hasError('required')">Email is
required</div>
                <div
*ngIf="registerForm.get('email').hasError('email')">Email must be a valid
email address</div>
        </div>

        // Password validation
        <div class="form-feedback"
                *ngIf="registerForm.get('password').errors &&
(registerForm.get('password').dirty ||
registerForm.get('password').touched)">
                <p
*ngIf="registerForm.get('password').hasError('required')">Password is
required</p>
                <p
*ngIf="registerForm.get('password').hasError('minlength')">Password must be
6 characters long, we need another
{{registerForm.get('password').errors['minlength'].requiredLength -
registerForm.get('password').errors['minlength'].actualLength}} characters
</p>
        </div>
```

The next rule is that the following `div` is used to show backend errors that may happen:

```
<div  *ngIf="error" class="alert alert-danger" role="alert">
        Ops: {{ error }}
</div>
```

Finally, the validation is set on the **Submit** button using the `[disabled]` directive:

```
<button [disabled]="!registerForm.valid" class="btn btn-lg btn-
  primary btn-block mt-5" type="submit">Register</button>
```

The final result of our form in action will look something similar to the following:

| Custom Bikes Garage | Bikes Builders Login **Register** |

Welcome

Motorcycle builders and road lovers

Name

```
Enter your name
```

Name is required

Email address

```
a
```

Email must be a valid email address

Password

```
•
```

Password must be 6 characters long, we need another 5 characters

```
Register
```

Register form validation

In the next screenshot, we can see the backend errors from where we tried to insert an email address that's already in use:

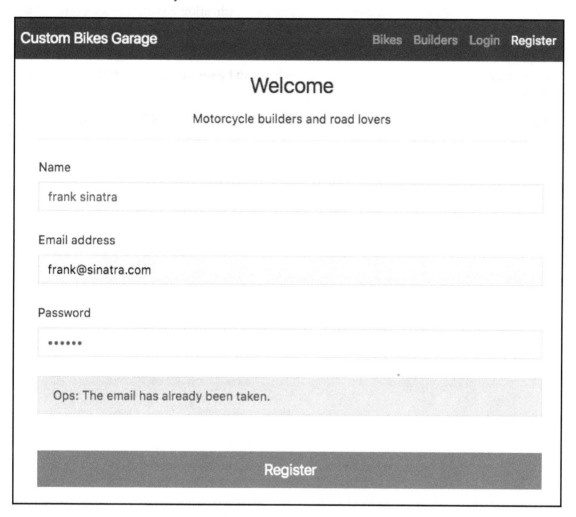

Backend error message

Summary

We have finished one more chapter, and our sample application has all the key points of a modern web application. We learned how to install, customize, and extend a Bootstrap CSS framework, and learned how to use `NgBootstrap` components.

We also understood how components and services can be set up together, form validation, and many other very useful techniques.

In the next chapter, we will see how to set up linters for SCSS and TS files and how to deploy using Docker images.

11
Building and Deploying Angular Tests

In the last chapter, you learned how to install, customize, and extend a Bootstrap CSS framework; how to use `NgBootstrap` components; and how to connect Angular services with components and UI interfaces. Now, let's look at another key point in Angular applications: tests.

Tests are a great way to check your application code to find issues. In this chapter, you will learn how to test Angular applications, how to configure application linters (for SCSS and TSLint files) to keep code consistency, and how to create `npm` build scripts. In addition, you will learn how to create a Docker image for a frontend application.

In this chapter, we will cover the following:

- Setting application linters
- Understanding Angular tests
- Writing unit and e2e tests
- Application deployment

Preparing the baseline code

First, we need to prepare our baseline code, a process very similar to that of previous chapters. Follow these steps:

1. Copy all of the content from the `chapter-10` folder.
2. Rename the folder `chapter-11`.
3. Delete the `storage-db` folder.

Now, let's make some changes to the `docker-compose.yml` file, to fit a new database and server containers.

4. Open `docker-compose.yml` and replace the contents with the following code:

```
version: "3.1"
services:
    mysql:
        image: mysql:5.7
        container_name: chapter-11-mysql
        working_dir: /application
        volumes:
            - .:/application
            - ./storage-db:/var/lib/mysql
        environment:
            - MYSQL_ROOT_PASSWORD=123456
            - MYSQL_DATABASE=chapter-11
            - MYSQL_USER=chapter-11
            - MYSQL_PASSWORD=123456
        ports:
            - "8083:3306"
    webserver:
        image: nginx:alpine
        container_name: chapter-11-webserver
        working_dir: /application
        volumes:
            - .:/application
            - ./phpdocker/nginx/nginx.conf:/etc/nginx/conf.d/default.
              conf
        ports:
            - "8081:80"
    php-fpm:
        build: phpdocker/php-fpm
        container_name: chapter-11-php-fpm
        working_dir: /application
        volumes:
            - ./Server:/application
            - ./phpdocker/php-fpm/php-ini-
              overrides.ini:/etc/php/7.2/fpm/conf.d/99-overrides.ini
```

Note that we changed the container names, the database, and the MySQL user:

- `container_name: chapter-11-mysql`
- `container_name: chapter-11-webserver`
- `container_name: chapter-11-php-fpm`

- MYSQL_DATABASE=chapter-11
- MYSQL_USER=chapter-11

5. Update the `.env` file with the following connection string:

```
DB_CONNECTION=mysql
DB_HOST=mysql
DB_PORT=3306
DB_DATABASE=chapter-11
DB_USERNAME=chapter-11
DB_PASSWORD=123456
```

6. Add the changes that we made to the Git source control. Open Terminal window and type the following command:

```
git add .
git commit -m "Initial commit chapter 11"
```

Setting application linters

All of us want a clean and consistent code base. Independent of the programming language adopted, it is very common to use linters for JavaScript and other languages. But, when we discuss CSS or SCSS/LESS, this practice is not very common; we rarely use a linter for our style sheets.

A **linter** is a tool that analyzes code and reports errors. We set the rules, and when a piece of code doesn't pass the rules defined in the linter's configuration, the linter reports an error. This feature is very useful when a team is growing and needs to keep the code base consistent.

If you don't have strict rules for coding style, code can become a mess very quickly. Even if you work alone, it is always a good practice to keep your code consistent.

In the following sections, you will learn how to apply a linter for SCSS and TypeScript files.

Adding stylelint for SCSS files

We will be using `stylelint`, a mighty, modern style sheet linter, supporting CSS, LESS, and SASS. `stylelint` has a lot of rules, available by default, and it is very easy to extend with our own rules, it's totally un-opinionated. Another advantage is that all rules are disabled by default, and we only enable the ones that we want to use. Let's see it in practice.

Open Terminal window inside of the `./Client` folder, and type the following commands:

```
npm install stylelint --save-dev &&
npm install stylelint-config-standard --save-dev &&
npm install stylelint-scss --save-dev
```

The preceding commands are very clear, right? We are installing the default configuration standard plugin, along with the SCSS plugin.

 You can read more about `stylelint` in the official documentation at `https://github.com/stylelint/stylelint`.

Adding new scripts to the package.json file

Open the `package.json` file at the root of the `./Client` folder and add the following code, right after the `lint` task:

```
    "sasslint": "./node_modules/.bin/stylelint \"src/**/*.scss\" --syntax
scss || echo \"Ops: Stylelint faild for some file(s).\"",
```

Note that we are using the `Stylelint` from our local `node_modules` folder. This helps us to ensure that the whole team uses the same plugin version, avoiding compatibility issues.

Adding the .stylelintrc configuration

Let's add our own rules, as follows:

1. Inside of `./Client`, create a new file, called `.stylelintrc`.

2. Add the following rules to the `./Client/.stylelintrc` file:

```
{
    "extends": ["stylelint-config-standard"],
    "rules": {
        "font-family-name-quotes": "always-where-
recommended",
        "function-url-quotes": [
            "always",
            {
            "except": ["empty"]
            }
        ],
        "selector-attribute-quotes": "always",
        "string-quotes": "double",
        "max-nesting-depth": 3,
        "selector-max-compound-selectors": 3,
        "selector-max-specificity": "0,3,2",
        "declaration-no-important": true,
        "at-rule-no-vendor-prefix": true,
        "media-feature-name-no-vendor-prefix": true,
        "property-no-vendor-prefix": true,
        "selector-no-vendor-prefix": true,
        "value-no-vendor-prefix": true,
        "no-empty-source": null,
        "selector-class-pattern": "[a-z-]+",
        "selector-id-pattern": "[a-z-]+",
        "selector-max-id": 0,
        "selector-no-qualifying-type": true,
        "selector-max-universal": 0,
        "selector-pseudo-element-no-unknown": [
            true,
            {
            "ignorePseudoElements": ["ng-deep"]
            }
        ],
        "unit-whitelist": ["px", "%", "em", "rem", "vw",
"vh", "deg"],
        "max-empty-lines": 2
    }
}
```

3. Note that you can use whatever rules you want; there's no right or wrong. It's just a matter of taste and team preference. For example, if your team chooses to use only px pixels for the entire project, your unit-whitelist configuration will be as follows:

```
"unit-whitelist": ["px"],
```

4. Let's perform a brief test to check that everything is going well. Open Terminal window at ./Client and type the following command:

```
npm run sasslint
```

The preceding command reports 77 errors in our project. How is that possible? We only have a few lines of code, and most of them are code indentation on a style.scss file. Well, this is expected, because this is the only file with SCSS. Remember that we didn't add any SCSS code to our components.scss files.

Installing the Stylelint plugin for VS Code

If you are using vs.code (and I hope you are), install the Stylelint plugin, as follows:

1. In VS Code, open the left extensions panel.
2. Type stylelint, on the search input field.
3. Choose stylelint extension.
4. Restart VS Code.

Setting VS Code for the new linter

Now, let's configure VS Code to only use stylelint rules; this will prevent us from seeing double error messages in the VS Code integrated Terminal (if you are using a different code editor, don't worry about it). The steps are as follows:

1. In VS Code, navigate to **Code | Preferences | Settings** in the top menu.

2. Add the following code in the right-hand panel:

```
{
        "css.validate": false,
        "less.validate": false,
        "scss.validate": false
}
```

To see the plugin in action, open the `style.scss` file
in `./Client/src/style.scss`. You will see the following in the bottom panel in
VS Code:

Errors logged by the stylelint extension

These are the same output errors we saw when using the `npm run sass-lint` command,
but here, we can navigate the files. If you are on macOS, use *Command* + mouse-click. If you
are on Windows or Linux, use *Ctrl* + mouse-click.

Applying stylelint rules on style.scss

It's pretty simple to validate the `style.scss` file. Let's read the error messages.

From lines 9 to 44, the errors are about indentation spaces, so let's remove the empty space.

Remove the space between `@import` and the left-hand side, for all Bootstrap imports.

Now, we have 41 errors. If you are inside VS Code, click on the error link on the bottom panel (on the **Problems** tab), and open the file right in the error, as shown in the following screenshot:

```scss
46    /* Sticky footer styles
47    ------------------------------------------------------- */
48    html {
49      position: relative;
50      min-height: 100%;
51    }
52    body {          You, 3 hours ago • initial commit
53      /* Margin bottom by footer height */
54      margin-bottom: 60px;
55    }
56    .footer {
57      position: absolute;
58      bottom: 0;
59      width: 100%;
```

PROBLEMS 41   OUTPUT   DEBUG CONSOLE   TERMINAL

styles.scss Client/src 41

⊗ [stylelint] Expected empty line before rule (rule-empty-line-before) (52, 1)
⊗ [stylelint] Expected empty line before rule (rule-empty-line-before) (56, 1)
⊗ [stylelint] Expected empty line before comment (comment-empty-line-before) (60, 3)
⊗ [stylelint] Expected empty line before rule (rule-empty-line-before) (65, 1)
⊗ [stylelint] Unexpected empty line before rule (rule-empty-line-before) (71, 3)
⊗ [stylelint] Unexpected qualifying type selector (selector-no-qualifying-type) (71, 3)
⊗ [stylelint] Expected newline after "," (selector-list-comma-newline-after) (71, 16)
⊗ [stylelint] Unexpected empty line before rule (rule-empty-line-before) (82, 5)
⊗ [stylelint] Expected empty line before rule (rule-empty-line-before) (85, 5)
⊗ [stylelint] Expected a leading zero (number-leading-zero) (87, 18)
⊗ [stylelint] Unexpected empty line before closing brace (block-closing-brace-empty-line-before)
⊗ [stylelint] Unexpected empty line before declaration (declaration-empty-line-before) (98, 3)
⊗ [stylelint] Expected newline after "," (selector-list-comma-newline-after) (102, 16)
⊗ [stylelint] Unexpected vendor-prefix "-webkit-animation" (property-no-vendor-prefix) (112, 3)
⊗ [stylelint] Unexpected empty line before declaration (declaration-empty-line-before) (112, 3)

VS Code stylelint plugin errors

If you are not using VS Code, the Terminal message after running `npm run sass-lint` will be the same, as shown in the following screenshot:

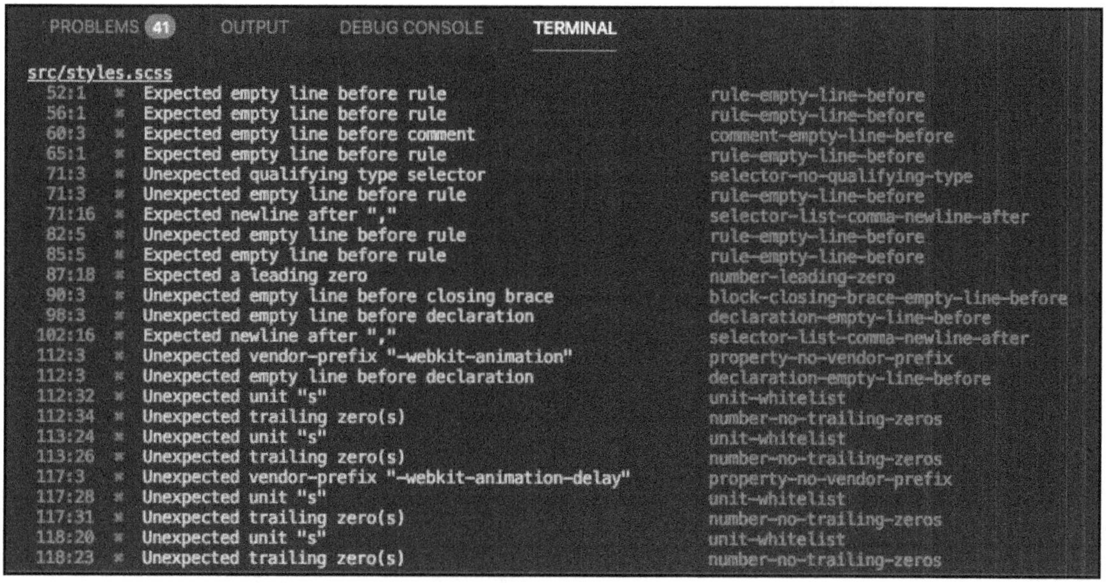

VS Code Terminal stylelint errors

Fixing SCSS errors

Let's fix all of the error messages in our `style.scss` file.

Open `./Client/src/style.scss` and replace the content after `@imports` with the following code:

```scss
/* Sticky footer styles
-------------------------------------------------- */
html {
    position: relative;
    min-height: 100%;
}

body {
    /* Margin bottom by footer height */
    margin-bottom: 60px;
}
```

```
.footer {
        position: absolute;
        bottom: 0;
        width: 100%;
        /* Set the fixed height of the footer here */
        height: 60px;
        line-height: 60px; /* Vertically center the text there */
        background-color: #f5f5f5;
}

main {
        padding-top: 3.5em;
}

form {
        .form-signin,
        .form-register {
                width: 80%;
                margin: 0 auto;
        }

        .form-group {
                height: 80px;
        }

        .has-error {
                .form-control {
                        border-color: red;
                }

                .form-feedback {
                        color: red;
                        font-size: 0.9rem;
                }
        }
}

// Loading spinner
.spinner {
        width: 40px;
        height: 40px;
        position: relative;
        margin: 100px auto;
}

.double-bounce1,
.double-bounce2 {
        width: 100%;
```

```
        height: 100%;
        border-radius: 50%;
        background-color: #333;
        opacity: 0.6;
        position: absolute;
        top: 0;
        left: 0;
        animation: sk-bounce 2 infinite ease-in-out;
}
.double-bounce2 {
        animation-delay: -1;
}
@keyframes sk-bounce {
        0%,
        100% { transform: scale(0); }
        50% { transform: scale(1); }
}
@keyframes sk-bounce {
        0%,
        100% { transform: scale(0); }
        50% { transform: scale(1); }
}
```

There are no errors now, and our project will be safe and consistent with our rules. Next, let's look at how to use the built-in TypeScript linter in our project.

Adding TSLint-angular to the package.json file

As we mentioned previously, code consistency is a key point for a successful project. By default, the Angular CLI has already added `tslint` to our project, as we can see in the `package.json` file and in the scripts tag, with the `ng-lint` command.

However, while we were writing this chapter, the Angular CLI had a small bug and reported the error message twice when we used the `ng-lint` command. To avoid that, let's add the following lines to our `package.json` file, right after the `sass-lint` script:

```
"tslint": "./node_modules/.bin/tslint --project tsconfig.json || echo
\"Ops: TSlint faild for some file(s).\"",
```

In the previous lines, we used the local `tslint` binary from the `node_modules` folder. This will help us to avoid compatibility issues.

As we are working in an Angular project, it will be very helpful for us to follow Angular's official style guide, as it has been adopted throughout the developer community.

 You can read more about the Angular style guide in the official documentation at `https://angular.io/guide/styleguide`.

To help us with the style guide, we will use a package called `tslint-angular`:

1. Open Terminal window and type the following command:

   npm install tslint-angular --save-dev

2. Now, open the `./Client/src/tslint.json` file and replace the contents with the following code:

```
{
        "extends": ["../tslint.json", "../node_modules/tslint-
angular"],
        "rules": {
                "angular-whitespace": [true, "check-interpolation",
"check-semicolon"],
                "no-unused-variable": true,
                "no-unused-css": true,
                "banana-in-box": true,
                "use-view-encapsulation": true,
                "contextual-life-cycle": true,
                "directive-selector": [
                        true,
                        "attribute",
                        "app",
                        "camelCase"
                ],
                "component-selector": [
                        true,
                        "element",
                        "app",
                        "kebab-case"
                ]
        }
}
```

Note that, in the previous code, we are using the `extends` property to extend the default configuration in `./Client/tslint.ts` and the `tslint-angular` from our `node_modules` folder.

> You can read more about recommended Angular rules at `https://github.com/mgechev/codelyzer#recommended-configuration`.

Creating linter tasks in package.json

Now, we will create some tasks to run the linters that we just set up.

Open `./Client/package.json` and add the following line before the `sasalint` script:

```
"lint:dev": "npm run sasslint && npm run tslint",
```

The preceding code will execute two commands: one for `sasslint` and another for `tslint`. So, we are ready to start testing our application and preparing the deployment.

> You can read more about TSlint-angular in the official documentation at `https://github.com/mgechev/tslint-angular`.

Understanding Angular tests

Tests are very important for any modern web application, and Angular includes some testing tools by default, such as Jasmine, Karma, and protectors for unit tests and end-to-end tests. Let's look at the main focus of each tool, in order to see the differences:

Unit Tests	End to End Tests
Test a single component, service, pipe, and so on.	Test the whole application
Test a single, specific behavior.	Test real-world situations
Require mocking the backend to test.	Test important features on complete applications
Test edge cases on the most detailed level.	Do not test edge cases

The preceding table is simple, but we can see all of the main differences between unit tests and end-to-end tests, also know as **e2e tests**. Also, both tools use the Jasmine framework, a **behavior-driven** development framework for testing JavaScript code.

 You can read more about Jasmine at `https://jasmine.github.io/`.

As mentioned previously, both tools are installed when we use the Angular CLI to generate the application.

For unit tests, we will use the Karma test runner; before we go further, let's look at `karma.conf.js` to better understand what we already have.

Open `karma.conf.js` inside the root of the `./Client` folder and check the `plugins` tag:

```
plugins: [
  require('karma-jasmine'),
  require('karma-chrome-launcher'),
  require('karma-jasmine-html-reporter'),
  require('karma-coverage-istanbul-reporter'),
  require('@angular-devkit/build-angular/plugins/karma')
],
```

By default, we already have some plugins installed, as we can see on the previous block of code.

 You can read more about the Karma test runner in the official documentation at `https://karma-runner.github.io/2.0/index.html`.

We also have the configuration for the browser that will be used in the tests; by default, we already have Chrome installed:

```
browsers: ['Chrome'],
```

What if you want to use a different browser to run the tests? It is very easy to do that; just install your favorite browser. The Karma test runner supports the most popular browsers, such as:

- Safari
- Firefox
- Internet Explorer

At this point, we are ready to start testing our application. Let's look at how everything works.

Writing unit and e2e tests

Now, you will learn how to run the tests so that you can better understand what happens to the application.

Before we start, let's run the command to execute the tests.

Open Terminal window and type the following command:

```
ng test
```

The preceding code will execute all of the unit tests; after that, we will see all of the errors in Terminal.

The last line will be very similar to the following line:

```
Executed 25 of 25 (18 FAILED) (1.469 secs / 0.924 secs)
```

Each test that fails is marked in red, and is followed by an error message, as you can see in the following excerpt:

```
AppHttpInterceptorService should be created FAILED
                Error:
StaticInjectorError(DynamicTestModule)[BuildersService -> HttpClient]:
                StaticInjectorError(Platform: core)[BuildersService ->
HttpClient]:
                        NullInjectorError: No provider for HttpClient!
```

With so many lines of output in Terminal, it is difficult to even see the tests that have passed. Note that there are seven of them.

Monitoring the tests in Terminal may not be the easiest task, so we can run the tests in the browser by using the following command:

```
ng test --watch
```

The preceding command will open Chrome and start the tests, but remember that you must have the Chrome browser installed on your machine. After the test is done, you can now see the results in a more effective way:

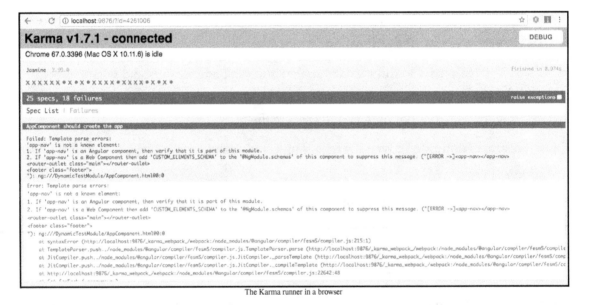

The Karma runner in a browser

The preceding screenshot is much better than the Terminal window, right? So, when we click on the **Spec List** tab menu, we can see the following:

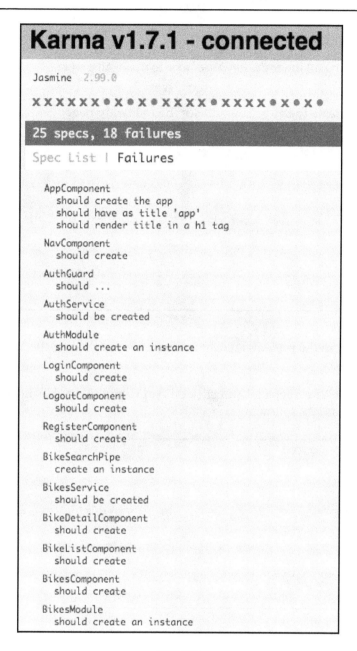

Karma v1.7.1 - connected

Jasmine 2.99.0

X X X X X X ● X ● X ● X X X X ● X X X X ● X ● X ●

25 specs, 18 failures

Spec List | Failures

AppComponent
  should create the app
  should have as title 'app'
  should render title in a h1 tag

NavComponent
  should create

AuthGuard
  should ...

AuthService
  should be created

AuthModule
  should create an instance

LoginComponent
  should create

LogoutComponent
  should create

RegisterComponent
  should create

BikeSearchPipe
  create an instance

BikesService
  should be created

BikeDetailComponent
  should create

BikeListComponent
  should create

BikesComponent
  should create

BikesModule
  should create an instance

Testing view

Also, it is possible to click on a test suite and check all of the related tests from that suite. Let's look at that feature in the next section.

Fixing unit tests

It's time to start fixing all the tests. Let's see how to make all green:

1. Still in the Chrome browser, click on the first test suite, called **AppComponent should create the app**. You will see the following page:

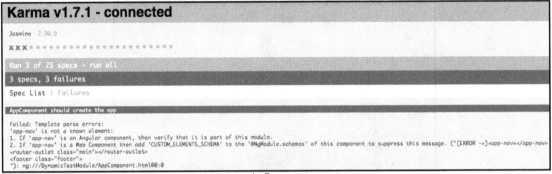

AppComponent

Note that, in the previous screenshot, you are only seeing the AppComponent – related tests.

2. Go back to the **Spec List** and click on **AppComponent should create the app**; you will see the following page:

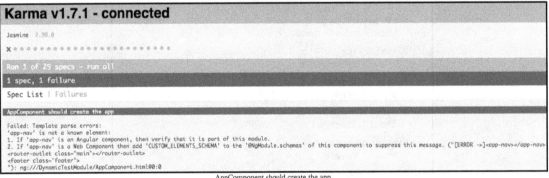

AppComponent should create the app

The preceding error message is very clear:

```
Failed: Template parse errors: 'app-nav' is not a known element:
1. If 'app-nav' is an Angular component, then verify that it is part of
this module.
2. If 'app-nav' is a Web Component then add 'CUSTOM_ELEMENTS_SCHEMA' to the
'@NgModule.schemas' of this component to suppress this message. ("[ERROR
->]<app-nav></app-nav> <router-outlet class="main"></router-outlet> <footer
class="footer">
```

We have a template error, and Angular suggests two ways to deal with it. The first suggestion is to check `app.module.ts`, to see if we added the `app-nav` component import. Let's check:

```
import { NavComponent } from './layout/nav/nav.component';
@NgModule({
declarations: [
        AppComponent,
        NavComponent
],
```

The preceding snippet was taken from the `app.module.ts` file, and we imported the `NavComponent`. Our action is to add `@NgModule.schemas` to our testing specs:

1. Open `./Client/src/app/app.component.spec.ts` and replace the contents with the following code:

```
import { TestBed, async, ComponentFixture } from
'@angular/core/testing';
import { RouterTestingModule } from '@angular/router/testing';
import { NO_ERRORS_SCHEMA } from '@angular/core';

// App imports
import { AppComponent } from './app.component';

describe('AppComponent', () => {
        let component: AppComponent;
        let fixture: ComponentFixture<AppComponent>;

        beforeEach(async(() => {
                TestBed.configureTestingModule({
                imports: [
                        RouterTestingModule
                ],
                declarations: [
                        AppComponent
                ],
```

```
                           schemas: [NO_ERRORS_SCHEMA]
                        }).compileComponents();
            }));

            beforeEach(() => {
                    fixture = TestBed.createComponent(AppComponent);
                    component = fixture.componentInstance;
                    fixture.detectChanges();
            });

            it('should create', async(() => {
                    expect(component).toBeTruthy();
            }));

            it('should render footer tag', async(() => {
                    const compiled =
    fixture.debugElement.nativeElement;
    expect(compiled.querySelector('footer').textContent).toContain('201
8 © All Rights Reserved');
                    }));
        });
```

Note that we added the `schemas` tag, and also our route module, so that the test would pass, as you can see in the next snippet:

```
TestBed.configureTestingModule({
        imports: [
                RouterTestingModule
        ],
        declarations: [
                AppComponent
        ],
        schemas: [NO_ERRORS_SCHEMA]
}).compileComponents();
```

Now, if we check the browser again, we will see the following results:

```
Jasmine  2.99.0

● ● ● ● ● ● ● ● ● ● ● ● ● ● ● ● ● ● ● ● ● ● ● ● ●

Ran 3 of 25 specs - run all

3 specs, 0 failures

    AppComponent
      should create
      should create router-outlet
      should render footer tag

    NavComponent
      should create

    AuthGuard
      should ...

    AuthService
      should be created

    AuthModule
      should create an instance

    LoginComponent
      should create

    LogoutComponent
      should create

    RegisterComponent
      should create

    BikeSearchPipe
      create an instance

    BikesService
      should be created

    BikeDetailComponent
      should create

    BikeListComponent
      should create

    BikesComponent
      should create
```

AppComponent success

The next test that failed is `NavComponent should created`; let's look at the error message:

```
Failed: Template parse errors:
Can't bind to 'routerLink' since it isn't a known property of 'a'.
```

Again, the error message is clear; we need to add `RouterTestingModule` to `nav.component.spec.ts`.

2. Open `./Client/src/app/layout/nav.component.spec.ts` and replace the contents with the following code:

```
import { async, ComponentFixture, TestBed } from
'@angular/core/testing';

import { NavComponent } from './nav.component';
import { RouterTestingModule } from '@angular/router/testing';
import { HttpClientModule } from '@angular/common/http';

describe('NavComponent', () => {
        let component: NavComponent;
        let fixture: ComponentFixture<NavComponent>;

        beforeEach(async(() => {
                TestBed.configureTestingModule({
                imports: [
                        RouterTestingModule,
                        HttpClientModule
                ],
                declarations: [ NavComponent ]
                })
                .compileComponents();
        }));

        beforeEach(() => {
                fixture = TestBed.createComponent(NavComponent);
                component = fixture.componentInstance;
                fixture.detectChanges();
        });

        it('should create', () => {
                expect(component).toBeTruthy();
        });
});
```

We can now see that our test for `NavComponent` works, as shown in the following screenshot:

```
Jasmine  2.99.0

● ● ● ● ● ● ● ● ● ● ● ● ● ● ● ● ● ● ● ● ● ● ● ● ● ● ●

Ran 1 of 24 specs - run all

1 spec, 0 failures

    AppComponent
        should create
        should render footer tag
    NavComponent
        should create
```

NavComponent works

Let's take a breath and consider the next lines.

The following steps are very similar to the steps that we have performed so far. We should mention that we are using routes in our application, so we need to add `RoutingTestingModule` to the `imports` tag in all of the tests, within the configuration of `TestBed.configureTestingModule`:

```
imports: [
        RouterTestingModule
        ...
    ],
```

In addition, we have to inject the same dependency into all of the components that use services (such as `BikeService` and `BuilderService`), as we did in the `components.ts` file.

In the next sections, we will replace the code of many files. Don't worry – when something is important, we will mention it.

Fixing authGuard tests

Open `./Client/src/app/pages/auth/_guards/auth.guard.spec.ts` and replace the contents with the following code:

```
import { RouterTestingModule } from '@angular/router/testing';
import { TestBed, async, inject } from '@angular/core/testing';
import { HttpClient, HttpHandler } from '@angular/common/http';
import { Router } from '@angular/router';
```

```
// App imports
import { AuthGuard } from './auth.guard';
import { AuthService } from '../_services/auth.service';

describe('AuthGuard Tests: ', () => {
const router = {
        navigate: jasmine.createSpy('navigate')
};

beforeEach(async(() => {
        TestBed.configureTestingModule({
        imports: [
                RouterTestingModule.withRoutes([
                {path: 'bikes:id'}
                ])
        ],
        providers: [AuthGuard, AuthService, HttpClient, HttpHandler, {
provide: Router, useValue: router } ]
        });
}));

it('should AuthGuartd to be defined', inject([AuthGuard], (guard:
AuthGuard) => {
        expect(guard).toBeTruthy();
}));

it('should AuthService to be defined', inject([AuthService], (auth:
AuthService) => {
        expect(auth).toBeTruthy();
}));

});
```

Note that we are injecting `AuthService` as a provider; don't worry about that now. Later on in this chapter, we will explain it more thoroughly. Let's just focus on the test.

Fixing authService tests

Open `./Client/src/app/pages/auth/_services/auth.service.spec.ts` and replace the contents with the following code:

```
import { TestBed, inject } from '@angular/core/testing';
import { AuthService } from './auth.service';
import { HttpClientModule } from '@angular/common/http';
import { RouterTestingModule } from '@angular/router/testing';
describe('AuthService', () => {
```

```
beforeEach(() => {
        TestBed.configureTestingModule({
        imports: [
                RouterTestingModule,
                HttpClientModule
                ],
                providers: [AuthService]
                });
}); it('should be created', inject([AuthService],
(service: AuthService) =>
 { expect(service).toBeTruthy();
})); 
});
```

Fixing login tests

Open `./Client/src/app/pages/auth/login/login.component.spec.ts` and replace the contents with the following code:

```
import { RouterTestingModule } from '@angular/router/testing';
import { HttpClientModule } from '@angular/common/http';
import { async, ComponentFixture, TestBed } from '@angular/core/testing';
import { FormsModule } from '@angular/forms';

// App imports
import { LoginComponent } from './login.component';
import { AuthService } from '../_services/auth.service';

describe('LoginComponent', () => {
let component: LoginComponent;
let fixture: ComponentFixture<LoginComponent>;

beforeEach(async(() => {
        TestBed.configureTestingModule({
        imports: [
                RouterTestingModule,
                FormsModule,
                HttpClientModule
        ],
        declarations: [ LoginComponent ],
        providers: [AuthService]
        })
        .compileComponents();
}));

beforeEach(() => {
        fixture = TestBed.createComponent(LoginComponent);
```

```
        component = fixture.componentInstance;
        fixture.detectChanges();
});

it('should create', () => {
        expect(component).toBeTruthy();
});
});
```

As we mentioned previously, practically all of the error messages are related to whether we included dependencies, such as services or direct Angular dependencies.

Fixing register tests

Open
`./Client/src/app/pages/auth/register/register.component.spec.ts` and replace the contents with the following code:

```
import { RouterTestingModule } from '@angular/router/testing';
import { async, ComponentFixture, TestBed } from '@angular/core/testing';
import { NO_ERRORS_SCHEMA } from '@angular/core';

// App imports
import { RegisterComponent } from './register.component';
import { HttpClientModule } from '@angular/common/http';
import { FormBuilder, FormsModule, ReactiveFormsModule } from
'@angular/forms';

describe('RegisterComponent', () => {
let component: RegisterComponent;
let fixture: ComponentFixture<RegisterComponent>;

beforeEach(async(() => {
        TestBed.configureTestingModule({
        imports: [
                RouterTestingModule,
                HttpClientModule,
                FormsModule,
                ReactiveFormsModule
        ],
        declarations: [ RegisterComponent ],
        schemas: [NO_ERRORS_SCHEMA],
        providers: [FormBuilder]
        })
        .compileComponents();
}));
```

```
beforeEach(() => {
        fixture = TestBed.createComponent(RegisterComponent);
        component = fixture.componentInstance;
        fixture.detectChanges();
});

it('should create', () => {
        expect(component).toBeTruthy();
});
});
```

Fixing bike service tests

Open `./Client/src/app/pages/bikes/_services/bikes.service.spec.ts` and replace the contents with the following code:

```
import { TestBed, inject } from '@angular/core/testing';
import { HttpClientModule } from '@angular/common/http';

// App imports
import { BikesService } from './bikes.service';
import { HttpErrorHandler } from '../../../shared/_services/http-handle-
error.service';

describe('BikesService', () => {
beforeEach(() => {
        TestBed.configureTestingModule({
        imports: [
                HttpClientModule
        ],
        providers: [
                BikesService,
                HttpErrorHandler
        ]
        });
});

it('should be created', inject([BikesService], (service: BikesService) => {
        expect(service).toBeTruthy();
}));
});
```

Fixing bike-detail tests

Open `./Client/src/app/pages/bikes/bike-detail/bike-detail.component.spec.ts` and replace the contents with the following code:

```
import { RouterTestingModule } from '@angular/router/testing';
import { async, ComponentFixture, TestBed } from '@angular/core/testing';
import { NO_ERRORS_SCHEMA } from '@angular/core';

// App imports
import { BikeDetailComponent } from './bike-detail.component';
import { FormsModule } from '@angular/forms';
import { HttpClientModule } from '@angular/common/http';
import { HttpErrorHandler } from '../../../shared/_services/http-handle-error.service';

describe('BikeDetailComponent', () => {
let component: BikeDetailComponent;
let fixture: ComponentFixture<BikeDetailComponent>;

beforeEach(async(() => {
        TestBed.configureTestingModule({
        imports: [
                RouterTestingModule,
                FormsModule,
                HttpClientModule
        ],
        declarations: [
                BikeDetailComponent
        ],
        schemas: [NO_ERRORS_SCHEMA],
        providers: [HttpErrorHandler]
        })
        .compileComponents();
}));

beforeEach(() => {
        fixture = TestBed.createComponent(BikeDetailComponent);
        component = fixture.componentInstance;
        fixture.detectChanges();
});

it('should create', () => {
        expect(component).toBeTruthy();
});
});
```

Fixing bike-list tests

Open `./Client/src/app/pages/bikes/bike-list/bike-list.component.spec.ts` and replace the contents with the following code:

```
import { RouterTestingModule } from '@angular/router/testing';
import { HttpClientModule } from '@angular/common/http';
import { async, ComponentFixture, TestBed } from '@angular/core/testing';
import { NO_ERRORS_SCHEMA } from '@angular/core';

// App imports
import { BikeListComponent } from './bike-list.component';
import { BikeSearchPipe } from '../_pipes/bike-search.pipe';
import { HttpErrorHandler } from './../../../shared/_services/http-handle-
error.service';


describe('BikeListComponent', () => {
let component: BikeListComponent;
let fixture: ComponentFixture<BikeListComponent>;

beforeEach(async(() => {
        TestBed.configureTestingModule({
        imports: [
                RouterTestingModule,
                HttpClientModule
        ],
        declarations: [
                BikeListComponent,
                BikeSearchPipe
        ],
        schemas: [NO_ERRORS_SCHEMA],
        providers: [HttpErrorHandler]
        })
        .compileComponents();
}));

beforeEach(() => {
        fixture = TestBed.createComponent(BikeListComponent);
        component = fixture.componentInstance;
        fixture.detectChanges();
});

it('should create', () => {
        expect(component).toBeTruthy();
});
});
```

Fixing bike tests

Open `./Client/src/app/pages/bikes/bikes.component.spec.ts` and replace contents with the following code:

```
import { async, ComponentFixture, TestBed } from '@angular/core/testing';
import { RouterTestingModule } from '@angular/router/testing';

// App imports
import { BikesComponent } from './bikes.component';

describe('BikesComponent', () => {
let component: BikesComponent;
let fixture: ComponentFixture<BikesComponent>;

beforeEach(async(() => {
        TestBed.configureTestingModule({
        imports: [
                RouterTestingModule
        ],
        declarations: [
                BikesComponent
        ]
        })
        .compileComponents();
}));

beforeEach(() => {
        fixture = TestBed.createComponent(BikesComponent);
        component = fixture.componentInstance;
        fixture.detectChanges();
});

it('should create', () => {
        expect(component).toBeTruthy();
});

});
```

Fixing builders service tests

Open
`./Client/src/app/pages/builders/_gservices/builders.service.spec.ts` and
replace the contents with the following code:

```
import { HttpClientModule } from '@angular/common/http';
```

```
import { TestBed, inject } from '@angular/core/testing';

// App imports
import { BuildersService } from './builders.service';
import { HttpErrorHandler } from '../../../shared/_services/http-handle-
error.service';


describe('BuildersService', () => {
beforeEach(() => {
        TestBed.configureTestingModule({
        imports: [
                HttpClientModule
        ],
        providers: [
                BuildersService,
                HttpErrorHandler
        ]
        });
});

it('should be created', inject([BuildersService], (service:
BuildersService) => {
        expect(service).toBeTruthy();
}));
});
```

Fixing builder-detail tests

Open ./Client/src/app/pages/builders/builder-detail/builder-
detail.component.spec.ts and replace the contents with the following code:

```
import { RouterTestingModule } from '@angular/router/testing';
import { HttpClientModule } from '@angular/common/http';
import { async, ComponentFixture, TestBed } from '@angular/core/testing';

import { BuilderDetailComponent } from './builder-detail.component';
import { HttpErrorHandler } from '../../../shared/_services/http-handle-
error.service';


describe('BuilderDetailComponent', () => {
let component: BuilderDetailComponent;
let fixture: ComponentFixture<BuilderDetailComponent>;

beforeEach(async(() => {
        TestBed.configureTestingModule({
```

```
        imports: [
                RouterTestingModule,
                HttpClientModule
        ],
        declarations: [
                BuilderDetailComponent
        ],
        providers: [HttpErrorHandler]
        })
        .compileComponents();
}));

beforeEach(() => {
        fixture = TestBed.createComponent(BuilderDetailComponent);
        component = fixture.componentInstance;
        fixture.detectChanges();
});

it('should create', () => {
        expect(component).toBeTruthy();
});
});
```

Fixing builder-list components

Open `./Client/src/app/pages/builders/builder-list/builder-list.component.spec.ts` and replace the contents with the following code:

```
import { RouterTestingModule } from '@angular/router/testing';
import { HttpClientModule } from '@angular/common/http';
import { async, ComponentFixture, TestBed } from '@angular/core/testing';

// App imports
import { BuilderListComponent } from './builder-list.component';
import { HttpErrorHandler } from '../../../shared/_services/http-handle-error.service';

describe('BuilderListComponent', () => {
let component: BuilderListComponent;
let fixture: ComponentFixture<BuilderListComponent>;

beforeEach(async(() => {
        TestBed.configureTestingModule({
        imports: [
                RouterTestingModule,
                HttpClientModule
        ],
```

```
        declarations: [
                BuilderListComponent
        ],
        providers: [HttpErrorHandler]
        })
        .compileComponents();
}));

beforeEach(() => {
        fixture = TestBed.createComponent(BuilderListComponent);
        component = fixture.componentInstance;
        fixture.detectChanges();
});

it('should create', () => {
        expect(component).toBeTruthy();
});
});
```

Fixing builders tests

Open `./Client/src/app/pages/builders/builders.component.spec.ts` and replace the contents with the following code:

```
import { RouterTestingModule } from '@angular/router/testing';
import { async, ComponentFixture, TestBed } from '@angular/core/testing';

// App imports
import { BuildersComponent } from './builders.component';

describe('BuildersComponent', () => {
let component: BuildersComponent;
let fixture: ComponentFixture<BuildersComponent>;

beforeEach(async(() => {
        TestBed.configureTestingModule({
        imports: [
                RouterTestingModule
        ],
        declarations: [
                BuildersComponent
        ]
        })
        .compileComponents();
}));

beforeEach(() => {
```

```
        fixture = TestBed.createComponent(BuildersComponent);
        component = fixture.componentInstance;
        fixture.detectChanges();
    });

    it('should create', () => {
        expect(component).toBeTruthy();
    });

});
```

Fixing home tests

Open `./Client/src/app/pages/home/home.component.spec.ts` and replace the contents with the following code:

```
import { TestBed , async, ComponentFixture } from '@angular/core/testing';
import { RouterTestingModule } from '@angular/router/testing';

// App imports
import { HomeComponent } from './home.component';

describe('HomeComponent', () => {
let component: HomeComponent;
let fixture: ComponentFixture<HomeComponent>;

beforeEach(async(() => {
        TestBed.configureTestingModule({
        imports: [
                RouterTestingModule
        ],
        declarations: [
                HomeComponent
        ]
        }).compileComponents();
}));

beforeEach(() => {
        fixture = TestBed.createComponent(HomeComponent);
        component = fixture.componentInstance;
        fixture.detectChanges();
});

it('should create', () => {
```

```
        expect (component) .toBeTruthy () ;
});


});
```

Fixing app tests

Open ./Client/src/app/app.component.spec.ts and replace the contents with the
following code:

```
import { TestBed, async, ComponentFixture } from '@angular/core/testing';
import { RouterTestingModule } from '@angular/router/testing';
import { NO_ERRORS_SCHEMA } from '@angular/core';

// App imports
import { AppComponent } from './app.component';

describe('AppComponent', () => {
let component: AppComponent;
let fixture: ComponentFixture<AppComponent>;

beforeEach(async(() => {
        TestBed.configureTestingModule({
        imports: [
                RouterTestingModule
        ],
        declarations: [
                AppComponent
        ],
        schemas: [NO_ERRORS_SCHEMA]
        }).compileComponents();
}));

beforeEach(() => {
        fixture = TestBed.createComponent(AppComponent);
        component = fixture.componentInstance;
        fixture.detectChanges();
});

it('should create', async(() => {
        expect(component).toBeTruthy();
}));
});
```

Fixing app interceptor tests

Open `./Client/src/app/shared/_services/app-http-interceptor.service.spec.ts` and replace the contents with the following code:

```
import { HttpClientModule } from '@angular/common/http';
import { TestBed, inject } from '@angular/core/testing';
import { RouterTestingModule } from '@angular/router/testing';

// App imports
import { AppHttpInterceptorService } from './app-http-interceptor.service';

describe('AppHttpInterceptorService', () => {
beforeEach(() => {
        TestBed.configureTestingModule({
        imports: [
                RouterTestingModule,
                HttpClientModule
        ],
        providers: [AppHttpInterceptorService]
        });
});

it('should be created', inject([AppHttpInterceptorService], (service:
AppHttpInterceptorService) => {
        expect(service).toBeTruthy();
}));
});
```

We have now fixed all of the tests, so let's add some more.

Adding unit tests

We've come a long way, and now, all of the tests are passing. So, it is time to create some new tests.

The following lines are very simple, and we have already followed this path in previous examples, so, if something new comes up, we will mention it at the end of the code block.

Let's create some unit tests in our application, as follows:

1. Open `./Client/src/app/app.component.spec.ts` and add the following code:

```
it('should create router-outlet', async(() => {
  const compiled = fixture.debugElement.nativeElement;
```

```
expect(compiled.querySelector('router-outlet')).toBeDefined();
}));
```

The preceding code will check the `router-outlet` tag inside
of `app.component.spec.ts`.

2. Open `./Client/src/app/pages/auth/_guards/auth.guard.spec.ts` and
   add the following code:

```
it('should AuthService to be defined', inject([AuthService], (auth:
AuthService) => {
 expect(auth).toBeTruthy();
}));
it('should not allow user to pass', inject([AuthGuard],      (guard:
AuthGuard) => {
expect(guard.canActivate(new ActivatedRouteSnapshot(),
fakeSnapshot)).toBe(false);
}));
```

Note that we are creating two new tests: one to check `AuthService`, and another
to check `AuthGuard`.

3. Open `./Client/src/app/pages/bikes/bikes.component.spec.ts` and
   add the following code:

```
it('should create router-outlet', async(() => {
 const compiled = fixture.debugElement.nativeElement;
 expect(compiled.querySelector('router-outlet')).toBeDefined();
}));
```

4. Open
   `./Client/src/app/pages/builders/builders.component.spec.ts` and
   add the following code:

```
it('should create router-outlet', async(() => {
 const compiled = fixture.debugElement.nativeElement;
 expect(compiled.querySelector('router-outlet')).toBeDefined();
}));
```

5. Open `./Client/src/app/pages/home/home.component.spec.ts` and add
   the following code:

```
it('should render title tag', async(() => {
 const compiled = fixture.debugElement.nativeElement;
 expect(compiled.querySelector('h1').textContent).toContain('Custom
Bikes Garage');
}));
```

6. Open `./Client/src/app/app.component.spec.ts` and add the following code:

```
it('should render footer tag', async(() => {
  const compiled = fixture.debugElement.nativeElement;
  expect(compiled.querySelector('footer').textContent).toContain('201
8 © All Rights Reserved');
  }));
```

We have now finished the sample unit tests. If we execute the tests using `ng test`, we will see the following results in Terminal:

```
Executed 24 of 24 SUCCESS (2.695 secs / 2.398 secs)
```

Fixing e2e tests

At this point, we are going to run the e2e tests, as we mentioned earlier in the chapter:

1. Open `./Client/e2e/src/app.e2e-spec.ts` and replace the contents with the following code:

```
import { AppPage } from './app.po';

describe('workspace-project App', () => {
    let page: AppPage;

    beforeEach(() => {
        page = new AppPage();
    });

    it('should display app title', () => {
        page.navigateTo();
        expect(page.getParagraphText()).toEqual('Custom
Bikes Garage');
    });
});
```

2. Open Terminal window and type the following command:

```
npm run e2e
```

The results of the preceding command will be similar to the following screenshot:

e2e test results

Remember, you need to run the Angular commands inside of the
./Client folder; otherwise, you will see an error message, because the Angular
CLI needs the angular.json file to execute the ng commands, and this file is
inside of the ./Client folder.

Application deployment

We have now finished all of the necessary steps to test our application. The tests can be
very comprehensive or quite simple; this will depend on the type of approach that you (or
your team) choose.

There are many debates about tests within the community. Some people defend the
development-oriented tests, such as **Behavior-Driven Development (BDD)** or **Test-Driven
Development (TDD)**.

Again, we will note that the most important thing is that your code, structure, and tests are
consistent, regardless of what type of development is adopted.

In this last section, we will look at how we can prepare our application to be published in
production. From the beginning of this book, we have been using Docker, and we would
not finish the book in any other way.

So, let's look at how we can prepare our application, using some Docker features.

Creating Docker images for frontend applications

As we discussed previously, we already have an environment configured with Docker, but
it only covers our backend application, since we run our frontend code using the Angular
CLI installed on our machine.

In the development environment, this is not a problem, since we need the code that we write in our host to update in our Docker container. However, when we are discussing deployment, we take into account the fact that our code is ready to run, without any changes to files.

Note that we are not talking about writing on the disk or data persistence; we will only mention changes in the source code of the application.

With that in mind, let's create an image of our frontend application using a Dockerfile.

Creating a Dockerfile

Create a new file called `Dockerfile` inside of the `./Client` folder, and add the following code:

```
FROM nginx:alpine

COPY nginx.conf /etc/nginx/nginx.conf

WORKDIR /usr/share/nginx/html
COPY dist/ .
```

The preceding code is very simple; we are using an image from `nginx:alpine`, a Linux distribution.

> You can read more about official Docker images at `https://hub.docker.com/explore/`.

Also, we are using a configuration file for the nginx server. Remember, the Angular application must be hosted by a web server.

Creating an nginx file

Create a new file called `nginx.conf` inside of the `./Client` folder, and add the following code:

```
worker_processes  1;

events {
        worker_connections  1024;
}
```

```
http {
        server {
                listen 81;
                server_name  localhost;

                root    /usr/share/nginx/html;
                index  index.html index.htm;
                include /etc/nginx/mime.types;

                gzip on;
                gzip_min_length 1000;
                gzip_proxied expired no-cache no-store private auth;
                gzip_types text/plain text/css application/json
application/javascript application/x-javascript text/xml application/xml
application/xml+rss text/javascript;

                location / {
                        try_files $uri $uri/ /index.html;
                }
        }
}
```

There's nothing new here – it's just a basic nginx configuration to serve the Angular files.

Creating npm building tasks

With the Dockerfile in place, we just need to create a building process using the npm that we have available.

Open ./Client/package.json and add the following code:

```
"build:docker":"npm run lint:dev && npm run test && npm run e2e && npm rum
build && npm rum docker:image",
 "docker:image":"./_scripts/create-docker-image.sh"
```

Let's explain what we did in the preceding code:

- Script tag: docker:image will use a bash script file to generate a Docker image; later, we will see this file in detail.
- Script tag: build:docker will execute the following steps:

    1. Run SASS listen.
    2. Run Tslint.
    3. Run unit tests.
    4. Run e2e tests.

5. Build the application.
6. Create a Docker image.

Before we go further, let's explain why we are using a bash file to create the Docker image.

Bash files are very useful in many places, and aren't different in any build processes as we will see on the following lines to execute some Docker commands. To avoid more complexity in npm packages, we will use a call to the `create-docker-image.sh` file that will execute the command necessary to generate our image.

Creating the bash script

Now, we are going to add a new directory in our frontend application, to store all of the bash script files that our application can have. In this example, we will only use one, but in real-world applications, this folder can store a series of bash files:

1. Inside of `./Client`, create a new folder, called `_scripts`.
2. Inside of the `./Client/_scripts` folder, create a new file called `create-docker-image.sh` and add the following code:

```
#!/bin/bash
set -e
# Docker command to create the front-end application
docker image build -t angular-laravel-book .
```

Note that you can use any name for your application; we are using `angular-laravel-book` for the book example.

Running npm build scripts

Now, let's make a small adjustment to the `angular.json` file; remove the `Client` folder from the `output` tag:

```
"outputPath": "dist",
```

The last step is to run the `build` command, to test and create our application.

Open Terminal window inside of the `./Client` folder, and type the following command:

```
npm run build:docker
```

The build process will take a few minutes; at the end, you will see a message similar to the following in Terminal:

```
> ./_scripts/create-docker-image.sh

Sending build context to Docker daemon  315.6MB
Step 1/4 : FROM nginx:alpine
 ---> ebe2c7c61055
Step 2/4 : COPY nginx.conf /etc/nginx/nginx.conf
 ---> Using cache
 ---> 5618c6694bab
Step 3/4 : WORKDIR /usr/share/nginx/html
 ---> Using cache
 ---> 9cf390101b82
Step 4/4 : COPY dist/ .
 ---> 5d94e018e758
Successfully built 5d94e018e758
Successfully tagged angular-laravel-book:latest
```

End-to-end tests

If you face errors with permissions, perform the following. Open Terminal window inside of the `./Client/_scripts` folder and type `chmod 755 create-docker-image.sh`.

Reviewing Docker commands

Here are some observations for the end of this chapter:

1. At the beginning of the book, we used Docker to create the development environment.
2. In this section, we created an image for our frontend application.

So, now is the right time to check over what we've done so far.

From `Chapter 4`, *Building the Baseline Application*, we have been using Docker to create the backend API application. In this chapter, we have been using Docker to turn the frontend Angular application into a Docker image. So, we can assume that we have an image for our backend with a server and a database, and another for the frontend application, also known as the client-side application.

This gives us the advantage of hosting the services separately, as we mentioned earlier in the book.

Remember that our backend API is totally independent of the frontend application.

Building the application for production

Let's make some adjustments in our `docker-compose.yml` file and add the image of the frontend application.

Open `./Client/docker-compose.yml` and add the following code:

```
appserver:
  image: 'angular-laravel-book'
  container_name: chapter-11-appserver
  # Build the image if don't exist
  build: './Client'
  ports:
    - 3000:81
```

Note the commented lines. As part of the `build` command, we are using the `angular-laravel-book` image created with the `npm run build:docker` command. So, if you forget to run the build script, every time you run the `docker-compose up -d` command, the image will be created (if it does not already exist).

Testing Docker images

Now it is time to check the Docker containers and images.

Attention, the next command, will erase all the Docker images and containers that you have in your machine. If you used Docker for other projects besides the book examples, we recommend that you only delete images and containers related to our example application.

The following command erases all images and containers in your machine:

```
docker system prune -a
```

Let's check the containers, as follows:

1. Open Terminal window and type the following command:

    docker ps -a

    The output returned will be an empty table.

2. Still in Terminal, type the following command:

    docker images -a

    At the end, you will again see an empty table.

3. Still Terminal, type the following command:

docker-compose up -d

    Congratulations! We have successfully built all of the images and containers.

4. Repeat step 1 to list all containers.

The result will be the following output:

Container ID	Image	Name
ContainerID	chapter-11_php-fpm	chapter-11-php-fpm
ContainerID	nginx:alpine	chapter-11-webserver
ContainerID	mysql:5.7	chapter-11-mysql
ContainerID	angular-laravel-book	chapter-11-appserver

Note that the container names are the same as those we chose in the docker-compose.yml file.

The following images represent our application:

*   **Frontend**: angular-laravel-book
*   **Backend**: phpdockerio/php72-fpm

We are now ready to deploy on the cloud.

Summary

We now have the necessary baseline code to put our application into production. The next steps are the most varied, because a multitude of cloud services are able to store Docker images for production websites and applications – and it often involves the use of a paid service. But we now have a robust and scalable application using the latest technology, namely Angular 6 and Laravel 5.

We have come a long way since the start of this book, explaining and introducing advanced web development techniques. You are now able to create an application from scratch, all the way to deployment.

Make sure to always keep yourself up to date, and keep in mind that consistent code can always help you.

Other Books You May Enjoy

If you enjoyed this book, you may be interested in these other books by Packt:

Full-Stack Vue.js 2 and Laravel 5
Anthony Gore

ISBN: 9781788299589

- Core features of Vue.js to create sophisticated user interfaces
- Build a secure backend API with Laravel
- Learn a state-of-the-art web development workflow with Webpack
- Full-stack app design principles and best practices
- Learn to deploy a full-stack app to a cloud server and CDN
- Managing complex application state with Vuex
- Securing a web service with Laravel Passport

ASP.NET Core 2 and Angular 5
Valerio De Sanctis

ISBN: 9781788293600

- Use ASP.NET Core to its full extent to create a versatile backend layer based on RESTful APIs
- Consume backend APIs with the brand new Angular 5 HttpClient and use RxJS Observers to feed the frontend UI asynchronously
- Implement an authentication and authorization layer using ASP.NET Identity to support user login with integrated and third-party OAuth 2 providers
- Configure a web application in order to accept user-defined data and persist it into the database using server-side APIs
- Secure your application against threats and vulnerabilities in a time efficient way
- Connect different aspects of the ASP. NET Core framework ecosystem and make them interact with each other for a Full-Stack web development experience

Leave a review - let other readers know what you think

Please share your thoughts on this book with others by leaving a review on the site that you bought it from. If you purchased the book from Amazon, please leave us an honest review on this book's Amazon page. This is vital so that other potential readers can see and use your unbiased opinion to make purchasing decisions, we can understand what our customers think about our products, and our authors can see your feedback on the title that they have worked with Packt to create. It will only take a few minutes of your time, but is valuable to other potential customers, our authors, and Packt. Thank you!

Index

A

Amazon Web Services (AWS) 212
Angular 6
  features 60
Angular application
  Angular service, creating 79
  component, adding 78
  creating 70
  deployment 84, 85, 86
  dotfiles 73
  environments 75
  module, adding 76
  package.json file 72
  route, adding 79
  sample application, executing 75
  structure 70
  template data binding 83, 84
Angular CLI
  baseline code, preparing 212
  directory structure, creating 215, 216
  installing 65, 67
  used, for scaffolding web application 212, 214
  used, for starting web application 209
Angular component
  life cycle 63
Angular forms
  about 334
  dealing with 332
  frontend form validation, adding 340
  reactive/model-driven forms 335, 337
  template-driven forms 335
Angular Language Service
  URL 67
Angular pipes
  dealing with 332
  pipe filter, creating 332, 333, 334

Angular routes
  authentication routes, creating 243
  dealing with 242
  home routing, creating 244
Angular services
  bike-detail methods, creating 321, 322, 324, 326
  bike-list methods, creating 326, 327, 328
  builder-detail methods, creating 328, 330
  builder-list methods, creating 330, 331, 332
  connecting, with application components 319
  environment configuration, adding 319
  navigation methods, creating 320
Angular Support
  URL 67
Angular templates
  template bindings, adding to bike-detail page 308
  template bindings, adding to bike-list page 312
  template bindings, adding to builder-detail page 313
  template bindings, adding to builder-list page 316
  template bindings, adding to login page 306
  template bindings, adding to navigation component 305
  template bindings, adding to register page 307
  writing, with Bootstrap CSS framework 304, 305
Angular tests
  about 361, 362
  end-to-end tests 361
  unit tests 361
Angular v5 Snippets
  URL 67
any type 49
application deployment
  about 387

Docker commands, reviewing 391
Docker images, creating for frontend application
 387
application linters
  linter tasks, creating in package.json file 361
  SCSS errors, fixing 357, 359
  setting 351
  stylelint rules, applying on style.scss 355, 356
  stylelint, adding for SCSS files 352
  TSLint-angular, adding to package.json file 359,
   360
Application Programming Interface (API) 7, 117
application routes
  protecting, with route guards 294
application
  components, adding 239, 242
Artisan command-line interface 21
auth service, HTTPClient module
  creating 270, 271
  getToken function, creating 274
  getUser function, creating 274
  handleError function, creating 275
  isAuthenticated function, creating 275
  Login function, creating 272, 273
  Logout function, creating 273
  Register function, creating 271
  setToken function, creating 274
authorization headers
  AppHttpInterceptorService, adding to main
   module 292, 294
  HTTP interceptor, creating 290, 292
  using 289, 290

B

base controller class 167
Bazel
  URL 60
Behavior-Driven Development (BDD) 387
bikes service, HTTPClient module
  creating 276
  CRUD functions, creating 277
  handleError function, creating 278
  voteOnBike function, creating 278
Blade template engine
  creating 36

boilerplate Angular components
  Auth routes, preparing 232, 233, 235
  bikes component, creating 229
  bikes module, creating 229
  builders component, creating 231
  builders module, creating 231
  creating 228
  home component, creating 228
  home module, creating 228
  layout component, creating 235
Bootstrap CSS framework
  Angular templates, writing 304, 305
  CSS import, removing 300
  installing 299, 300
  SCSS imports, adding 301
  variables, overriding 302, 303
Bugsnag
  reference 284

C

child routes
  app.component.html, refactoring 248
  bikers child routes, adding 246
  builders child routes, adding 245
  configuring, for details page 245
class
  about 53
  creating 52
command-line interface (CLI) 20, 59
components
  adding, to application 239, 242
Composer
  installing 9
controllers
  creating 149
  functions, creating 149, 153, 159, 163
  functions, updating 149, 153, 159, 163
Create, Read, Update, and Delete (CRUD)
  creating, with resource flag 33
Cross-Origin Resource Sharing (CORS)
  about 297
  Laravel CORS, setting up 318
  reference 317
  setting up, on Laravel backend 317

D

database seed
  creating 29, 104, 106
  Workbench table view, exploring 108
database
  Blade template engine, creating 36
  connecting with 27
  migrations file, creating 29
  resource flag, used for creating CRUD methods
    33
  seed, creating 29
  setting up, inside Docker container 27
details pages
  child routes, configuring 245
directory structure
  creating 215, 216
Docker commands
  application, building for production 392
  reviewing 391
Docker Compose foundation
  creating 88
  docker-compose configuration file, creating 90,
    92
  nginx, configuring 88
  php-fpm, configuration 90
  php-fpm, configuring 89
Docker images
  bash script, creating 390
  creating, for frontend applications 387
  Dockerfile, creating 388
  nginx file, creating 388
  npm build scripts, executing 390
  npm building tasks, creating 389
  reference 388
  testing 392, 393
Docker
  installing 9
  URL 9
domain models 265
dotfiles 73

E

e2e tests
  fixing 386

  writing 363, 364
Eloquent ORM relationship
  about 129, 130
  database, querying with Tinker 144, 145, 146,
    147, 148
  database, seeding 139, 141, 142, 143
  many-to-many relationship 134, 135, 136, 138
  one-to-many relationship 134
  one-to-one relationship 131, 132
  URL 130
enum
  using 50
environment
  Composer package manager, installing 9
  Docker, installing 9
  Laravel, setting up 12
  PHPDocker, setting up 12
  PHPDocker.io, configuring 11
  setting up 8
  VS Code text editor, installing 15
error messages
  handling 167, 168

F

frontend form validation
  adding 340
  on reactive/model-driven forms 342, 346, 347
  on template-driven forms 340, 342
frontend views
  bike-detail template, creating 255
  bike-detail view, creating 255
  bike-list template, creating 253
  bike-list view, creating 253
  bikes router-outlet, creating 252
  builder-detail template, creating 257
  builder-detail view, creating 257
  builder-list view, creating 256
  building 248
  home template, creating 251
  home view, creating 251
  login template, creating 258
  login view, creating 258
  navigation component, creating 249, 250
  register template, creating 259
  register view, creating 259

routes, testing 260
template, creating 256
testing 260

G

generic functions
  creating 55
generics 55
Git
  installing 64
  URL 65
GitLens Plugin
  URL 68
GitLens
  URL 68

H

HOMESTEAD
  URL 8
HTTP status code 169
HTTPClient module
  auth service, creating 270, 271
  bikes service, creating 276
  builders service, creating 279
  XHR requests, dealing with 269, 270
HttpErrorHandler service
  bikes service, refactoring 287
  builders service, refactoring 285
  dealing with 282
  handler error service, creating 282, 283, 284
  importing, into app.module.ts 284, 285

I

interface
  declaring 54

J

Jasmine
  reference 362
JavaScript code
  any type 49
  enum, using 50
  never type, using 51
  null type 52

tuple, creating 46
undefined type 52
void type, using 48
writing, with static types 46

K

Karma test runner
  reference 362

L

L5-Swagger library
  installing 110, 111
Laravel Application lifecycle
  about 19
  URL 20
Laravel application
  executing 97, 98
  scaffold, creating 95
  scaffolding, with PHP Composer 94
  setting up 12
Laravel applications, architecture
  about 16
  directory structure 16
  MVC workflow 18
Laravel CORS
  setting up 318
Laravel documentation
  URL 8
Laravel resources
  adding, to controllers 194, 197, 199, 207
  BikesResource, creating 190
  BuildersResource, creating 191
  ItemsResource, creating 192
  ratingResource, creating 193
  working with 190
Laravel, with Docker
  about 88
  application container, building 92, 94
  Docker Compose foundation, creating 88
linter 351

M

MAMP
  URL 8
master detail page 245

methods 53
migrations
  boilerplate, creating 104, 105
  creating 104
  files, creating 29
Model View Controller (MVC)
  about 7, 23
  controllers, creating 24
  model, creating 24
  routes, creating 25
  URL 16
  views, creating 25
models
  Bike class model, creating 268, 269
  builders class model, creating 266, 267
  User class model, creating 266
modern web applications
  Angular, building block 61
  developing, with Angular components 60
modules
  class export feature, using 57
  external classes, importing 58
  external classes, using 58
  working with 57
MySQL database
  .env file, configuring 99, 101
  external client, using 101, 102
  setting up 98
  storage folder, adding 98

N

never type
  using 51
ng add
  used, for adding PWA features 218
Node Package Manager (NPM) 9

O

Object Relational Mapping (ORM) 118
Object-Oriented Programming (OOP) 52

P

package.json file
  about 72
  URL 73

PHP Composer
  used, for scaffolding Laravel application 94
PHPDocker.io
  configuring 11
PHPDocker
  setting up 12
PHPDOCKER
  URL 8
Progressive Web Application (PWA)
  about 60, 209
  Angular service 223, 224
  baseline, building 217
  debugging 225, 227
  executing, in production mood 222
  features, adding with ng add 218
  key files 218
  reference 217
  working with 219, 221, 222

R

Reactive Extensions Library for JavaScript (RxJS)
  272
reactive/model-driven forms, Angular
  about 337
  register form component, reviewing 337
  register form template, reviewing 337
reactive/model-driven forms
  form validation, dealing with 342, 346, 347
Representational State Transfer (REST) 117
request validation
  dealing 167
  using 168
RESTful API
  API URLs, checking with Swagger UI 173, 174
  content, adding to migration files 125, 127, 128,
    129
  controllers validation, implementing 169, 171
  controllers, creating 149
  custom error handling, adding 171, 173
  Eloquent ORM relationship 129
  error messages, handling 167
  files, refactoring 119, 120
  HTTP status code 169
  Laravel resources, working with 190
  migration files, creating 123, 125

models, creating 123, 125
overview 120, 122
preparing 118, 119
record, obtaining by ID 175
records, obtaining 175
request validation, using 167
response errors, checking 176, 177
routes, creating 149
summary 122, 123
token-based authentication 177
route guards
  application routes, protecting 294
  creating, for bike-detail 295, 296
routes
  about 23
  API routes, creating 164, 165
  creating 25, 149
RxJS library
  reference 272

S

Search engine optimization (SEO) 226
Single Page Applications (SPAs)
  about 237
  baseline code, preparing 237, 239
static types
  JavaScript code, writing 46
stylelint
  .stylelintrc configuration, adding 352
  reference 352
  scripts, adding to package.json file 352
  Stylelint plugin, installing for VS code 354
  VS Code, setting 354
Swagger framework
  API documentation 109, 110
  API documentation, generating 112
  API documentation, publishing 112
  application API controller, creating 111
  definitions, adding 113, 115
  L5-Swagger library, installing 110, 111
Swagger UI documentation
  generating 165

T

template-driven forms, Angular
  about 335
  form validation, dealing with 340, 342
  login form component, reviewing 335, 337
  login form template, reviewing 335, 337
Test-Driven Development (TDD) 387
Tinker
  used, for querying database 144, 145, 146, 147
token-based authentication
  about 177
  API routes, protecting 187
  auth guard, setting up 180
  authController, creating 181, 186
  tymon-jwt-auth, installing 178
  User model, updating 179
  user routes, checking 187, 189
  user routes, creating 186
TSLint-angular
  adding, to package.json file 359, 360
  reference 361
tuple
  creating 46
tymon-jwt-auth
  installing 178
TypeScript
  advantages 43
  class, creating 52
  generic functions, creating 55
  installing 40
  interface, declaring 54
  project, creating 41

U

unit tests
  adding 384, 386
  app interceptor tests, fixing 384
  app tests, fixing 383
  authGuard tests, fixing 371
  authService tests, fixing 372
  bike service tests, fixing 375
  bike tests, fixing 378
  bike-detail tests, fixing 376
  bike-list tests, fixing 377

builder-detail tests, fixing 379
builder-list components, fixing 380
builders service tests, fixing 378
builders tests, fixing 381
fixing 366, 369, 370, 371
home tests, fixing 382
login tests, fixing 373
register tests, fixing 374
writing 363, 364

V

Visual Studio Code (VS Code)
  installing 15
  references 15
void type
  using 48
VS Code Angular plugins
  Angular Language Service 67
  Angular Support 67
  Angular v5 Snippets 67

GitLens 68
GitLens Plugin 68
installing 67

W

WAMPSERVER
  URL 8
web application
  baseline code, preparing 210
  scaffolding, with Angular CLI 212, 214
  starting, with Angular CLI 209
webpack 60

X

XAMPP
  URL 8
XHR requests
  dealing, with HttpClient module 269
  reference 270

www.ingramcontent.com/pod-product-compliance
Lightning Source LLC
Chambersburg PA
CBHW060649060326
40690CB00020B/4575